Explorations
in
Strategy

EXPLORATIONS IN STRATEGY

Colin S. Gray

Westport, Connecticut
London

The Library of Congress has cataloged the hardcover edition as follows:

Gray, Colin S.
    Explorations in strategy / Colin S. Gray.
        p.   cm.—(Contributions in military studies. ISSN 0883–6884
    ; no. 164)
    Includes bibliographical references and index.
    ISBN 0–313–29510–7 (alk. paper)
    1. Strategy.   I. Title.   II. Series.
    U162.G69   1996
    355.4—dc20   95–50524

British Library Cataloguing in Publication Data is available.

A hardcover edition of *Explorations in Strategy* is available from
Greenwood Press, an imprint of Greenwood Publishing Group, Inc.
(Contributions in Military Studies, Number 164; ISBN: 0–313–29510–7).

Library of Congress Catalog Card Number: 95–50524
ISBN: 0–275–96256–3 (pbk.)

First published in 1996

Praeger Publishers, 88 Post Road West, Westport, CT 06881
An imprint of Greenwood Publishing Group, Inc.
Printed in the United States of America

The paper used in this book complies with the
Permanent Paper Standard issued by the National
Information Standards Organization (Z39.48–1984).

10 9 8 7 6 5 4 3 2 1

To my father,
Bill Gray,
in memory

Contents

Part IV: Conclusions   233

Tables and Figures

Preface

Explorations in Strategy was conceived some years ago as a project which would enable me to share the process of strategic investigation with interested readers. Although each chapter and even each cluster of chapters (Parts I–IV) has its own integrity and can be read by those particularly interested in, say, air power or special operations, the book really is about what its title proclaims, strategy.

I am grateful to the various individuals and offices in the U.S., and more recently in the British, government who have licensed and encouraged me to explore their particular concerns from a broad strategic perspective. If the results were not always what they anticipated, that is a feature of strategic exploration; one finds what one finds and then one reports honestly.

Specifically, I am pleased to acknowledge permission of the editors of *Joint Force Quarterly* to use a later revision of my article on "The Limits of Seapower: Joint Warfare and Unity of Conflict" (published in their issue no. 6, Autumn/Winter 1994/95) as Chapter 2 for this book. Also, I am grateful to my friend Professor Williamson Murray for the editing skill which he applied to the manuscripts which have become Chapters 7 and 8 of *Explorations in Strategy*.

I am grateful to Greenwood Press for their patience during the lengthy gestation of this book. Its writing happened to coincide with my transition from the think-tank world of Washington, D.C., to the calmer waters of a British university. Hopefully, the end result is a happy blend of both perspectives.

My family, as always, provided vital support in tolerating yet another of my ventures into the arcane realms of strategy. They know how well I appreciate them.

Introduction

Explorations in Strategy is designed to enrich and extend understanding of the nature and purpose of strategy. The text can be viewed quite legitimately as providing contributions to several of the highways and byways of contemporary strategic studies, but the whole—I intend and hope—is greater than the sum of its parts. The central thread which links the several chapter topics most comprehensively is the persisting contrast between, on the one hand, the pull of geographically or functionally distinctive concerns and, on the other hand, the push of strategic logic.

For example, naval warfare and air warfare have both generated huge specialized literatures, just as both are massively unforgiving of tactical incompetence. Naval warfare and air warfare, though tactical and arguably operational subjects in their own rights, are given instrumental meaning only by the direction provided by strategy. Definitions of tactics and strategy abound; when applied with a little intelligence, those supplied by Carl von Clausewitz are as good as any and far better than most. The great man advises that "tactics teaches *the use of armed forces in the engagement;* strategy, *the use of engagements for the object of the war.*"[1] Tersely expressed, tactics and operations serve strategy, as strategy serves policy, and as policy should serve some vision of the desirable.

So fascinating are the geographically and functionally distinctive branches of military activity that it can be difficult to peer through the absorbing behavior in question (aerial combat, commando raids, nuclear threats) to reach the elevated realm of strategic meaning. Technical, logistical, or tactical failure easily can mean strategic failure. If airplanes fall out of the sky because they are structurally unsound, or if they lack the fuel, ammunition, bases, and skilled aircrews necessary for success in combat, the brilliance or otherwise of their higher strategic direction will be strictly moot. Tactical failure typically, though not invariably, means strategic failure. But, tactical success most likely will be effort wasted if it comprises victory in engagements whose winning contributes not at all positively to the course and outcome of the war at issue.[2]

~

Of this book's three intimately connected binding themes and arguments, the ubiquity of strategy is the first and by far the most important. All forms of combat and defense preparation inherently are connected by strategy to the essential unity that is the enterprise of deterrence or war (regardless of policy motive or ultimate political vision—strategy is an equal opportunity guide). There is a strategic meaning to military "engagements," whether or not that meaning is discerned, let alone intended. Poor or negative and unintended strategic effect still lies within the scope of strategy. Troops and equipment wasted in the expensive pursuit of unworthy tactical or operational objectives—frequently the case in the U.S. war in Vietnam, for a painful example[3]— still have an effect upon the course and outcome of the war. The poverty or absence of explicit strategy does not halt the workings of strategy. Tactically abused forces may be strategically wasted, but that waste still can matter strategically. The United States did not evade strategic failure in Vietnam by failing to function in a strategically purposeful manner; indeed, quite the contrary was the case.

My second theme is the thoroughly politically correct argument that preparation for, and the actual conduct of, war has to be pervasively *joint*, which is to say interservice or multiservice in character. Such preparation and conduct also often need to be *combined* in framework, which is to say multinational,[4] though with careful provision for the technical feasibility of a wide range of unilateral national military behavior. The synergistic benefits to be derived from truly joint planning for land, sea, air, and now space operations are as obvious in principle as they are often neglected in practice. The terms of relative advantage between land and sea power (and air power) certainly have shifted from one historical era and geographical arena to another, but their interdependence is illustrated by ancient, medieval, and modern practice. Joint sea-land operations enabled a resurgent Byzantine Empire to stage a dramatically successful "D-Day" to reconquer Crete on 13 July 960.[5] No less dramatic an example of joint operations enabled German air-land (the sea element was sunk) operations to conquer Crete on 28–31 May 1941.

I will not belabor the obvious. Indeed, today the challenge is not so much to stand up for a proper jointness in planning and operations as it is to be prepared to stand out against a mindless mantra of the credo of jointness.[6] The necessary unity of war and the undeniable interdependence of geographically and functionally specialized forces should not be allowed to obscure lead or key roles that particular kinds of forces should play in particular circumstances. It is no sin against jointness to argue simultaneously for a possible "key role" for land power (early phases of an erstwhile NATO–Warsaw Pact conflict), sea power (the Pacific War of 1941–45 or the Falklands conflict of 1982), air power (the Gulf War of 1991),[7] special operations (many low-intensity conflicts, arguably including Vietnam from 1959 to 1963), and—for a functional contribution to the list—"strategic" nuclear forces in the late phases of any armed conflict between nuclear-armed states.[8] To recognize the necessity for a jointness in military operations that can provide the overall strategic effectiveness required for success in the unity that is war should not be to deny key or lead roles in unique geostrategic contexts to one or another element of military power. From time to time there will be occasions when air forces, naval forces, conventional land forces, or special operations forces are able virtually unaided by the others to generate the total strategic effectiveness required by policy.

The third theme of *Explorations in Strategy* is that each form of military power (to extend the domain of the argument, each instrument of grand strategy) has its distinctive advantages and limitations. Logically this point is integral to my second theme, on the necessity for a joint approach to strategy. In practice, however, the mixed merits and demerits of distinguishable forms of military power warrant separate recognition because defense debate is dominated by subcommunities dedicated to the promotion of favored geographically or functionally specialized capabilities. A joint approach to defense planning and to the conduct of war is mandated by the fact that the capabilities in each dimension (sea or space, for example) have distinctive strengths and limitations. "Dimension-pure" solutions to military problems, which is to say intended solutions that are, again for example, wholly naval or air in character, tend to have the advantages of relative simplicity[9]—a considerable military virtue—but the disadvantages of a lack of robustness in the face of setbacks (*inter alia*). Mixed solutions to problems usually will prove stronger than will pure solutions.

The necessity for jointness is recognized today in American and British military cultures as never before. Nonetheless, the trail toward a truly unified vision of defense preparation and war has been long, sometimes interrupted by substantial roadblocks and diversions, and remains incomplete. The Goldwater-Nichols Defense Reorganization Act of 1986 was an important milestone on the jointness trail, as was the British decision in 1994 at long last to create a permanent joint headquarters for the armed forces.[10] An important motive for this British innovation would appear to have been financial, but that apparent fact should not detract from appreciation of the strategic merit in the move. By way of the laying down of a professional marker of no small symbolic significance, in 1993 the National Defense University in Washington, D.C., launched a new journal, unambiguously titled *Joint Force Quarterly*.

Although *Explorations in Strategy* is strongly supportive of jointness as a goal,[11] there is a caveat which helps inform this text. No matter how strong is the top-down policy insistence upon joint approaches to defense behavior, that behavior actually has to be in the hands of organizations specialized to operate in unique geographical contexts. No matter how "purple" (i.e., jointly interservice or multiservice) higher headquarters may be, the great organizations that turn resources of many kinds into military, then strategic, effectiveness are armies, navies, and air forces. A certain, even a certain necessary, parochialism is built into the nature of the principal mission of an army, a navy, and an air force. The first charge upon an air force, for example, is likely to be that it achieves air superiority. If such superiority cannot be secured, then the air force's joint value must be severely restricted, at best. The caveat, therefore, amounts to the recognition of large military organizations that are relatively narrowly focused in geographic scope. Armies, navies, air forces—thinking land, sea, and air—exist and will long continue to exist, no matter how strong the tide flows for jointness. Regarded positively, my caveat on the limits of jointness expresses the attitude that the basis for effectively joint, and jointly effective, forces has to be forces that in the first instance are excellent in their own environmental domain.

~

This is not a work of advocacy. Different dimensions of war, and the forces specialized for their conduct, are explored strategically here. In particular I examine at some length what air power and special operations forces can and cannot contribute to national security, but this book seeks only to advance strategic understanding, not the relevant budgets. Acting as a politically engaged citizen, I am not at all averse either to lobbying for programs in which I believe or to writing the occasional polemic to make a case that I believe needs to be made.[12] *Explorations in Strategy*, however, is not a lobbyist's tract, a lawyer's brief, or in any sense a polemic.

Methodologically, my approach may best be characterized as (strategic) theoretical with historical illustration. I do not theorize or argue by means of history, as if history objectively could resolve matters in need of explanation, but I do theorize and argue from history. Experience—or, if you prefer, historical experience—is always unique, but strategic experience I believe to be a unity through all of time.

Those readers puzzled as to how a book can aspire to intellectual coherence when it has chapters on topics as apparently divergent as sea power, air power, special operations forces, and nuclear deterrence are invited to recall Clausewitz's definition of strategy: "the use of engagements for the object of the war." By way of threat, or in actual execution, military behavior of all kinds is strategic in the effect that it has on the course and outcome of the conflict as a whole. Air power, sea power, land power, space power, nuclear deterrence, special operations forces, all have a strategic dimension in the consequences of their threat or action. With such a clear strategic understanding in mind, historical, geographical, or functional diversity can be regarded from a common viewpoint for assessment.

~

Explorations in Strategy has four parts. Part I explains the relevance to the problem of security of a distinctively strategic form of thinking. This mission is accomplished by examining the ever growing complexity of the security environment over the past one hundred years (Chapter 1); by looking closely at the promise and perils of joint operations from the perspective of the limitations of sea power (Chapter 2); and by explaining the likely effectiveness of deterrence as a framework for strategy in this post–Cold War era (Chapter 3).

Parts II and III, the twin cores or centers of gravity of the book,[13] pursue in detail the strategic effectiveness that can be generated by air power and by special operations forces. Part II identifies the advantages and limitations of air power (Chapter 4); examines what it means to be an air power (Chapter 5); and explores the ways in which air power can support the national interest, possibly to "decisive" effect (Chapter 6).

Part III, on "Strategy and Special Operations," explores the all but unknown territory of the strategic value of special operations forces. The discussion examines the character of special operations and of special operations forces (Chapter 7); explores when, how, and why special operations forces can (and cannot) make a strategic difference to the course of events (Chapter 8); and considers the potential value of special operations in support of foreign policy after the Cold War (Chapter 9). Part III is important both as an exploration in strategy that happens to focus upon special operations and as a strategic analysis of military capabilities that often escape strategic consideration. For every thousand pages in the literature which recount the deeds of derring-do, there is scarcely one page that troubles to ask whether those deeds made much of a difference to the course and outcome of a conflict. One part of one book alone cannot correct for that lack of strategic appraisal, but it can make a useful beginning. For all the mass of publications on special operations, commando raids and the like, serious endeavors to probe the strategic meaning of such phenomena are distinguished by their exceptional rarity.

Part IV picks up on the leading themes and arguments of the book and offers some thoughts on the emergence of "information warfare" in relation to my broad themes (Chapter 10). The discussion concludes with some suggested advice to improve strategic performance and with a brief reflection upon the state of understanding of the Cold War decades.

~

Explorations in Strategy is written in defiance, not in ignorance, of some modern and "postmodern" critiques of strategic studies.[14] Those studies are criticized from one perspective as being less and less important as the security agenda alters,[15] and from another as handling political-military issues inadequately. In the words of a leading critical theorist, "questions of war and peace are too important to leave to students of Strategic Studies."[16] It is a little ironic that the ideas of so-called "critical theory" that now generally are out of favor in their disciplines of origin (philosophy and literary theory) should find devotees among students of politics.[17] There is some consolation in the fact that in the past strategic studies have suffered assault from—or even been enriched by, if one prefers—bodies of fashionable theory considerably more powerful than is the current postmodernist vogue among academics.[18]

Explorations in Strategy treats the world as it is, notwithstanding the claims of those who would deconstruct what strategic theorists and commentators long have taken as their realist working assumptions.[19] Critical theory is intellectual fun, but basically it is not serious. What is serious is the enduring, value-charged "reality" of civilization on trial.[20] Civilized values, as understood by this necessarily culture-bound scholar-citizen, need to be protected and if possible advanced in the face of challenge by the thugs who would, if allowed, put the lights out. That is my perspective. If it biases the explorations in this book, so be it.

NOTES

1. Carl von Clausewitz, *On War*, ed. and trans. Michael Howard and Peter Paret (Princeton, NJ: Princeton University Press, 1976; first pub. 1832), p. 128 (emphasis in original).

2. The dialogue between tactical performance and operational, strategic, and higher political performance is illustrated fairly convincingly in Paddy Griffith, *Battle Tactics of the Western Front: The British Army's Art of Attack, 1916–18* (New Haven, CT: Yale University Press, 1994). Contrary to still-fashionable opinion among military historians, the British Army of 1916–18 vintage was tactically formidable. The problem lay in the operational, strategic, and political use made of that tactical competence. For views strongly critical of British proficiency, see Martin Samuels, *Doctrine and Dogma: German and British Infantry Tactics in the First World War* (Westport, CT: Greenwood Press, 1992); and Tim Travers, *How the War Was Won: Command and Technology in the British Army on the Western Front, 1917–1918* (London: Routledge, 1992).

3. See Ronald H. Spector, *After Tet: The Bloodiest Year in Vietnam* (New York: Free Press, 1993), for powerful illustration of my argument.

4. Multinational combined operations should not be confused with "combined arms," which "means coordinated action by elements of different combat arms. The term is usually used in relation to combat activities at the tactical level, up to and including the division." Trevor N. Dupuy, ed., *International Military and Defense Encyclopedia*, vol. 2 (Washington, DC: Brassey's [US], 1993), p. 574.

5. See Gustave Schlumberger, *Un empereur Byzantin au dixième siècle: Nicephore Phocas* (Paris: Librairie de Firmin-Didot, 1890), chap. 2.

6. See Chapter 2 of this book.

7. The idea of a "key force" is introduced and explained well in John A. Warden III, *The Air Campaign: Planning for Combat* (Washington, DC: Pergamon-Brassey's, 1989; first pub. 1988), pp. 123–27. The concept does not deny the importance of all contributing forces in a joint operation, but it asserts that one kind of force can be "key" in a particular, unique context.

8. In theory it makes no sense to call any forces "strategic" as by existential ascription. *All* forces are strategic in their impact upon the course and outcome of events. Nonetheless, singlehandedly I cannot consign terminological sins to the garbage heap of history. The fact that some actions, by definition tactical, have greater strategic consequences than do others does not render them inherently strategic. However, bowing to common usage, I recognize that nuclear weapons married to delivery vehicles of long range generally are regarded as a "strategic" type of weapon— that is to say a weapon likely to have a major effect upon the course and outcome of a conflict.

9. "Simplicity contributes to successful operations by reducing the possibility of misunderstanding and confusion." John I. Alger, *Definitions and Doctrine of the Military Art, Past and Present* (Wayne, NJ: Avery Publishing, 1985), p. 11. The U.S. Army persistently has favored including simplicity among "the principles of war."

10. See Ministry of Defence, *Front Line First: The Defence Costs Study* (London: HMSO, 1994), pp. 16–17.

11. On jointness, see General Colin L. Powell, "A Word from the Chairman," *Joint Force Quarterly*, no. 1 (summer 1993): 5.

12. Colin S. Gray, *House of Cards: Why Arms Control Must Fail* (Ithaca, NY: Cornell University Press, 1992), for example, was written as a polemic. In *House of Cards* I sought to indict the theory and much of the practice of arms control. Some book reviewers chided me for not being "balanced" in my arguments, when I had not sought to make the opposing case, although I did state and review that case at some length.

13. "A certain center of gravity develops, the hub of all power and movement, on which everything depends. That is the point against which all our energies should be directed" (pp. 595–96). On center of gravity, as on so much else, see Clausewitz, *On War*, pp. 595–97.

14. For postmodernism in general, see David Harvey, *The Condition of Postmodernity: An Enquiry into the Origins of Cultural Change* (Oxford: Blackwell, 1990).

15. Ken Booth informs us that "[v]iolence, without doubt, will continue to be a pervasive feature of the world scene; what we are now seeing is the replacement of the 'grand narrative' of nuclear theory by a pattern of post-modern violence which is both more localized and not easily definable as 'internal' or 'external.' " "Strategy," in A. J. R. Groom and Margot Light, eds., *Contemporary International Relations: A Guide to Theory* (London: Pinter Publishers, 1994), p. 119. Also see Ken Booth, ed., *New Thinking about Strategy and International Security* (London: HarperCollins Academic, 1991); and Barry Buzan, *People, States and Fear: An Agenda for International Security Studies in the Post–Cold War Era*, 2nd ed. (Boulder, CO: Lynne Rienner, 1991).

16. Bradley S. Klein, *Strategic Studies and World Order: The Global Politics of Deterrence* (Cambridge: Cambridge University Press, 1994), p. 3.

17. For a useful survey see Chris Brown, "Critical Theory and Postmodernism in International Relations," in A. J. R. Groom and Margot Light, eds., *Contemporary International Relations: A Guide to Theory* (London: Pinter Publishers, 1994), pp. 56–68.

18. In particular, economics, organization theory, and psychology all had their devotees among strategic thinkers in the 1950s, 1960s, and 1970s. History and cultural anthropology, unfortunately, have been less frequent visitors to the field, in the United States at least.

19. See Klein, *Strategic Studies and World Order*; and Michael C. Williams, "Neo-Realism and the Future of Strategy," *Review of International Studies* 19, no. 2 (April 1993): 103–21.

20. See Arnold J. Toynbee, *Civilization on Trial* (New York: Oxford University Press, 1948); Samuel P. Huntington, "The Clash of Civilizations," *Foreign Affairs* 72, no. 3 (summer 1993): 22–49; and Colin S. Gray, *Villains, Victims and Sheriffs: Strategic Studies and Security for an Inter-War Period, An Inaugural Lecture* (Hull, England: University of Hull Press, 1994).

Part I
The Challenge of Strategy

Chapter 1

On Strategic Performance

It has become almost a commonplace to observe that in the two world wars of the twentieth century the Germans proved that they were good at fighting, but not very good at waging war.[1] A similar judgment applies to the French and to the U.S. experience of war in Indochina. One of the better books on the U.S. adventure in Vietnam concluded that "[i]n the end, the American failure was a failure of understanding and imagination. The American leaders did not see that what for them was a limited war for limited ends was, for the Vietnamese, an unlimited war of survival in which all the most basic values—loyalty to ancestors, love of country, resistance to foreigners—were involved."[2]

President Lyndon B. Johnson, Secretary of Defense Robert S. McNamara, and the commander of U.S. Military Assistance Command Vietnam, General William C. Westmoreland—to name but three of the more guilty parties—had not read or understood, let alone applied, the wisdom of a long-dead Prussian soldier-theorist. Carl von Clausewitz wrote that "[t]he first, the supreme, the most far-reaching act of judgment that the statesman and commander have to make is to establish by that test [of war as an instrument of policy] the kind of war on which they are embarking; neither mistaking it for, nor trying to turn it into, something that is alien to its nature. This is the first of all strategic questions and the most comprehensive."[3] Clausewitz also advises:

No one starts a war—or, rather, no one in his senses ought to do so—without first being clear in his mind what he intends to achieve by that war and how he intends to conduct it. The former is its political purpose; the latter its operational objective. This is the governing principle which will set its course, prescribe the scale of means and effort which is required, and make its influence felt throughout down to the smallest operational detail.[4]

In all four historical cases cited—Germany in the two world wars and France and the United States in Indochina—somewhat inchoate visions of the politically desirable inspired scarcely more orderly sets of high policy goals which had to serve as dim and swaying guiding lights for military effort. In each of these cases political ambition exceeded the military means and the strategic skill available. Germany, France, and the United States all lacked the multidimensional assets necessary to achieve some approximation to political success. Whether or not a plausible facsimile of victory was attainable in any of these cases is distinctly debatable. What is not debatable is that Germany, France, and the United States all failed strategically. Each failed to wage war in such a manner or to such a degree that the more important policy goals were secured.

Explorations in Strategy is sensitive to, but not cowed by, the possible charge that too much is revealed with the wisdom of hindsight. Also, it is not to be denied that there is much in the history of U.S. statecraft that is strategically admirable. U.S. victory in the Cold War was a success for strategy of which any polity could be proud. Although there is usually more to be learnt from failure than from success, these explorations in strategy are not biased in favor of the study of failure, early impressions perhaps notwithstanding. Furthermore, this analysis is not unsympathetic to the people and organizations which must generate strategic effectiveness in the face of real-world friction. Indeed it is the very difficulty of providing consistently high strategic performance that yields much of the interest of this subject to the scholar. Also, if the scholar is to have anything to say that should merit attention in the world of practice, he has to seek empathy with the constraints of that world.[5]

THE MEANING OF STRATEGY

The book is called "explorations in strategy" because it addresses the value for policy of sea power, nuclear deterrence, air power, and special operations forces, rather than the activities per se of those instruments of policy. My subject is not the goals of policy, nor is it the means to which grand strategy can turn to support policy; it is, instead, the relationship between means and ends—the realm of strategy.

The virtue of Clausewitz's definition of strategy is that it is crystal clear upon the critical distinction between its subject and other matters. Specifically, to repeat the formula quoted in the Introduction, strategy is "the use of engagements for the object of the war." Because tactics have just been defined as "the use of armed forces in the engagement,"[6] the distinction could hardly be clearer.

Virtually without exception, well-meaning attempts to improve upon Clausewitz's definition of strategy have not proved successful.

For example, a justly well regarded American military theoretician, writing in a no less justly well regarded series of quasi-official textbooks, invites acceptance of strategy as "the planning for, coordination of, and concerted use of the multiple means and resources available to an alliance, a nation, a political group, or a commander, for the purpose of gaining advantage over a rival."[7] John I. Alger, the theorist at fault here, seems not to appreciate that there is merit in parsimony, that clarity in definition depends upon uncluttered identification of the essence of the subject, and that speculation on the purpose of the subject is irrelevant at best and misleading at worst. Alger's definition is not wholly without merit, but it quite needlessly muddies water that was clear enough in its Clausewitzian formulation.

Nonetheless, Alger's definition shines by comparison with the rather casual and not useful one offered by the noted historian Martin van Creveld. He speaks of "strategy, the method by which those armed forces [the military organization created by the state] wage war."[8] Lest there be any misunderstanding, "the method by which those armed forces wage war" is actually the realm of tactics or even of doctrine. Doctrine is guidance on how to fight, tactics is what forces do, while strategy is the meaning of what forces do for the course and outcome of a conflict.

What may be called the "strategy test" applied to behavior reduces usefully to the question "so what?" Tactical discussion should focus upon what force, or threats of force, did or might have done. Strategic discussion, by contrast, should consider what difference the use, or threat of use, of force would make to the course of events.

There is a sense in which all levels of conflict have strategic features, as Edward N. Luttwak notes persuasively.[9] For the purposes of this book, however, the Clausewitzian approach outlined already is preferred. In order to avoid undue apparent pedantry, the terms naval strategy, air power strategy, space strategy, and even nuclear strategy will be employed occasionally, though only with particular and consistent meaning. For example, naval strategy will refer to the use of naval engagements for the object of war at sea; that object has to be the right to use the sea at will or the ability to deny such use to the enemy. Maritime strategy, by contrast, refers to the use of prowess at sea for the course of events in a conflict as a whole.[10]

Providing the means-ends reasoning which is the core of the meaning of strategy is never forgotten, common sense and a little care should preclude the necessity for undue punctiliousness in precision of usage. Scholars tend to be good at making distinctions. Indeed doing so is crucial for the generation of the theory that should help explain, and perhaps even understand, events.[11] The drawing of distinctions needs to be complemented, however, by the recognition of important connections, even of what one could call a systemic framework.

A HOLISTIC APPROACH AND THE PERILS OF REDUCTIONISM

A cardinal virtue of strategic theory, reasoning, or planning is that it brings together, it connects, activities which otherwise easily could be treated as though they were autonomous realms.[12] Absent a holistic approach to conflict assisted by the central idea of strategy, the universe of possible concern is a series of frequently disconnected loose ends. In the absence of a strategic framework of instrumental thinking and planning, how can defense behavior be governed rationally? People fight on land, at sea, and in the air; they also wage low-intensity, mid-intensity, and perhaps high-intensity conflict; while in geopolitical reality they deter or fight in Korea, Indochina, the Falkland Islands, the Persian Gulf and so forth. Of those three kinds of classification, the first (the geographic) is inadequate because it excludes the purposes of the policy in question. To harken back to Clausewitz yet again, if "the object of the war" is politically truly heroic, while friendly forces are able to perform only modestly in those "engagements" that the strategist must "use," then strategic failure is all but certain.[13]

Clausewitz exaggerates slightly, though only slightly, when he observes that "[t]he conduct of war, in its great outlines, is therefore policy itself, which takes up the sword in place of the pen, but does not on that account cease to think according to its own laws."[14] Also he expresses the unexceptionable opinion that "a certain grasp of military affairs is vital for those in charge of general policy."[15] Given his continentalist Prussian strategic culture, it is not surprising that Clausewitz should risk erring on the side of assuming a unity of purpose between policy and strategy. It might be more accurate to say that he elected not to dwell at length or in detail upon the divergent paths that policy and strategy could pursue. As an interpreter of Napoleonic warfare with the perspective of a staff officer trained to revere the genius of Frederick the Great,[16] Clausewitz would not be likely to notice the friction that may arise between strategy and high policy, a relationship in which strategy necessarily is subordinate. When the duties of head of state, head of government, and principal field commander all devolve upon one person, plainly the prospects for harmony between policy and military action are maximized. Had Clausewitz been geostrategically broader in his education, he might have learnt from the British experience of war how a maritime polity can have difficulty coordinating political, economic, and military interests.[17]

The adoption of a holistic approach to strategy does not require the foolish embrace of a strictly nominal coordination of political intent and military action. A holistic approach, as here, recognizes that political goals and military capabilities may be poorly matched. Clausewitz was constrained by his mission to prescribe what ought to be—this book suffers from no such limiting consideration. I insist that a holistic approach to my subject is the correct one. I insist that a vision of a politically desirable condition should inspire policy choices which should be supported by a strategy which makes proper use of an operational competence founded upon tactical excellence. In practice, tactical performance will be less than excellent, operational skills may be slim, and strategic planning may lack political guidance worthy of the name.[18] As for the political vision which ought to propel the entire process, it may lack all practical connection to behavior in the field (as, for example, with the vision of a united Ireland for the Irish Republican Army). Holism captures or corrals the whole; it does not assume a perfect coordination of the whole. For example, Clausewitz's sensible advice on the proper relationship between political ends and military means was not invalidated by the political-military malpractice of 1914–18. Quite to the contrary, those years demonstrated just how important it is for high policy and its military instrument to be mutually empathetic.

A holistic approach to strategy operates vertically and horizontally. Vertically viewed, our subject encompasses all aspects of peace with security, from political vision down to tactical military performance; horizontally considered, our mandate must include land, sea, air, and space power, together with "strategic" nuclear and special operations forces. It is important that this dual-axis holistic appreciation should be accepted before challenges in detail are offered.

Those in search of simple solutions to apparently complex problems are pejoratively termed reductionists. Advocates of one or another kind of military power are wont to argue that land power, sea power, air power, (would-be) nuclear deterrence, or special operations forces "can do it." The strategic problem in question reduces to a task which, purportedly, a favored military capability can fulfill. *Explorations in Strategy* seeks to chart the perilous channel between a holistic inclusiveness and a reductionist exclusivity. It is not necessarily reductionist in a pejorative sense to recognize that there are conflicts to which a geographically or functionally specific "key force" is strategically most appropriate. For example, Northern Ireland is obviously a special operations, low-intensity-conflict case, as the Falklands was a maritime problem.[19]

Northern Ireland "reduces" both to a complex political problem and to an irregular form of warfare, but it can be difficult to draw the line soundly between an analysis which penetrates to the heart of the problem (i.e., which reduces it to its key element or elements) and an analysis which reduces a complicated reality to an oversimplified, much more manageable reality-as-task. This book offers no universal panaceas, but it does recommend that one should not be afraid to assert the identity and strategic significance of a key force. In other words, notwithstanding the complexity of an issue, there is likely to be a particular kind of power, probably military power, that is most appropriate to a specific context.[20]

It is well to be suspicious of reductionism or essentialism.[21] Also it is well to be open to the suggestion that one or another kind of power should attempt to function as the cutting edge of policy. To say that air power was the key force in the Gulf War of 1991 is not to be reductionist; it is to be sensible. Similarly, to claim that the threats implicit in U.S. nuclear forces were key to the frustration of Soviet policy over Berlin and Germany in 1948–49 and 1958–61 is not to be reductionist, but rather to be realistic. To recognize geographical and functional variety in strategic matters—ipso facto—is to recognize the possible variety of key elements.

WHY STRATEGY IS DIFFICULT

As the great man wrote, "[e]verything in strategy is very simple, but that does not mean that everything is very easy."[22] It should be useful to recognize why strategy is difficult, but it is scarcely less useful to recognize also why explanation need not contribute to practical solution. By analogy, some of the more mechanistic aspects of strategy, like art, can be taught, but people cannot be taught reliably how to be great strategists any more than they can be taught to be great artists. There is room, indeed a requirement, for creativity in both professions that defies pedagogical programming. The intellectual mastery of purportedly permanent "principles of strategy" is probably helpful rather than unhelpful, but is no guarantee of success.[23]

Why is strategy difficult? With some grateful borrowing and adaptation from Clausewitz, I find six connected reasons which more than suffice to explain why superior strategic performance is difficult to achieve, let alone sustain.

First, competence in strategy requires mastery of a particularly challenging complexity. Strategy, after all, is the bridge that connects the threat and use of force with policy or politics. The strategist needs to understand what is tactically and operationally possible in all geographical environments; what success or failure in each environment (or on each functional dimension) contributes to performance in the other environments; what that all means for military performance writ large; and what general military performance means for policy (and vice versa). Moreover, whereas in 1900 the strategist had to master the combined meaning only of land and sea-surface forces, today his counterpart has to master the synergistic meaning of land, sea, air, and space (and nuclear) forces.

Strategy has always been difficult, but the growing complexity of the subject renders it more difficult today than it was a century ago. At its core, strategy has not altered, of course. Strategy is still about "the use of engagements for the object of the war," or—if you prefer, for a modern translation—about the threat and use of force for political reasons. As the character of the possible engagements, or use of forces, has diversified, however, the task of the strategist has grown ever more difficult in practice.

Second, by its very nature strategy is more demanding of the intellect and perhaps the imagination than is any structurally more simple activity—policy, operations, tactics, or logistics, for prominent examples. Excellence in strategy requires the strategist to transcend simple categories of thought. The strategist's task is not to create wise policy or successful schemes of military action, but rather to build and repair the bridge that connects the two. On the one hand, policy will be wise only if it proves (in this case, militarily) feasible. On the other hand, brilliant military schemes can be irrelevant or worse if they promise to achieve politically inappropriate objectives.

Third, it is extraordinarily difficult to train people to be competent, let alone outstanding, strategists. It is all very well for Clausewitz to claim rather glibly, and misleadingly, "that war is simply a continuation of political intercourse, with the addition of other means"[24] or to argue that "in the highest realm of strategy . . . there is little or no difference between strategy, policy, and statesmanship."[25] In the real world of the late twentieth century, military and political careers tend to be massively distinctive, even exclusive in many political cultures. There is little in the training either of professional politicians or professional soldiers that would equip them well for strategic responsibilities. By and large, the military professional learns how to fight and then, as he or she is promoted, how to organize others to fight in ever larger, *militarily* more inclusive formations. The military professional is not taught how engagements should be used "for the object of the war." Similarly, the rising politician is promoted for reason of his or her growing seniority and maturing *political* skills. At no point in an outstanding political career is there likely to be anything resembling more or less explicit training in strategy.

Fourth, strategy places unique physical and moral burdens on the would-be strategist. The demands of high command in time of crisis and war can age a person as surely as can a wasting disease. For illustration of this point, readers are invited to compare film footage of Adolf Hitler in 1939 with that in 1944 (even before the bomb attempt at Rastenburg on 20 July) or 1945, or film footage of President Jimmy Carter in 1976 with that in January 1981. It was with good reason indeed that in Book One of *On War* Clausewitz emphasized the impediments to good strategic performance provided by such broad factors as danger, fatigue, and anxiety born of uncertainty. The burdens of command naturally increase with the level of responsibility. As a person is promoted from tactical, through operational, to strategic realms of individual responsibility, so the potential physical and moral hindrances to sound performance can increase also.

Fifth, it is worth itemizing separately what Clausewitz termed "friction," even though the fourth point could be seen as encompassing aspects of this phenomenon. Clausewitz advises that "[f]riction, as we choose to call it, is the force that makes the apparently easy so difficult."[26] He notes that "[f]riction is the only concept that more or less corresponds to the factors that distinguish real war from war on paper."[27] Friction is not by any means unique to the strategic realm, but it is likely to be uniquely pervasive and uniquely debilitating in its cumulative effects in that realm. As modern chaos theory suggests, unpredicted and unwanted changes of state that are initially very small can have massively nonlinear consequences downstream.[28]

Clausewitz argues that "[e]verything in war is very simple, but the simplest thing is difficult. The difficulties accumulate and end by producing a kind of friction that is inconceivable unless one has experienced war."[29] So many and so potentially synergistic are the sources of friction in war and preparation for war that it is little short of amazing that great military enterprises can be organized and carried through at all.[30] One has to remember that friction impedes all parties in war.

The fundamental reason why friction can be so damaging at the strategic level is because, by definition, that level must accommodate, integrate, and direct all of the activities that constitute war. The strategist will encounter the effects of friction from the world of policy and from all of the geographically and functionally specialized armed forces that are performing tactically, logistically, and operationally. Stated bluntly, at the strategic level of performance there is more that can go wrong.

Sixth and finally, success in strategy calls for a quality of judgment that cannot be taught. Although there is certainly scope for individual "genius" at the tactical and operational levels of war, sound training for consistently superior military performance at those levels—friction permitting—can be provided. Strategic excellence cannot be taught the same way or to anything like the same degree. Strategy inherently requires understanding of the terms of the two-way relationship between military power (perhaps, following Clausewitz, as "engagements," or more loosely as the use and threat of force) and political purpose ("the object of the war," or policy). In addition, strategy requires understanding of how very different kinds of armed force can generate the effectiveness that will yield politically useful consequences. These necessary truths about strategy are almost too easy to state; they can be abominably difficult to put into consistently successful practice.

Many apparently well educated generals have lacked the personal qualities necessary for success in the highest of high commands. One thinks of General Charles B. McLellan in 1862, for example, or, for the British Army, of Field

Marshal Sir Ian Hamilton at Gallipoli in 1915 or General (later Field Marshal) Sir Archibald Wavell in the Western Desert in 1941.[31] As well as a large element of luck and bigger battalions, success in strategy most typically requires (*inter alia*) constitutional fortitude (physical and mental),[32] a sophisticated grasp of political essentials, and the ability to make and adhere to judgments in the face of gross uncertainties. Education should help, but there is a strong element of truth in the claim that strategists are born rather than made. General William C. Westmoreland could be trained to direct troops efficiently; he could not be trained to perform with strategic excellence in the wise conduct of an unusually difficult war.

THE WORKING OF STRATEGIC EFFECT

Strategic performance is inescapable. The old saying that "you may not be interested in strategy, but strategy is interested in you" expresses an enduring verity. The alternative to good strategic performance can only be fair or poor strategic performance, not no strategic performance. "Engagements" of any and all kinds, conducted by every variety of armed force, have consequences for the course and outcome of a conflict; that is to say, they have a strategic effect, or they generate some quantity of strategic effectiveness. That is how strategy "works." Because some polities at some times behave as if strategy and strategists were an optional extra to fighting, and because strategy from its Greek origins (the art of the general)[33] implies purposeful and skillful direction, the true ubiquity of the phenomenon of strategic effect can evade notice.

Unplanned or ill-conducted engagements must have some influence upon the general progress, or lack of progress, registered on behalf of "the object of the war." Not only do the tactical and operational levels of war implement strategy, but even when there is no strategic direction worthy of the name, tactical and operational behavior has strategic effect, albeit one that is undirected centrally. This is not to downplay the significance of strategy, but it is to claim that strategic performance can only rest upon tactical performance. One need not, indeed should not, endorse all of Clausewitz's argument to appreciate the strength in his claim "that only great tactical successes can lead to great strategic ones; or as we have already said more specifically, *tactical* successes are of *paramount importance* in war."[34] My point is that whether or not enemy forces actually are destroyed or comprehensively defeated, indeed whether or not success attends our arms, tactical activity must have strategic effect.

NOTES

1. For example, H. P. Willmott, *The Great Crusade: A New Complete History of the Second World War* (New York: Free Press, 1989), p. xi.

2. Ronald H. Spector, *After Tet: The Bloodiest Year in Vietnam* (New York: Free Press, 1993), p. 314. Spector is a Marine Corps veteran of Vietnam.

3. Carl von Clausewitz, *On War*, ed. and trans. Michael Howard and Peter Paret (Princeton, NJ: Princeton University Press, 1976; first pub. 1832), pp. 88–89.

4. Ibid., p. 579.

5. See Colin S. Gray, "New Directions for Strategic Studies? How Can Theory Help Practice?" *Security Studies* 1, no. 4 (summer 1992): pp. 610–35.

6. Clausewitz, *On War*, p. 128.

7. John I. Alger, *Definitions and Doctrine of the Military Art, Past and Present* (Wayne, NJ: Avery Publishing, 1985), p. 5.

8. Martin van Creveld, *Nuclear Proliferation and the Future of Conflict* (New York: Free Press, 1993), p. 1.

9. Edward N. Luttwak, *Strategy: The Logic of War and Peace* (Cambridge, MA: Harvard University Press, 1987), p. 69.

10. See Julian S. Corbett, *Some Principles of Maritime Strategy* (Annapolis, MD: Naval Institute Press, 1988; first pub. 1911), pp. 10–11. The distinction between naval and maritime strategy is developed and exploited admirably in Jan S. Breemer, "Naval Strategy Is Dead," U.S. Naval Institute *Proceedings* 120, no. 2 (February 1994): pp. 49–53. Breemer argues that naval strategy (for the U.S. Navy) is dead because for the next few years, at least, there is no other navy in the world capable of menacing U.S. sea control. But circumstances will change. See the final point in Chapter 2 of this book.

11. See Martin Hollis and Steve Smith, *Explaining and Understanding International Relations* (Oxford: Clarendon Press, 1991).

12. For an earlier raid upon the topic discussed in this section, see Colin S. Gray, *War, Peace, and Victory: Strategy and Statecraft for the Next Century* (New York: Simon and Schuster, 1990), chap. 10, "Seeing the Problem Whole."

13. Consider French political goals in Indochina from 1946 to 1954 in relation to French political-military assets. The grim story may be approached most usefully via Bernard B. Fall, *Street Without Joy* (New York: Schocken Books, 1972; first pub. 1964); and *Hell in a Very Small Place: The Siege of Dien Bien Phu* (New York: Da Capo; first pub. 1967).

14. Clausewitz, *On War*, p. 610.

15. Ibid., p. 608.

16. See Peter Paret, *Clausewitz and the State* (New York: Oxford University Press, 1976).

17. As with modern Israel, Clausewitz's Prussia was awkwardly shaped geopolitically and lacked robust natural frontiers. The biasing influence of Prussia's distinctly continentalist geostrategic circumstances upon Clausewitz's theory of war has, in my opinion, yet to receive anything close to adequate recognition in commentaries upon the great man's thought. For example, Christopher Bassford, *Clausewitz in English: The Reception of Clausewitz in Britain and America, 1815–1945* (New York: Oxford University Press, 1994), generally is excellent, but it fails to consider properly the lack of a maritime dimension to Clausewitz's theorizing.

18. Colin S. Gray, *Weapons Don't Make War: Policy, Strategy, and Military Technology* (Lawrence: University Press of Kansas, 1993), chap. 4.

19. The geography of the Falkland Islands as a theater of war mandated a maritime strategy, but the military style of the British reconquest had the general character of "a commando operation writ large." Edward N. Luttwak, Steven L. Canby, and David L. Thomas, *A Systematic Review of "Commando" (Special) Operations, 1939–1980* (Potomac, MD: C and L Associates, 24 May 1982), p. P-2.

20. To acknowledge the merits of, indeed the necessity for, jointness and the importance of capabilities for military action in all geographical environments is not to be blind to the enduring fact of a maritime or continental tilt in a polity's strategic culture. I develop these thoughts in my book *The Navy in the Post–Cold War World: The Uses and Value of Strategic Sea Power* (University Park: Pennsylvania State University Press, 1994), chap. 4.

21. See Gray, *War, Peace, and Victory*, pp. 323–24; and David Hackett Fischer, *Historians' Fallacies: Toward a Logic of Historical Thought* (New York: Harper and Row, 1970), pp. 172–75.

22. Clausewitz, *On War*, p. 178.

23. Allegedly "immutable principles of strategy" are presented in Antoine Henri de Jomini, *The Art of War* (London: Greenhill Books, 1992; first pub. 1862), pp. 327–35.

24. Clausewitz, *On War*, p. 605.

25. Ibid., p. 178.

26. Ibid., p. 121.

27. Ibid., p. 119.

28. See David Ruelle, *Chance and Chaos* (Princeton, NJ: Princeton University Press, 1991); Stephen H. Kellert, *In the Wake of Chaos: Unpredictable Order in Dynamical Systems* (Chicago: University of Chicago Press, 1993); and Alan Beyerchen, "Clausewitz, Nonlinearity, and the Unpredictability of War," *International Security* 17, no. 3 (winter 1992/93): pp. 59–90.

29. Clausewitz, *On War*, p. 119.

30. For a wonderful case study of friction, and the overcoming of friction, in war, see John France, *Victory in the East: A Military History of the First Crusade* (Cambridge: Cambridge University Press, 1994). France concludes that it was the "growth of the coherence and experience of the crusader host as a whole which was the key to their military success" (p. 371). The crusaders won notwithstanding the superiority of their foes in weaponry, organization, logistics, and familiarity with terrain and climate. "But the divisions of their enemies meant that their weaknesses were never exposed fully and they were given time in which they became more and more experienced" (ibid).

31. Unlike Charles B. McClellan, who was way over his head as general-in-chief, Ian Hamilton and Archibald Wavell were both exceptionally able soldiers who were trapped in contexts exceptionally unforgiving of error, weakness, and plain bad luck. On Ian Hamilton, see E. K. G. Sixsmith, *British Generalship in the Twentieth Century* (London: Arms and Armour Press, 1970), chap. 8; and Eliot A. Cohen and John Gooch, *Military Misfortunes: The Anatomy of Failure in War* (New York: Free Press, 1990), chap. 6. Ian Beckett, "Wavell: Field-Marshal Earl Wavell," in John Keegan, ed.,

Churchill's Generals (New York: Grove Weidenfeld, 1991), chap. 4, is fair and persuasive.

32. Clausewitz believes that the determination necessary for success by a commander flows more from a "strong" than from a "brilliant" mind. *On War*, p. 103. Intelligence, even knowledge, and strength of character are not synonymous.

33. In Greek, *strategos* is a general; hence strategy means generalship. See Luttwak, *Strategy*, pp. 239–41.

34. Clausewitz, *On War*, p. 228 (emphasis in original).

Chapter 2

The Advantages and
Limitations of Sea Power:
British Defense in a Joint World

Jointness is the spirit of this age, but what does it mean for defense planning and military action? Strategic effect is the output, the universal currency, into which all tactical and operational behavior must be converted, but what does it imply for a particular country with a unique political-strategic culture? This chapter develops further some of the ideas introduced earlier, as well as some new ones, and explores their strategic meaning for Britain in the 1990s. The choices both of Britain and of the advantages and limitations of sea power are not arbitrary, but neither are they particularly significant. This discussion is an exploration in strategy that happens to focus upon the advantages and limitations of sea power for Britain. These specific points of reference should be viewed principally as illustrative, rather than determining. The important arguments presented here about balanced forces, the perils of defense planning, and the distinctive advantages and limitations of an environmentally specific form of military power, all lend themselves to a more general application.

My theme is a hardy, perennial one; indeed it was well aired in 1929 by Major-General Sir Frederick Maurice when he wrote:

> If, as the Field Service Regulations say, the prime object of the Army in war is "in cooperation with the Navy and the Air Force, to break down the resistance of the enemy's armed force in furtherance of the approved plan of campaign," it follows that the Army can be most effectively employed and our military power as a whole be most effectively exercised when our Army is within comparatively easy reach of the coast. Therefore in choosing the object of a war, when we have any liberty of choice, that particular feature of our power must be ever in our minds, and we should

be very chary of going far inland unless circumstances leave us no option in the matter.[1]

Those words must have made particularly poignant reading in the last weeks of May 1940.[2] Reorganized in question form, my theme reappears as the challenge, Should Britain's strategy and armed forces have a maritime "tilt"?

It is politically correct, as well as strategically prudent, to observe that today the prevention, and if need be the conduct, of war are both massively and invariably joint and typically combined in character. So much is both true and even obvious. Rather less obvious is what this joint military truth implies for a British military establishment that is ever more constrained in its resources. As always, the first challenge is to identify the right question.

The question is not how best to shape British defense policy, strategy, and military capabilities for the distinctly transitional conditions of the 1990s, essential though that is for immediate requirements. The complex question, rather, is how to shape British defense policy, strategy, and military capabilities so that they both yield the necessary strategic effect for the transitional period of the 1990s and provide a strategic legacy suitable for the future. Designs effected in this transitional period should be such as to provide a sound basis upon which the British strategic contribution to the next great balance-of-power struggle can be founded; that is the strategy challenge of most interest here.

History does not repeat itself, at least not in detail. Nonetheless, Britain in the 1990s, strategically viewed, is more than casually reminiscent of Britain in the peaceable Locarno era of the mid-1920s. As so often in defense debates, assumptions about the relevant time dimension are an underrecognized factor molding attitudes and opinions. Is the problem for British defense planners the military servicing of foreign policy in the 1990s, or is it preservation of the ability to respond tolerably promptly to the strategic consequences of this period? For a related thought, I suggest that the challenge today is not to reform NATO so that it becomes well crafted to cope with the deeply unsettled conditions of the 1990s. Truly NATO is far too important to risk the expending of its scarce political capital all but frivolously on Balkan quarrels. NATO should be reformed when we know how to reform it; which is to say, when we can discern the shape of the return of threats to our vital security interests.[3] The task today is to keep the NATO framework sufficiently alive so that it can be purposefully revived when bad times return, as surely they will.[4]

Whether or not a country—in this case, Britain—should have a maritime (or land or air) emphasis in its defense preparation, the whole character and circumstances of choice need to be considered holistically. The advantages and limitations of sea power (for Britain), therefore, are analyzed in an extensive prior discussion of the many dimensions of war, popular demands for "balanced forces," and the general challenges that make life difficult for defense planners.

DIMENSIONS OF WAR

The strategic history of the twentieth century can be deployed to illustrate many propositions, but one of the more striking contrasts is that between the complexity of the defense planner's world in the 1890s and today. A century ago the strategic world effectively was two-dimensional—to ignore the faint glimmer of more extensive possibilities—the land and the surface of the sea. By way of sharp contrast, today the defense planner must contend with five geographically distinctive dimensions of war, as well as with what could amount to a nuclear "wild card" that could trump otherwise successful nonnuclear performance. Today, therefore, the designs of the defense planner must accommodate the possibilities of conflict on land, at sea, in the air, in space, and on the electromagnetic spectrum. The need that Julian Corbett recognized and underlined for war at sea and war on land to be coordinated by preponderantly maritime or continental strategy[5] was a need frequently honored in the breach. How much more difficult it is today both to coordinate defense plans for the expanded dimensions of war and also to understand just what military prowess in one geographical medium implies for combat power elsewhere and for strategic effectiveness overall.

Contemporary sea power, for example, has so far co-opted the more maritime-relevant air power that it is a matter of choice to distinguish where the one ends and the other begins. Slowly, but inexorably, sea power is recognizing also that it must co-opt space power if it is to be competent on the frontier of information-age warfare.[6] It is difficult today to assess the relative military effectiveness, and hence the strategic potency, of sea power. Navies both fuse with air and space forces, as they always have done with amphibious forces, and are able to perform traditional naval tasks much more effectively because of the enabling action taken, say, in an air—and one day a space—campaign.

Defense analysis that declines to assume an end-to-end character from high policy to deployed forces and that has a noticeably truncated view of the sources of military effectiveness can fail to comprehend much of the joint nature of modern war. Sharp-end analysis, for example of the strategic bombing campaigns conducted in Europe and the western Pacific in World War II or of the air campaign against Iraq in 1991, can neglect to notice that those generally land-based air campaigns were, in effect, conducted as extensions of superior sea power.

Land power, sea power, air power, and space power are distinguishable, even though the potency of each typically depends upon the performance of one or more of the others; each (with the exception of space power) embraces well-established activities that would appear to belong more properly to another (e.g., navies with their own small armies and air forces); and each contributes more or less strategic effectiveness overall to the course and outcome of deterrence and war. It is possible to recognize the uncertainty of the margins between, say, sea power and air power, or land power and air power, as well as the many synergisms for improved performance that exist among the geographically specialized forces. It is also important, however, that appreciation of the scope for strategic choice should not be lost amidst such wise-sounding military ecumenicalism.

Uncertain margins duly recognized and the synergisms of "jointness" granted, still there are possibilities for choice among geostrategic emphases. The facts, for example, that all warfare ultimately must have landward reference, and that navies since 1940–41 could not perform their tasks in the absence of a tolerably benign air environment (cover for their overhead flank), most emphatically do not mean that sea power or maritime strategy now is bereft of identity or meaning. Even in the most challenging of cases for the tidy-minded theorist—that of superpower conflict wherein land-based intercontinental ballistic missiles (ICBM's) could threaten to function as very long-range artillery able to conduct barrage attacks against naval task forces and submarine-launched ballistic missiles (SLBM's) could threaten to neutralize the most continental of target arrays—still it makes sense to distinguish maritime from continental strategies.

J. F. C. Fuller insisted that of the five principal characteristics of a weapon, its range of effective action was by far the most significant.[7] In order to discuss the limitations and advantages of sea power, it is essential to acknowledge first that today both land power and sea power occasionally can find the reach to grasp each other's center of gravity ashore and afloat. Second, there can be no evasion of the complication posed by the emergence of a mature air power that truly has global range (though not for a sustained campaign, as contrasted with a raid or two). It is usual to compare maritime with continental strategies and, similarly, to think of national strategic-cultural orientation in terms of that binary choice. In the view of some commentators, however, a third choice finally has appeared. Early in 1991 some U.S. Air Force buildings displayed banners proclaiming "Douhet was right!" (Giulio Douhet, 1869–1930, was an Italian air power theorist who predicted victory through the use of air power). To quote the immortal words of the principal author of the 1991 Gulf War strategic air campaign, "[t]he world has just witnessed a new kind of warfare—hyperwar. It has seen air power become dominant."[8]

In a slightly less triumphalist view, Edward N. Luttwak proclaimed that "[a]irpower had finally done it."[9] Air power theorists in the United States have continued to seek vindication of service independence in the form of unmistakable evidence that independent action in and from the air can achieve decision in war.[10] This somewhat curious, and typically strategically forlorn, ambition may not be unique to air forces, but it is certainly strongly characteristic of them. The fact is that air power is important in virtually all conflicts and occasionally just might be the military executive agent for decisive success. More to the point, perhaps, air power's potency over an increasing range of operational contexts (not just over the desert or the sea on a clear day) implies a growing ability to function as the key force in deterrence or defense, the key force to which land, sea, and space elements strictly have only adjunct status. Nonetheless, the limitations and advantages of sea power find ample parallels in the actuality and even the potential of air power. For example, Rear Admiral J. C. Wylie may not be entirely correct when he writes that "*[t]he ultimate deterrent in war is the man on the scene with a gun*,"[11] but one knows what he means and one can appreciate what speed, altitude, and distance can mean for tenuousness of local control.

Politically, strategically, operationally, and tactically, each of the geographically distinctive dimensions of war enhances the performance of the others. Indeed, the strategic challenge often is to find ways to transmute excellence and success in one environment into good enough performance in one or more of the others. As Donald Kagan observed:

> The Peloponnesian War was one of those classic confrontations between a great land power and a great naval power. Each entered the war hoping and expecting to keep to its own element and to win a victory in a way that conformed to its strength at a relatively low cost. Within a few years events showed that victory would not be possible that way for either side. To win, each had to acquire the capacity to fight and succeed on the other's favorite domain.[12]

The virtues of jointness suggested by fashion and good manners, as well as by common sense, can, however, be overstated. It is true to claim that because the seat of political purpose must rest on land, sea power, air power, and space power typically will play enabling roles, which is to say military roles that enable conflict to be concluded successfully on land. But contrary to the apparent implication of that point, advantage at sea, in the air, or in space literally may provide a decisive edge in war overall.

To grasp the joint nature of warfare is all very well, but general truths can be less than compelling when applied to particular historical choices in policy and defense planning. It is one thing to assert the essential unity of deterrence and war and the many synergisms that work among their different dimensions; it is quite another to know what that should mean for actual historical choices.[13] Not all policymakers and defense planners find much comfort in

Carl von Clausewitz's conclusion that "[t]heory cannot equip the mind with formulas for solving problems, nor can it mark the narrow path on which the sole solution is supposed to lie by planting a hedge of principles on either side. But it can give the mind insight into the great mass of phenomena and of their relationships, then leave it free to rise into the higher realms of action."[14]

Typical scholarly evasion, one might think. The scholar explains the structure of the problem and thereby helps educate the minds of those who must make discrete choices on policy, on forces, or on the taking of action. The great man was correct, of course, though not in a way that busy officials find most useful. The rather bounded utility of Clausewitz's reasoning helps explain the longstanding popularity of the more positivist view of theorizing represented by Baron Antoine Henri de Jomini,[15] a tradition continued by Alfred Thayer Mahan[16] and—in our time—perpetuated and perpetrated by "stability theorists" from the intellectual stable of the RAND Corporation in the 1950s and after.[17]

The sheer complexity of the multidimensionality of war poses puzzles for peace with security. It may be true that the five dimensions of war function synergistically for the enhancement of strategic effectiveness overall, but what does it mean? If everything enhances everything else, what should one buy? A helpful guide through what otherwise can be an impenetrable thicket of ideas on jointness and combined arms lies in a sensible approach to the long-familiar concept of balanced forces.

BALANCED FORCES

Balanced forces is a familiar item in the credo of politically correct modern strategic thinking: "I believe in the principle of jointness, and in balanced forces that sometimes will be combined," and so on. Rarely is it entirely self-evident just what is meant, let alone implied, by the endorsement of balanced forces. It sounds like a politician's concept. Few people are inclined or willing to stand up for *unbalanced* forces; indeed, if you are sufficiently careful in your lack of precision, you will never need to do so. In common with stability, the notion of balance can mean virtually whatever you wish it to mean. Since the superpowers negotiated about strategic weapons off and on for more than twenty years without benefit of an agreement on what was stabilizing and what was not,[18] perhaps the indeterminacy of balanced forces should not be cause for surprise. I will attempt to advance the argument by suggesting five nonexclusive meanings for the concept of balanced forces.

First, forces need to be balanced for their external strategic integrity rather than their internal beauty. The latter is not to be despised, but it stands to external integrity much as tactical prowess stands to strategic effect. Whatever their composition, the armed forces exist primarily to serve as a more or less complex instrument of the grand strategy of the state; they are not funded to function as a well-oiled machine that is an end in itself. Military power, therefore, should be balanced against best estimates of the country's need for it. Not for nothing is mass, or concentration, cited as a principle of war: numbers matter. A naval establishment may be wonderfully balanced internally among its constituent parts—in a happily clockwork strategic universe—but there may be too little of it to deter, and if need be fight, the queen's enemies.

Second, and to be more respectful of a clockwork universe, armed forces do need to be balanced as a military machine. Land-based elements for the conduct of an air campaign may require the supply of fuel and ordnance by sea; naval forces operating far beyond ready sustenance from shore establishments require the assistance of a fleet train;[19] and so forth. Whatever the mix chosen among environmentally specialized forces, whatever the trend in joint doctrine and combined arrangements, the country's armed forces have to "work" in combat if they are to serve the national or coalition security well enough. It is essential, however, that the understandable fascination in peacetime with the internal integrity of forces, so that they can work well tactically and operationally, should not unduly obscure their strategic function.

Third, the armed forces need to be balanced against the calculated demands that could be placed upon them across a more or less extensive range of conflict scenarios. Most profoundly, this is a matter for judgment in foreign policy. It is not for the armed forces to try to decide how intense may be the national interests possibly engaged here or there in the future. Nonetheless, the armed forces, suitably joint in orientation and hopefully combined usefully with the forces of other polities, have to be developed so as to be balanced for deterrence or defense vis-à-vis several different kinds of conflicts, most probably in diverse geographical contexts. The spectrum of conflict extends from the unpleasantness that can attend humanitarian intervention, through local and regional quarrels, up to and including the appearance of yet another balance-of-(great)-power struggle.

Fourth, the armed forces should be balanced for tolerable fit with unique national strategic preferences and needs, as well as to exploit national strengths and provide suitable cover for national weaknesses. In other words, consistent with the generation of an overall strategic effectiveness adequate to support foreign policy, the British armed forces should be balanced expediently for comfort and convenience with British strategic culture: they should reflect British geostrategic circumstances, traditions, habits of mind, and proven effective practices.[20] That may sound unduly conservative, romantic even, or both; really it is just prudent. One does not have to endorse a particular view of British strategic culture that Julian Corbett derived significantly from his study of the Seven Years' War,[21] or that Basil Liddell Hart latched upon in his repudiation of Britain's continental role during World War I,[22] to find value in the concept of a British way of war. Similarly, the exaggeration of the maritime dimension in British policy and grand strategy by Corbett and Liddell Hart should not blind us to the exaggeration of the continental dimension that one finds in the analyses of such distinguished scholars as Paul Kennedy and Sir Michael Howard.[23] Even if one does not theorize about this century, assuredly one theorizes from this century. This century has, of course, underlined the periodically appalling scale of the continental dimension to Britain's security problems.

Fifth and finally, the armed forces need to be balanced by strategic reasoning, rather than arithmetically. The principle of balance could suggest scales that measure equal weights. Plainly, the country should not seek to invest in armed forces neatly balanced among themselves in terms of resource inputs or even performance outputs. Who cares whether service budgets are arithmetically equal, any more than whether or not British land power, sea power, and air power all generate like amounts of combat power? These standards would be absurd. The armed forces need balance to meet the strategic demands of such conflicts that foreign policy insists they enter.

I have not suggested here that Britain's forces should be so balanced for comfortable fit with dominant national strategic culture that they become massively specialized (indeed overspecialized) for operation in and from one geographical environment only. Having said that, I must add that what might be called "full service" armies, navies, and air forces can provide an impressive flexibility in their ability to influence military events in the other environments. Often there are alternative military ways of performing tasks for foreign policy. Land power, sea power, air power, and one day even space power are no more rigorously mutually distinctive than are land powers, sea powers, or, putatively, air powers or space powers. Most polities have some land, sea, and air power. The questions are how much of each do they have and is there a dominant geostrategic orientation for each of them?

It is useful to descend from the great abstractions in order to cite two significant caveats. First, grand theory, no matter how valid at its own elevated level of analysis, is always vulnerable to embarrassment in particular historical cases. The trends in events that could produce conflicts which Britain would decide it must join in some capacity would be no more random than would the pertinent British foreign policy decisions. Nonetheless, the future can only be anticipated by classes of possibilities; it cannot be predicted in detail. One can always point to the truly exceptional conflict that might generate strategic demands the country could meet only by monumentally adaptive military practices. (A particularly clear example is the size, scale, and duration of Britain's continental commitment in the Great War).[24] If so much is granted, still the country should not, indeed politically could not, "balance" its defense preparation to fit the emergence of what would amount to a truly *super* threat.[25]

The second caveat is that just because one can identify a range of possible conflicts of more than passing interest to Britain, and just because competent military performance in those conflicts would require a joint style of operation of a most testing kind, it does not follow necessarily that Britain either needs to intervene at all or would need to intervene with decisively effective British forces in all environments. These thoughts introduce the subject that can be deferred no longer, policy guidance and defense planning.

THE PERILS OF DEFENSE PLANNING

I am enough of a positivist to be suspicious when I read that the leitmotif for defense planning is the need to cope with the unexpected or to manage uncertainty. It used to be said that the coronation of uncertainty as a strategic principle governing NATO's concept of flexible response was all too appropriate, given the mental confusion in NATO capitals. If NATO's response was unpredictable even to itself, how much more uncertain must it have seemed to Soviet statesmen?

It is all very well to speak seemingly wisely and prudently about preparing for the unexpected, but what does, or should, that mean in terms that could lend themselves pragmatically to assist the defense planner? Where are the boundaries of the unexpected? Are they an asteroid strike from space; a nuclear-armed ultranationalist like Vladimir Zhirinovsky insecurely in command of the Russian ship of state; a United States which decides it has done its duty often enough in this century for the balance of power and world order?

There is a wide menu of options for the conduct of defense and force planning; there is a methodology to suit most tastes.[26] All defense planning methodologies, however, lack a quality that is key to the purposeful integrity of the enterprise. Namely, political guidance expressing foreign policy judgment has to be provided as an input for defense planning. Defense planning does not have integrity unto itself.

Field Marshal Sir Nigel Bagnall writes that "over the centuries identifying a nation's future strategic priorities has proved to be a very imprecise art, and as a result peacetime force structures have seldom proved relevant when put to the test of war."[27] That is a harsh judgment, but one that is probably correct and certainly well worth worrying about. There is no magical elixir that a defense planner can imbibe that will allow him to distinguish the fanciful from the real future. Nonetheless, it is possible to offer some general thoughts that approximate in spirit, at least, what Clausewitz identified as the character and purpose of theory: "Theory exists so that one need not start afresh each time sorting out the material and plowing through it, but will find it ready to hand and in good order. It is meant to educate the mind of the future commander or, more accurately, to guide him in his self-education, not to accompany him to the battlefield."[28]

First, an approach suitable to cope with the unexpected, with uncertainty, excludes the foolish and impracticable pursuit of surprise avoidance. The future is full of surprises, some pleasant (the collapse of the evil empire of the U.S.S.R.), some unpleasant (the persistence and violence of intra-Balkan hatreds), most of which will carry little, if any, obvious meaning for British defense policy. However, although one cannot plan against surprise, one can plan against many of the worst of predictable surprise effects.[29] For example, the precise identity and timing of a modestly scaled, but possibly not modestly armed, ballistic missile threat either to British forces or to Britain itself at home cannot be predicted; British policymakers will be surprised in detail. Nonetheless, those policymakers can prepare prudently and quite effectively to neutralize the effects of such surprise.

Although history is inconveniently more than cyclical but less than arrowlike,[30] still a great deal about the future that should be of interest to the defense planner is identifiable in general terms. With a suitable bow to the fashionable chaos theory that alerts us to possible nonlinearity in events,[31] the continuities in the conditions that shape statecraft and strategy remain impressive and are worth recalling. For the leading example, geography in all its aspects and implications for policy, as well as culture and the preferences it teaches and expresses, means that the defense planner and his political masters do not confront a tabula rasa when they wonder what the late 1990s may bring. It is an instructive exercise to identify what is known in useful detail, and what is unknown in useful detail, in order to see what information is available as a planning aid. Needless to add, perhaps, one will be aware that it may be an unknown that poses the most severe of challenges. The world of nuclear planning was troubled time after time by the discovery of hitherto unknown or underappreciated weapon effects. The defense planner cannot know exactly what will be demanded of the armed forces or when; but he should have a reasonable idea concerning the why, the where, the who, and even—in general, but still useful, terms—the kind of what.

Second, it so happens that we do know important things about the future security environment. We know, for example, that bad times return; perhaps the 1990s will disprove this dictum, but the smart money is on the continuing validity of the lessons of the better part of three millennia. Also, we know that the purportedly novel primacy of issues of economic and environmental (and other types of) security over traditional matters of military security almost certainly reflects the confusion of an extraordinary, temporary period, with some permanent "sea change" in the security affairs of humankind. Of necessity, military power is built on economic power, but at any particular historical juncture, military power will come up trumps: guns outrank fat purses.

Third, a British policymaker or defense planner cannot know precisely when, where, or by whom British interests will be in peril. But, following as much of Sun Tzu's wise counsel as should prove practicable, he can know himself and his own society in advance of certain knowledge of the enemy.[32] He can specify the hierarchy of national interests—from those of a "survival" down to an "other" category—which, in descending order, are more and then less likely to require military support. It is interesting, but not crucial, for defense planners to acquire improved understanding of the unfolding character of the global security environment. The crucial question is, what does this unfolding character mean for Britain? A national-interest discriminator has to be applied by the makers of foreign policy.

Fourth, Britain remains very much a maritime country. The international trade upon which the prosperity of its industrial society depends overwhelmingly is, as it always has been, a maritime international trade. For heavy or bulky goods, Mahan remains authoritative in his 1890 judgment that "both travel and traffic by water have always been easier and cheaper than by land."[33] Married to the continuity of the seas and oceans and the continuing comparative advantage of sea transportation in ton-mile costs, Britain's insular geostrategic condition all but ensures the necessity for a maritime framework to its foreign security endeavors. Unless allies are most logistically competent and accommodating or the mission has the character of a special operation (which is to say it is very small in scale, brief, and stealthy), the center of gravity for British strategic effectiveness has to remain maritime.

Fifth, whatever statesmen may prefer by way of policy logic in guidance for their defense planners, there is, following Clausewitz, a "grammar" to military affairs that can and should impose itself upon defense plans.[34] For example, if Luttwak is correct in his judgment that "air power had finally done it" in the Gulf War in 1991, what, if anything, does that imply for the relative weight of investment that air power merits in our defense future? Although it is unwise to draw sweeping conclusions and to rewrite doctrine on the basis of one campaign that may or may not have lessons of wider validity, surely it would be unwise to ignore relationships visible in the latest active passage of arms on a large scale. Just because every war is waged in unique conditions, it does not follow that its military meaning is utterly distinctive.

The joint and combined arms stories evolve. Defense planners need to monitor evidence and argument concerning the relative combat prowess and significance of both the different dimensions of war and the different components to each dimension. A trouble with revolutions in military affairs is that they are never historically precisely bounded, nor are they universal in their authority. Consider the longstanding debate over the survivability of surface ships.[35] Strategic, operational, and tactical contexts are everything. The tactical relationship between surface ships and their foes must alter with the political identities of the adversaries (whose surface ships and whose weapons menace them?) and the highly variable geography of potential combat. Similarly, debate over the future of "heavy" land forces in the army needs to be informed by awareness of the trends in net tactical advantage between armored fighting vehicles and their enemies (antitank guns, helicopters, infantry antitank missile systems, mines, and new unconventional weapons). But a general trend that plainly leans to the tank's disadvantage may well mean little in a particular place, at a particular time, against a particular enemy not well equipped to neutralize tanks and armored personnel carriers.

The strategic history of this century shows that defense planning is a perilous enterprise. More often than not, those providing defense guidance and the planners themselves were significantly in error. This is not the place in which to explore why that should be so, but it is the place to register the fact. Why were Field Marshal Helmuth von Moltke (the elder) and Lord Kitchener so lonely in their prescience about the probable duration of World War I? A systematic study of the better and the worse among prewar expectations would be a worthwhile enterprise—even though most probably it would reveal no common methodology producing success, but rather the statistical point that someone had to get it right.

THE ADVANTAGES AND LIMITATIONS OF SEA POWER

Those who engage in public debate over strategy are painfully aware of the significance of context (theoretical, political, strategic, operational, tactical) for authority of argument. Good ideas instantly can become bad ideas if they are shifted from a general concept of operations to alleged operational propositions. For example, would the U.S. Navy charge far into the Norwegian Sea with irreplaceable aircraft carriers against a Cold War–era Soviet foe with his defenses unattrited and fully prepared; in short, would the navy attempt a maritime "charge of the Light Brigade"?[36] To win the battle of the context for debate is to win the debate itself.

Five arguments or points serve to close this discussion. First, each kind of geographically focused armed force has distinctive general advantages and limitations, albeit advantages and limitations that carry different weights in different cases of conflict. The limitations of sea power are summarized in Table 2.1.

For positive contrast, the advantages granted by superior sea power are itemized tersely in Table 2.2.

For the sake of comparison, similar lists can be developed for the other forms of military power. When thinking about the general limitations and advantages pertaining to each form of military power, it is instructive to conduct a four-way analysis. Specifically, land power, sea power, air power, space power, special operations, and nuclear forces can each be analyzed in terms of what it

Table 2.1
Limitations of Sea Power

1. Essentially an enabling agent
2. Difficulty gripping continental foes
3. Strategically slow in operation
4. Tactically relatively slow
5. High expense of platforms means few platforms and therefore modest-scale distribution of value
6. Weather

Table 2.2
Advantages of Sea Power

1. Flexibility, mobility, adaptability
2. Endurance on station
3. Enables global strategy
4. Noncommitting, continuous presence
5. Places strategic frontier close to enemy's coastline
6. Provides means to bind together global coalition and provides interior lines of communication

uniquely can perform; cannot perform at all; tends to perform well; and tends to perform poorly.

Second, the armed forces plan to perform jointly and in combined arms contexts precisely so as to offset their distinctive limitations. The whole point in developing a variety of armed forces is that a country can enjoy the benefits both of specialization and of complementarity.

Third, if Britain is obliged to choose where the balance should lie among the several geographically focused dimensions of war, the limitations of sea power are more bearable and culturally and strategically more tolerable than would be the limitations of land power or air power as the leading edge of military prowess.[37]

Fourth, this analysis has had as its center of gravity the question of sea power in relation to land power and air power for Britain today. The subject here is not the strategic utility of sea power versus land power versus air power versus space power, at some abstract, free-floating level of strategic assay.

Fifth and finally, the argument here has avoided contention over sea control vis-à-vis power projection, in good part because there is not much worthy of discussion in that realm. Jan Breemer is wrong. Naval strategy is not "dead;"[38] rather, it is resting pending the next call to action when bad times return to world politics, as surely they will.

NOTES

1. Frederick Maurice, *British Strategy: A Study of the Application of the Principles of War* (London: Constable, 1927), pp. 85–86.

2. The bulk of the British Expeditionary Force was very nearly definitively cut off from the sea on 22 May 1940. The actual order to evacuate from Dunkirk was not issued by the British government until 26 May. Amidst a huge literature, I recommend Gregory Blaxland, *Destination Dunkirk: The Story of Gort's Army* (London: Military Book Society, 1973); Michael Glover, *The Fight for the Channel Ports, Calais to Brest 1940: A Study in Confusion* (Boulder, CO: Westview Press, 1985); and Telford Taylor, *The March of Conquest: The German Victories in Western Europe, 1940* (Baltimore, MD: Nautical and Aviation Publishing Company of America, 1991; first pub. 1958).

3. Charles L. Glaser, "Why NATO Is Still Best: Future Security Arrangements for Europe," *International Security* 18, no. 1 (summer 1993): 5–50, generally is sound.

4. See Colin S. Gray, *Villains, Victims, and Sheriffs: Strategic Studies and Security for an Inter-War Period, An Inaugural Lecture* (Hull, England: University of Hull Press, 1996).

5. Julian S. Corbett, *Some Principles of Maritime Strategy* (Annapolis, MD: Naval Institute Press, 1988; first pub. 1911).

6. A thesis I develop in "Vision for Naval Space Strategy," *U.S. Naval Institute Proceedings* 120, no. 1 (January 1994): 63–68.

7. An argument advanced in J. F. C. Fuller, *Armament and History: A Study of the Influence of Armament on History from the Dawn of Classical Warfare to the Second World War* (London: Eyre and Spottiswoode, 1946).

8. John A. Warden III, "Employing Air Power in the Twenty-First Century," in Richard H. Shultz, Jr., and Robert L. Pfaltzgraff, Jr., eds., *The Future of Air Power in the Aftermath of the Gulf War* (Maxwell Air Force Base, AL: Air University Press, July 1992), p. 81.

9. Edward N. Luttwak, "Air Power in U.S. Military Strategy," in Richard H. Shultz, Jr., and Robert L. Pfaltzgraff, Jr., eds., *The Future of Air Power in the Aftermath of the Gulf War* (Maxwell Air Force Base, AL: Air University Press, July 1992), p. 19.

10. Carl H. Builder, *The Icarus Syndrome: The Role of Air Power Theory in the Evolution and Fate of the U.S. Air Force* (New Brunswick, NJ: Transaction Publishers, 1994), is a fascinating near inside examination of the soul of the U.S. Air Force.

11. J. C. Wylie, *Military Strategy: A General Theory of Power Control* (Annapolis, MD: Naval Institute Press, 1989; first pub. 1967), p. 72 (emphasis in original).

12. Donald Kagan, *The Fall of the Athenian Empire* (Ithaca, NY: Cornell University Press, 1987), p. 423.

13. See Michael D. Hobkirk, *Land, Sea or Air? Military Priorities, Historical Choices* (London: Macmillan, 1992).

14. Carl von Clausewitz, *On War*, ed. and trans. Michael Howard and Peter Paret (Princeton, NJ: Princeton University Press, 1976; first pub. 1832), p. 578.

15. Antoine Henri de Jomini, *The Art of War* (London: Greenhill Books, 1992; first pub. 1862); John I. Alger, *The Quest for Victory: The History of the Principles of War* (Westport, CT: Greenwood Press, 1982); and Michael I. Handel, *Masters of War: Sun Tzu, Clausewitz and Jomini* (London: Frank Cass, 1992), are useful.

16. Alfred Thayer Mahan, *The Influence of Sea Power upon History, 1660–1783* (London: Methuen, 1965; first pub. 1890).

17. See Marc Trachtenberg, *History and Strategy* (Princeton, NJ: Princeton University Press, 1991), chap. 1; and Colin S. Gray, "The Holistic Strategist," *Global Affairs* 7, no. 1 (winter 1992): 171–82.

18. "While negotiating START in 1987–91, the parties were not operating on any mutual understanding of the meaning of 'stability.' . . . only at the final stages of talks did the Americans and Soviets arrive at a common definition of strategic stability, albeit a general and vague one." Alexei G. A. Arbatov, "We Could Have Done Better," *Bulletin of the Atomic Scientists* 47 (November 1991): 37.

19. See Geoffrey Marcus, *Quiberon Bay: The Campaign in Home Waters, 1759* (London: Hollis and Carter, 1960), p. 66.

20. For example, David French, *The British Way in Warfare, 1688–2000* (London: Unwin Hyman, 1990). A more skeptical view is A. D. Harvey, *Collision of Empires: Britain in Three World Wars, 1793–1945* (London: Hambledon Press, 1992).

21. Julian S. Corbett, *England in the Seven Years' War: A Study in Combined Strategy*, 2 vols. (London: Longmans, Green, 1918; first pub. 1907); and *Some Principles of Maritime Strategy*.

22. Basil Liddell Hart, *The British Way in Warfare* (London: Faber and Faber, 1932), chap. 1; and *History of the First World War* (London: Pan Books, 1972; first pub. 1930).

23. Paul Kennedy, *The Rise and Fall of British Naval Mastery* (New York: Charles Scribner's Sons, 1976); and Michael Howard, *The Causes of Wars and Other Essays* (London: Counterpoint, 1984; first pub. 1983), pp. 189–207, "The British Way in Warfare: A Reappraisal." More recently, Paul Kennedy has noted that "[t]his further swing in the historiography [toward the continental aspect of British grand strategy], if continued, suggests that the danger may soon, or already, be that scholars become too dismissive of the influence of sea power upon history and thus explain away the popularity of Mahan's ideas as being simply due to the heady expectations of that 'age of navalism' which occurred in the two decades prior to the First World War." "The Influence and the Limitations of Sea Power," *International History Review* 10, no. 1 (February 1988): 7.

24. See Michael Howard, *The Continental Commitment: The Dilemma of British Defence Policy in the Era of the Two World Wars* (London: Temple Smith, 1972), especially p. 57.

25. I pursue this thought in my *Weapons Don't Make War: Policy, Strategy, and Military Technology* (Lawrence: University Press of Kansas, 1993), pp. 95–99, "Super Threats."

26. The contemporary bible comprises the three-volume set edited by the Force Planning Faculty, Naval War College, *Fundamentals of Force Planning*, vol. I, *Concepts*; vol. II, *Defense Planning Cases*; vol. III, *Strategy and Resources* (Newport, RI: Naval War College Press, 1990–1992).

27. Field Marshal Sir Nigel Bagnall, foreword to Hobkirk, *Land, Sea or Air?*, p. x.

28. Clausewitz, *On War*, p. 141.

29. Liddell Hart, *History of the First World War*, p. 325.

30. I am grateful to Stephen Jay Gould, *Time's Arrow, Time's Cycle* (Cambridge: Harvard University Press, 1987).

31. For bold ventures into strategic application, see Stephen R. Mann, "Chaos Theory and Strategic Thought," *Parameters* 22, no. 3 (autumn 1992): 54–68; and David Nicholls and Todor D. Tagarev, "What Does Chaos Theory Mean for Warfare?" *Airpower Journal* 8, no. 3 (fall 1994): 48–57.

32. Sun Tzu, *The Art of War*, trans. Ralph D. Sawyer (Boulder, CO: Westview Press, 1994), p. 179. "[O]ne who does not know the enemy but knows himself will sometimes be victorious, sometimes meet with defeat."

33. Mahan, *Influence of Sea Power upon History, 1660–1783*, p. 25.

34. Clausewitz, *On War*, p. 605.

35. For an unpersuasive, though then trendy, belief in an "empty ocean," see John Keegan, *The Price of Admiralty: The Evolution of Naval Warfare* (New York: Viking Penguin, 1989; first pub. 1988), pp. 266–75.

36. See Jack Beatty, "In Harm's Way," *Atlantic*, May 1987, pp. 37–46, 48–49, and 52–53. Robert S. Wood, "Fleet Renewal and Maritime Strategy in the 1980s," in John B. Hattendorf and Robert S. Jordan, eds., *Maritime Strategy and the Balance of Power: Britain and America in the Twentieth Century* (New York: St. Martin's Press, 1989), pp. 330–55, provides an effective reply.

37. I recognize that this is an assertion. In this chapter I have not sought to demonstrate the plausibility of the claim. My purpose here has been restricted to exploration of the strategic challenge posed by the limitations of one kind of military power. For the record, I believe that maritime—not continental or aerial—strategy provides the most appropriate framework for British defense planning in the future, notwithstanding the fact that the strategic world is both joint and combined in nature.

38. Jan S. Breemer, "Naval Strategy Is Dead," U.S. Naval Institute *Proceedings* 120, no. 2 (February 1994): 49–53.

Chapter 3

Is Deterrence Reliable?

No book aspiring to present explorations in strategy could be complete without some extended treatment of deterrence. I bow to common usage and refer to deterrence as a strategy. In fact, deterrence is the desired effect of strategy; it is not strategy itself. Deterrent effect is indirect influence over the behavior of others.[1] Direct effect would be actual physical coercion. Whether or not a particular strategic bridge between means and ends produces deterrence must always be in some measure uncertain.

Because deterrence, particularly so-called stable deterrence,[2] was the center-piece of nuclear-age strategic thought and intended practice for more than forty years of superpower Cold War, it is a subject of theoretical, and even some empirical, enquiry that is relatively mature. Indeed, deterrence is a subject on which probably far too many words have been written already.[3] From that admittedly unpromising beginning, this exploration in strategy ventures to attempt a nonroutine "physical" on the health of the patient.

Such confidence as one had in deterrence in the context of East-West strategic relations in the Cold War looks distinctly optimistic for these post–Cold War years. Moreover, even if one is confident that deterrence is robust, it is only prudent to assume that that is not the case, given the potential costs of an erroneous assumption.

How good, which is to say how useful, is the strategic theory of deterrence? How do we know how good the theory of deterrence has proved to be? How much of the common knowledge on the working of deterrence is perilously narrow in its basis of historical evidence? Finally, if deterrence is not adequately reliable, what might, perhaps should, be done to offset the possible consequences of that claimed fact? One needs to beware of counsels of perfection. The reliability of deterrence is a quality that can be assessed only subjectively and it applies on a sliding scale. Deterrence is not a phenomenon with a simple binary structure, reliable or unreliable. Similarly, threats intended to deter do not divide neatly into credible and incredible.

ON DETERRENCE: SOME BASICS

Conceptual confusion is responsible for a great deal of misunderstanding of deterrence. The most important point to appreciate is that, almost paradoxically, deterrence embraces a cooperative relationship that works through contingent explicit or implicit menaces. Deterrence works when a person, organization, or state decides not to take a particular course of action because the net consequences are judged likely to be unduly negative. In deterrence one is dealing with a would-be "deterrer" and an intended "deterree." The intended deterree, the designated partner in a deterrence relationship, has a choice and in fact is likely to have several choices. He may choose not to be deterred. Or, assuming that there are transaction costs for the would-be deterrer, the intended deterree may seek to bargain and comply only partially with the demand issued with menaces. To neglect the cooperative dimension of deterrence is to miss much of the action in the argument over reliability. Deterrence is not, and cannot be, reliable in part because the intended deterree has to agree to be deterred. If the intended deterree is either unwilling or unable to be deterred, then deterrence cannot work.

The concept, the theory, and the practice of deterrence are not unique to the nuclear age, to the Cold War, or to nuclear issues.[4] There is no doubt, however, that the explicit elevation of deterrence to the status of key idea was an intellectual and policy innovation of the post-1945 world order as viewed from the West.[5] It remains an open question whether prenuclear or even contemporary and future nonnuclear contexts for deterrence differ radically from nuclear cases. The extraordinary character of nuclear weapons, weapons which allegedly disconnect policy from military power,[6] arguably may so distort debate over the efficacy of deterrence as to render uncertain the general validity of evidence, insights, and conclusions derived narrowly from nuclear circumstances. To repeat, that is an open question. If nuclear weapons have the "crystal ball" effect of allowing no sane, sober, and halfway prudent statesman to entertain daydreams of politically meaningful victory,[7] what might that imply for the predictive or explanatory value of nuclear cases of deterrence for nonnuclear cases? Most likely the answer is that intellectually nothing changes, but the practical implications potentially are extensive. There are many reasons why deterrence can be unreliable, but a massive reduction in the scale of damage that could be suffered, or at least a massive increase in the time scale required to wreak extensive damage, could not help but enhance that unreliability. Deterrence theory, preferably an intellectually superior deterrence theory, should be relevant to all eras and climes,[8] but it is going to lend itself to effective practical application more in some contexts than in others.

Cooperation for Deterrence

Several of the more common confusions about deterrence need to be eliminated at the outset of this discussion. Because deterrence flows from a relationship, it cannot reside in unilateral capabilities, behavior, or intentions. Anyone who refers to *the* deterrent plainly does not understand the subject. It is but common sense to affirm that nuclear-armed aircraft and missiles have functioned in some unquantifiable measure as "the great deterrent,"[9] but intended deterrees may believe, rightly or wrongly, that "the great deterrent" would not be unleashed upon them. No less important, the intended deterrees may decide that national death is preferable to dishonor. The targets of nuclear threats intended to deter may believe, on a rational basis, that their country can best serve the cause of historical progress by taking its nuclear punishment. For example, a Soviet army engineer, Colonel Semykin, has written about the 1962 Cuban missile crisis that "[t]he Cubans really insisted we use our weapons. 'Why else did you come here? Use your weapons. Fire.' They were ready for war. Maybe they believed so strongly, they were ready to sacrifice themselves. They would say, 'Cuba will perish, but socialism will win.' They were ready to sacrifice themselves."[10] Military capabilities that reasonable people, which is to say "us," believe should deter—matched with contingent plans to employ them—in fact may not deter. Nothing is inherently deterring.

Deterrence does not have to be packaged as a purposeful strategy in order to work. Whether or not we think of our forces and describe them as a deterrent, indeed whether or not we have consciously sought to establish a relationship of deterrence, still we may deter. What matters is what the other party chooses to believe and then do or not do. The quality of our forces for deterrence is decided abroad, not at home.

Deterrence and Defense

Confusion persists about the respective meanings of deterrence and defense (or denial, in practice generally a synonym for defense).[11] Defense, or denial, is a theory of deterrence. Broadly, there are two theories of deterrence, punishment or denial. In principle, a candidate enemy may be deterrable either by the threat to punish him in ways that hurt him very badly or by the threat to defeat his armed forces in the field and thereby deny him achievement of his objectives. The theory of deterrence by defense or denial often is called, or miscalled, a "war-fighting" theory.[12]

The war-fighting label can mislead people into believing that alternatives to it somehow are of a non-war-fighting kind. In practice, anybody who endorses the contingent use of (nuclear) weapons, no matter what theory of deterrence informs his targeting preferences, also endorses a war-fighting philosophy. Whether one elects to fight a war by bombing cities or bombing military targets—if the two are distinguishable—is beside the point.

Common Security, Common Deterrence, and Security Dilemmas

It has become fashionable, and probably it is orthodox now among professors, to argue that the real meaning of the nuclear revolution must include the key insight that deterrence, like security, is now common, rather than mutual, let alone unilateral.[13] The peril lies in the context of the nuclear revolution. The details of a potential or actual enemy's military posture pale into insignificance compared with the awesome and awful fact of nuclear danger. The relevant image might be of two people fighting with open-flame torches in a room soaked in gasoline or strewn liberally with gunpowder. The fine-grained detail of difference between the combatants' lit torches matters scarcely at all in comparison to the common peril guaranteed by the gasoline- or gunpowder-impregnated battlefield.

The thesis of a common deterrence is cited because it contains obvious merit, because it has become a politically significant argument, and because it has important implications for public policy and, ipso facto, for the proper terms of debate about that policy. Overall, however, I find the thesis of a common deterrence and a common security less than thoroughly compelling. The more vociferous advocates of these notions tend to be people whose judgment on defense matters I do not greatly respect. Undoubtedly there are people who could be trusted with a common-deterrence or common-security perspective, but those are not the people in the front rank with this thesis.

One may recall the well-known postulate of the so-called security dilemma.[14] The dilemma, purportedly, lies in the unfortunate paradox that by endeavoring to increase my security, I may decrease your security. That unhappy consequence will prompt you, in your turn, to take unilateral steps to increase your security which, inexorably, must reduce my security, and so on. The logic of the security dilemma is elegant, simple, and persuasive, yet fraught with traps for the unwary. Writings on the security dilemma by scholars such as Robert Jervis in the United States and Barry Buzan and Ken Booth in Britain should carry a public-policy health warning. Security-dilemma thinking, along with the common-deterrence and common-security postulates, neglects to distinguish politically and ideologically among the state or coalition players. In short, this way of thinking about the rough world of international security is liable to miss the action that really matters.

The peril, according to security-dilemma logic, is that state players thinking unilaterally and for the short term inadvertently will stimulate other polities into taking unilateral and short-term decisions on defense, to the disadvantage of them all. The real peril, however, is not that states foolishly will diminish their security as the unintended consequence of attempting to improve it, but rather that would-be rogue states will not be adequately opposed. The logic of the security dilemma is a relatively minor problem compared with the danger of underpreparation by the forces of order. Moreover, the elegant simplicity of the security dilemma can work to discourage a prudent recognition of the need to deter and deny an aggressor. If our strategic culture is permeated with sophisticated anxiety about security dilemmas, guess who is unlikely to take early and appropriate action on behalf of civilized values?[15]

The logic of the security dilemma, like the logic of a common security and a purportedly common deterrence, would be entirely suitable were the international world inhabited solely by well-intentioned short-term thinkers who might stumble into a common catastrophe. Unfortunately, there are some real thugs and opportunistic cadet thugs out there who are entirely untroubled by security dilemmas. Indeed, they work to enhance the insecurity of others in the hope that they can gain advantage as a result.

General and Immediate Deterrence

This section of the discussion pursues further sets of popular distinctions among types of deterrence and between deterrence and coercion. First, it is probably important to distinguish between general and immediate deterrence—a distinction developed usefully by Patrick Morgan.[16] For example, nuclear armament in support of a broad superpower political commitment to the security of allies in Europe helped provide a general deterrence that discouraged Soviet adventure. But one could never be certain that that general deterrence would translate into the immediate deterrent effect that might be needed to protect a specific interest. In other words, one could describe in general terms the reasons why East and West in the Cold War were respectful of each other, but then wonder just how much deterrence would be needed, say, to keep East German and Soviet troops out of West Berlin in 1961 or to discourage Soviet troops from reentering self-liberated Hungary in the fall of 1956.

The connections between the general and the immediate are always uncertain and subject to resolution only by field tests of resolve. An object or principle in political contention is worth whatever the defender and the aggressor are prepared to pay to protect or acquire it. Generalized descriptions of the capabilities and political will of two sides will say surprisingly little about respective bargaining strengths at specific times over specific issues.

Existential and Postexistential Deterrence

Second, there are ample references in the scholarly literature to existential and even to postexistential deterrence. Existential deterrence is a concept popularized, though certainly not invented, by McGeorge Bundy, who was national security adviser to President John F. Kennedy.[17] The thesis is that the very existence of nuclear weapons commands widespread deterrent effect. In this popular view, nuclear weapons are not weapons, nuclear strategy is not strategy, and nuclear war could not be war in any military, instrumental sense that Clausewitz would acknowledge.[18] Happily, on this logic, the truly revolutionary character of nuclear weapons does not fatally inhibit their political value, because the general fear of nuclear disaster that the mere presence of these so-called weapons generates suffices to secure all the deterrence necessary. The proximate danger, in this view, lurks in the ideas and behavior of people and organizations who cling atavistically to a wholly outdated Clausewitzian approach to nuclear weapons.[19] The details of comparison of one state's nuclear arsenal with another's are completely irrelevant. It is the existence of nuclear arsenals per se which deters.

For those who find the existential postulate overly hawkish, not to say expensive and perhaps even accident prone—after all, even an existential nuclear arsenal might "go off"[20]—there is the ingenious idea of postexistential deterrence. The key notion in the theory of postexistential deterrence is that weapons need not actually exist in order to cast a giant dissuasive shadow. The logic of postexistentialism is that if the mere existence of nuclear weapons can deter, why should not the prospect of the introduction or reintroduction of nuclear weapons into the arsenal also deter? Following the logic pioneered by Jonathan Schell in his clever 1984 book, *The Abolition*,[21] antinuclear sentiments could be indulged in the form of a policy favoring total nuclear abolition, confident in the residual deterrent value of a capability for nuclear mobilization.

There is a serious problem with postexistentialism. Specifically, an enemy might decide he need not be deterred by a theoretical ability to rebuild nuclear strength if he could achieve preclusive military victory in the short run. States and coalitions which plan cunningly to win long wars in an elegant fashion have been known to neglect unduly the problem of short-term survival.

Deterrence and Compellence

The third set of popular distinctions which requires prompt attention is that between deterrence and what Thomas C. Schelling called "compellence" in his

1966 classic, *Arms and Influence*.[22] Deterrence leans heavily upon what is recognized as the defender's advantage. The hypothesis is that people and states care more about holding what they have than they do about gaining more. This reasonably historically well attested thesis translates as an uneven playing field tilted beneficially on behalf of the status quo. Alas, it can be the case that once an aggressor has seized his ill-gotten gains, he then becomes the defender. Whereas deterrence seeks to dissuade a would-be aggressor from committing aggression, compellence is the far more demanding mission of persuading an aggressor to disgorge his ill-gotten gains. It is one of the several paradoxes of Western policy and strategy that a defensive policy requires an offensive strategy and operational style because Western states, by and large, will be seeking to turn an aggressor out of his conquests.

Desert Storm provides a perfect illustration of the point. The problem in 1990–91 was not recognized in time to be one of deterrence; therefore it became a problem in compellence. Iraq had to be compelled to disgorge Kuwait, as a minimum goal of coalition policy. Ideally, Iraq would be so damaged by the course of that compulsion that it would be structurally uninterested in regional aggression for many years to come. There was a massive triple U.S. failure over Iraq in 1990–91 that should fuel scholarly contemplation. There was a failure to attempt to deter Saddam Hussein prior to August 1990, when he invaded Kuwait. Next, there was a complete failure of nonlethal coercive diplomacy to compel Hussein to abandon Kuwait. Finally, the coalition won the military campaign but did not win the war in a politically definitive manner by toppling Saddam Hussein's regime.

Deterrence and compellence are different ideas and probably require different military postures. This important distinction is not one that drives much of the argument in the works of the existentialists and postexistentialists. The existential deterrer simply assumes away the problem of compellence, or coercion, by hypothesizing the existential success of deterrence. Whether or not a nuclear posture suitable to deter would also be appropriate to compel is left in a convenient silence.

Extended Deterrence

Fourth, the theory and the attempted practice of deterrence have been shaped significantly by the implications of the distinction between the deterrence of hostile acts against the national homeland and the deterrence of such acts against the homelands of close friends and allies. In his 1960 masterpiece, *On Thermonuclear War*, Herman Kahn distinguished among what he termed Type I, Type II, and Type III deterrence.[23] Kahn's Type I deterrence was deterrence of hostile acts against our homeland, Type II was the deterrence of hostile acts against our allies, while Type III was a catch-all category covering the deterrence of other acts that we would judge to be hostile.

In recent decades, particularly since the 1970s, Type II and perhaps Type III deterrence has been known as extended deterrence.[24] The idea is that a guardian state or coalition extends its protection over other, probably geographically distant, states. The focus of most theoretical and practical attention has been the extending of protection by contingent and often deliberately ambiguous promises of nuclear-weapons use on behalf of allies menaced by nuclear threats. Extended deterrence does not have to mean extended nuclear deterrence, but that is the context in which the concept has been developed. In fact, as Edward Luttwak has argued, it is in the nature of great and super powers to protect client states against rival great and super powers.[25]

The problems of extended deterrence drove debate after debate on NATO's strategy and military posture. How could a nuclear-armed adversary be persuaded that the United States would assume any and all risks on behalf of friends and allies? Some critics of modern strategy argue that many of the problems of credibility discussed or anticipated by professional strategic theorists really are not problems at all.[26] It is a commonplace to notice that ideas which work logically often do not work well in the less permissive world of experience. By contrast, in the realm of nuclear strategy and deterrence much would seem to work in practice that does not work at all well as theory. For a prominent example, NATO's central strategic concept from 1967 until 1991, "flexible response," elevated uncertainty to the status of a master principle, no doubt to the beneficial confusion of the alliance's enemies.[27] Flexible response was a recipe for confusion, if ever there was one. As theory, it was all but nonsensical. Without the means or the probable will to achieve escalation dominance,[28] how could NATO possibly lead, to its net advantage, a process of ever more-desperate nuclear risk-taking?

Beyond Deterrence

The attractions of deterrence are obvious. Deterrence of war is always cheaper than war, prevention is preferable to cure, while a debate focused upon the estimated requirements of deterrence serves usefully to preclude the paying of what could be embarrassing attention to the prospective conduct of war. Since many people have always been optimistic about the chances for success in deterrence, they have never been strongly motivated to pierce the veil of war and explore its possible dynamics.[29] Indeed, to worry about the conduct of war, especially nuclear war, suggests to many people an inappropriate or even possibly dangerous pessimism about the prospects for deterrence.

Understandably enough, psychological avoidance techniques enable many strategic theorists to evade the necessity of considering the actual conduct of war. Unless one adheres to the distinctly contestable and certainly politically incorrect notion that probable prowess in defense or denial should enhance prewar deterrence, then the best approach to the conduct of war is probably to ignore it. One should not be peremptorily dismissive, let alone disdainful, of this popular view. After all, if nuclear war is judged likely to be a common catastrophe, rather than an instrument of policy or "a continuation of political intercourse, with the addition of other means,"[30] there is little to be gained by focusing upon its prospective conduct, course, and outcome. In that perspective, policy and strategy will have failed if a decidedly noninstrumental nuclear war ensues.

By way of an imperfect analogy, great amphibious expeditions tend to be so difficult to mount that planning staffs typically exhaust themselves solving the myriad problems involved in throwing an army upon a hostile shore, securing a beachhead, and then winning the logistical battle of the rival buildups. Imaginative planning for the prosecution of the campaign beyond the beachhead simply is overwhelmed by the far more pressing problem of just getting an army safely ashore. The literature on modern strategy shows a similar unwillingness, perhaps inability, to think beyond deterrence or to relate the prospects for success in deterrence convincingly to ideas and plans for the conduct of operations should deterrence fail. The analogy breaks down, of course, in that the theorists of deterrence know that if deterrence succeeds, there will be no subsequent military campaign.

HOW DETERRENCE WORKS

Any discussion skeptical of the reliability of deterrence lends itself readily to misunderstanding and even misrepresentation. It is the contention here that deterrence theory, unlike arms control theory,[31] is not wrong; rather, its ability to describe and prescribe successfully for the real world of statecraft is distinctly limited. Furthermore, to suggest the unreliability of deterrence is not to argue for its wholesale abandonment in favor of alternative themes in grand strategy and military strategy. Bribery and defense also are unreliable.

Deterrence should do whatever it can, but wise statecraft will have other strands to its grand strategy. A mixture of positive with negative sanctions short of the use of force and a powerful war-fighting instrument backstopping the array of menaces begins to provide the range for policy choice suitably tolerant of unpleasant surprises.

It is important that criticism should be targeted accurately and that by implication it should not hold deterrence to an unreasonably heroic level of successful performance. There are problems for this discussion both in identifying traditional deterrence theory fairly and in assessing the quality of performance in practice of ideas on deterrence over the past fifty years. The *theory of* deterrence frequently is confused with *theories for* deterrence and with advocacy positions linked to favored weapon systems and military postures.[32] To aid clarification, the following points state in the barest essentials how mutual deterrence works.

Two states or coalitions in a relationship of more or less acute political hostility

- reason consequentially and strategically in a rational manner about the probable implications of their behavior
- understand well enough their own and each other's political wishes, policy goals, and domestic constraints
- are able to communicate intentions and anxieties in ways that will be understood accurately enough by the recipients
- will have operational control of the salient military forces
- will have military forces reasonably congruent with the scope and character of the contingent threats that are issued
- will not only understand each other's positions, purposes, and general situation well enough, but also share some key values (e.g., abhorrence of war)[33]

This list can be expanded, contracted, or conflated to suit individual taste, but it captures the point raised earlier that a relationship of deterrence, be it bilateral, multilateral, or common, necessarily is cooperative. The intended deterree, if he recognizes himself as such, strictly does not have to comply with the more or less overt commands that are issued.

The overwhelming difficulty in attempts to assess the performance of deterrence as theory or policy is that the evidence can only be negative. If war did not occur, was it because of successful deterrence? Perhaps the parties involved did not require much deterring? Of late there has been a marked tendency by liberal-minded commentators to have resort to dubious judgment by historical hindsight. The argument proceeds thus: because the evil empire of the Soviet Union collapsed so precipitately in 1989–91, it must always have been rotten to the core, a "house of cards" if you will, and not the worthy superpower adversary it was long believed to be. Similarly, because there was no World War III between East and West, while since October 1962 there was not even a crisis slide which plausibly might have led to such a conflict (to discount the October War of 1973 in the Middle East and the acute Soviet anxieties of 1981–84), deterrence between the superpowers must have been easy to achieve. It follows, on this logic, that virtually any nuclear force posture would have sufficed to ensure all the existential deterrence that circumstances may have required.[34] Apart from historical interest for its own sake, we have to assess the quality of deterrence in the Cold War because we need to know how deterrence may function, or malfunction, differently in the new post-Soviet era.

Contrary to much popular pontification, it so happens that the unexpected and certainly unexpectedly comprehensive fall of the Soviet empire, along with the absence of apparent occasions for superpower deterrence in recent decades, proves absolutely nothing about the working or requirements of deterrence. All that is known for certain about deterrence in the Cold War is that whatever needed deterring in order to prevent World War III, or even a major regional conflict, plainly was deterred. Western policy, strategy, and defense allocations unarguably were good enough to do what needed doing. The question of most interest is just what it was that needed doing. The political avalanche of 1989–91 certainly showed that the Soviet Union would have been massively vulnerable politically in any protracted military conflict,[35] but those events tell us little about the true scale of Soviet military menace in, say, 1975 or 1980.

Often I find myself in agreement with colleagues who are deeply skeptical over the real importance of the detail of targeting plans, of military posture, and of the feasibility of politically responsive nuclear operations. Where I differ from those colleagues is in the conclusions that I draw for statecraft and for defense planning and force structure. It is plausible to argue that politicians of any culture or strategic inclination are going to be terrified by the prospect of nuclear war writ large, not of anticipated nuclear-weapon effects tailored to endanger purported national centers of gravity.[36] It is not difficult to be persuaded that an attempt to use nuclear weapons in limited and controlled ways for carefully constrained policy purposes would prove utterly impossible.[37] Those points notwithstanding, should one plan and posture forces capable of effecting only the most indiscriminate actions? Is it prudent, or moral, to render the strong likelihood of general catastrophe a certainty?

Policymakers from the United States and some from its allies have behaved as if deterrence could be difficult to achieve, for the excellent reason that that is the only responsible position to adopt; it is a position more tolerant of fault. Administration after administration in the United States chose larger rather than smaller strategic nuclear forces and elected to posture them diversely rather than simply, for the same reason that Winston Churchill, the new first lord of the admiralty, insisted on 27 July 1911 upon placing military guards around the Royal Navy's only two cordite magazines. In his memoirs Churchill wrote that "the incident was a small one, and perhaps my fears were unfounded. But once one had begun to view the situation in this light [war with Germany as a distinct possibility], it became impossible to think of anything else."[38] Herman Kahn once commented in almost identical terms upon the need for U.S. strategic forces to be deployed beyond reach of a Soviet first strike. Kahn did not think that the Soviet Union would have attacked the United States, even if U.S. forces had been concentrated all together in Times Square.[39] But no U.S. government that was serious about national security could afford to take the admittedly small chance. What if it was wrong?

The argument that follows cannot be proved; it is very much a hypothesis. People should be as careful drawing lessons for the future from Cold War experience as they need to be in interpreting Cold War experience itself. In large part because of that general deterrence cited earlier—a general deterrence induced by U.S. nuclear as well as other military and fundamentally economic strength—in comfortable retrospect it is plausible to assert that the Soviet Union never needed much immediate deterring from, say, the Berlin blockade of 1948–49 to the fall of Mikhail Gorbachev. The correlation of forces between the Soviet and American-led worlds, though long anticipated to shift significantly in the Soviet favor almost certainly ruled out general war as a viable, purposeful instrument of policy for the U.S.S.R. Naturally, the Soviet Union would have sought to win had it been obliged to fight. But war was an instrument of policy that the U.S.S.R. never would have chosen to wield, save in the most desperate of circumstances.

Even if this is plausible, it does not follow that deterrence was easy and that Western policymakers should have been relaxed about their military posture. In the first place, viewed contemporaneously rather than with hindsight, the events might lend themselves to the opposite interpretation. Second, had war nonetheless erupted between East and West, even though rationally it should not have done so, the detail of military preparation could have made the difference between a survivable disaster and an irretrievable catastrophe. Third, no one can be certain that via general deterrence the weight and quality of Western military forces did not dissuade Soviet leaders from ever pressing a claim to the point where the adequacy of immediate deterrence would be a potent topic. Finally, had there been an acute crisis of a war-in-sight variety, larger rather than smaller Western forces, married to a suitable quality of perceived political will, could have made the difference for peace with security.

Deterrence works either on the ragged edge of feasibility or scarcely at all. This theory applies to the Cold War as well as to the post–Cold War period. Both rational defense analysis and popular political-military commentary tend to misunderstand the working of deterrence because they misunderstand the occasions for its applicability. When one examines the stream of "stability" (i.e., forces' vulnerability) studies generated by the Glenn Kent (or RAND) school of numerical analysis, one notices that the strength of political motivation to act or misbehave—to fight—is missing from consideration.[40] The result is a political, indeed an apolitical (which is to say a real-world), nonsense. The popular political-military commentary errs no less in that typically it declines to empathize with a realistic context for deterrence. A decent, humane, rational theorist looks out from a context of deep peace and judges deterrence to be either easy to achieve or thoroughly irrelevant. Similarly, such a person is likely to deem war, let alone nuclear war, abhorrent; that belief is unlikely to encourage insight suitable for the guidance of policy when deterrence is hard to achieve.

A general deterrence functions pervasively but untraceably to support civility in international relations.[41] Further, the immediate deterrence of overt military acts is required only rarely. But, like air bags for safety in cars, when it truly is needed nothing else will do. It follows all but inevitably that military posture is doomed to fall into the apparently inappropriate range. Day by day, even during much of the Cold War, it was exceedingly unlikely that the Soviet Union needed to be deterred. Of course, that judgment may well largely reflect the healthful influence of a general deterrence. Nonetheless, day by day, week by week, the country's military posture is likely to appear grossly overdesigned for any clear and present danger. Needless to add perhaps, this point applies far more obviously today than it did during the Cold War. When the country is not actively and specifically menaced, deterrence can appear easy. This is a persisting case of the confusion of an absence of need for deterrence with ease of deterrence performance.

For two centuries and certainly since 1918, let alone since 1945, major war generally has been regarded with more or less severe apprehension by policy-makers of widely differing political cultures. War has been viewed neither merely as a continuation of politics nor in any sense casually. It follows that when deterrence is needed, it is likely to be difficult to effect. If war is a live policy option, which is to say if deterrence is relevant, the requirements of deterrence probably will be exacting at least. Careful peacetime analysis of the needs of a so-called stable deterrence tends radically to misassess the implications of a strong political motivation to fight. As a general rule, defense posture will be too large for the security needs of order on the regular day, month, and year, yet it will fall significantly short of the requirements of deterrence on the only occasions when deterrence is relevant.

To move rapidly from when deterrence applies to the subject of how to make the most of what one has, it is useful to comment on political will and social strength contrasted with, and as a complement to, military (and economic) capability. Deterrent effect cannot flow from military forces per se. The intended deterree has to believe both that our forces would be used and that they would be used to the degree of causing pain and damage in excess of his threshold of acceptability relative to the issues at stake. An economical approach to deterrence holds that one should substitute will and skill for mere military muscle.

Clausewitz reminds us that "*[w]ar is thus an act of force to compel our enemy to do our will.*"[42] He also emphasizes that "war is nothing but a duel on a larger scale." In other words, war is—*inter alia*—a duel of two (or more) wills. There can be no guarantee that our political will must outweigh or outlast a foe's political will, which is why numbers and brute force are so important. Democracies can be implacable in war, but so can dictatorships. No matter how one explains the outcomes of the two world wars, the social dimension of strategy does not contain the key to understanding.[43]

Overall, in endeavoring to assess the record of nuclear-age deterrence to date, it is difficult to know whether the West was clever or lucky or both. It is probably fortunate that the adequacy for deterrence of U.S. and NATO's political will, military posture, and strategy was never field-tested severely. Horror stories of varying credibility abound concerning the nearness of major East-West war at various times and from various causes from 1948 until 1989,[44] but one should be in no doubt about the factors and conditions that helped make for a peaceful outcome to the Cold War. By way of the briefest of summaries, they are as follows:

- The two superpowers found little in direct, specific, and concrete dispute between them (e.g., West Berlin, like the Polish corridor in 1939, was an excuse for crisis, not a serious cause for war after the fashion of Alsace-Lorraine or Manchuria and Korea).

- The "rogue" superpower challenger, the Soviet Union, generally adhered patiently to a theory of inevitable long-term success in statecraft (the reverse of the gambler character of Hitler's perilously personal Third Reich).[45]

- The superpower strategic relationship had a useful, and probably stabilizing, simplicity in its bilateral nature. Third parties had nuisance value, but only modest alliance value.

- The East-West standoff was cartographically clearly demarcated, a fact which meant that areas of exclusive Soviet or U.S. influence were understood by all key players.

- The Cold War was understood on both sides to be a balance-of-(great)-power struggle over relative global standing. The generality of the contest, married to the asymmetrical geopolitics of the two sides, meant that there could be no political flexibility in the intensity of national interests asserted in all areas of contact in Europe. This fact reduced the danger of miscalculation of commitment.

- In their lonely shared preeminence, the superpowers trained each other in the practice of prudent behavior for deterrence. Communication occasionally could be poor and understanding of intent less than perfect, but the years of intense study and practical engagement did yield a modus operandi that worked well enough. Deterrence may have come close to failure or irrelevance once or twice in the early 1960s and early 1980s—one cannot be sure. But the test of policy and strategy, as contrasted with the test of theory, is how well it did work.[46] On the record of what did and did not happen, and with reference to what can be surmised reasonably about what might have happened, there are grounds for satisfaction.

- The nuclear element in the Soviet-U.S., East-West, strategic contest was so pervasive as to damp down any and every reasonable expectation of easy military, hence political, gain at the other's expense. When all courses of political-military adventure appear pregnant with nuclear peril, indeed when one side elevates nuclear risk as the basis of its security policy (NATO's "strategy"), even Pyrrhic victory looks unattainable. The influence of nuclear weapons for the peaceful outcome to the Cold War is debatable,[47] but there can be no reasonable doubt that nuclear armament helped discourage whatever inclination to policy excitement needed discouragement.

If Soviet leaders needed to be deterred, they were deterred. Self-congratulation should be qualified, however, with recognition of the factors just mentioned that rendered success likely, perhaps probable, though not certain.

THE FUTURE OF DETERRENCE

The theory of deterrence requires little amendment for changing times. The problem lies in the relevance and application of policies intended to produce deterrent effect. The argument I develop here is that, of the three broad policy avenues nominally available—deterrence, bribery, and physical discipline—both deterrence and bribery (leaning upon negative or positive sanctions, respectively) are of sharply lower reliability now than was the case in the Cold War. That is the bad news, though far from all of the bad news. The main items of good news are, first, that the "rogue" polities that cannot be deterred reliably in the 1990s tend to lie much lower on the scale of capability than did yesterday's superpower Soviet Union. Second, because the 1990s-era rogues are relatively minor players, the consequences to the United States and NATO of failures to deter will be eminently survivable events.

Overall judgment on deterrence after the Cold War therefore has to be careful to take due account of several competing strands of conclusions. For example, deterrence will be less reliable, but there is solid cause to care less about such failures. With a focus most particularly upon the United States, but also to some degree upon NATO broadly, there are at least five reasons why deterrence will decline in reliability over the years immediately ahead.

First, there is growing uncertainty over the identity and intensity (survival, vital, major, and other) of national interests. If one is not clear over the relative importance of issues and events, how can one communicate credible contingent menaces for deterrence in their regard?

Second, and closely related to the first point, whatever the national-interest analysis of government may discover in the heat of rapidly unfolding regional events, it is a near certainty that the social dimension of strategy will decline to cooperate. The general publics in Western popular democracies in the 1990s will not endorse the issuing of credible threats, let alone the taking of expensive and painful action, in dubious enterprises.[48]

Third, it is all but certain that ethnocentrism and other maladies will impede that cultural empathy which is often necessary for the accurate targeting with effective threats of vulnerable alien centers of gravity. As a general rule, the U.S. and NATO grasp of the political and strategic cultures of likely wrongdoers in the 1990s will be so inadequate as to render much, if not all, of the theory of deterrence simply irrelevant. One will not know whom to deter, when, over what, or by which threats. Illustration of this argument was provided in 1990 over Iraq, as indeed it was in the 1950s, 1960s, and 1970s in U.S. endeavors to deter, and then to compel, North Vietnam. In the inimitable words of General Maxwell Taylor in 1972, "we knew very little about the Hanoi leaders other than Ho Chi Minh and General Giap and virtually nothing about their collective intentions."[49] In such a context, U.S. success with deterrence or compellence would have to be accidental. If one does not have a robust grasp of what an enemy values highly or of his intentions, how can one proceed rationally to pose threats that his consequentialist logic should judge worthy of triggering compliant behavior?

Fourth, as Cold War anxieties fade into history, the politically correct cognoscenti will gaze into their crystal balls and find the future to be a surprise-free projection from today; they will find it peaceful. In these already emerging circumstances our ready military capabilities deteriorate rapidly. Of course, the United States will be able to cobble together sufficient air power to conduct a punitive raid or two, but a sustained campaign will be difficult to threaten credibly. It takes years, even decades, to build a first-rate military force, but it takes only months, a year or two at most, to ruin that force for all save minor enterprises. In fact, as the 1970s and early 1980s demonstrated, when a military establishment degrades its capacity for the larger cases of possible conflicts, it tends to degrade in the small-war cases also. It is the hope in the U.S. military that the emerging military revolution of "information-age" warfare will allow fewer forces to accomplish far more.[50] The aspirations for information-age war are not wholly unreasonable, but they risk placing American faith unduly in machines at the expense of the human factors that traditionally make for high military effectiveness—to cite one problem among many possible.[51]

Fifth and finally, deterrence after the Cold War is rendered unreliable by a host of typically unpredictable factors of which deterrence theory takes, perhaps can take, but little account. Specifically, there are rigidities, even irrationalities, accidents and the like, which detract from the reliability of deterrence. This somewhat catch-all final class of factors owes something to Clausewitz's concept of "friction," something to Yehezkel Dror's 1971 speculative monograph on "crazy states,"[52] and a great deal to commonsense appreciation of the rich variety of possible dysfunctional behavior by individuals, groups, and organizations.

By the late 1980s, the United States and NATO had been purposively seeking to deter whatever might need deterring in Soviet behavior for more than forty years. Accidents, human and mechanical/electronic, as well as bizarre behavior, were always possible—indeed, they happened—but there was a substantial framework of shared experience, common—commonly understood, not necessarily agreed-upon—ideas, and very detailed knowledge on a large number of relevant subjects, which to some unknown degree helped fireproof (but did not guarantee) East-West strategic relations against deterrence failure. It is when one contrasts erstwhile Soviet-U.S. relations with, say, NATO-Serbian or U.S.-Iraqi or U.S.-North Korean or even U.S.-Indian relations that one can begin to appreciate just how few are the safety features pertaining to these newly more significant connections.

A LAST WORD

In direct reply to the central question posed, Is deterrence reliable? the answer is, first, that the value of deterrence during the Cold War is somewhat uncertain. Second, such unreliability as attached to it in those years assuredly is multiplied several times over in would-be deterrence relations in this post–Cold War era. The more uncertain the political and strategic maps, the less reliable must be a strategy of deterrence. The good news proclaimed earlier—that failures of deterrence or failures to attempt deterrence in time should matter less in the future than in the recent past—ought not to promote unconstrained relief. If anyone needs to be reminded, we are now in an interwar, which means a prewar, period, as well as a post–(Cold) War period. Apparently minor failures in deterrence can have thoroughly unpredictable consequences for a slide toward the next great balance-of-power struggle.

NOTES

1. Lawrence Freedman, "Terrorism and Strategy," in Freedman et al., *Terrorism and International Order*, Chatham House Special Paper (London: Routledge for the Royal Institute of International Affairs, 1986), pp. 60–61, 71, is particularly useful on the subject of indirect influence. Also see his insightful analysis of "Strategic Studies and

the Problem of Power," in Freedman, Paul Hayes, and Robert O'Neill, eds., *War, Strategy, and International Politics: Essays in Honour of Sir Michael Howard* (Oxford: Clarendon Press, 1992), pp. 279–94.

2. For some basics of stability theory, see Thomas C. Schelling, *Arms and Influence* (New Haven, CT: Yale University Press, 1966), chap. 6.

3. The literature on deterrence is vast and generally arid. For the essentials see William W. Kaufmann, "The Requirements of Deterrence," in Kaufmann, ed., *Military Policy and National Security* (Princeton, NJ: Princeton University Press, 1956), pp. 12–38. For the state of intellectual play approximately thirty to thirty-five years on, as the Cold War was winding down, see Roman Kolkowicz, ed., *The Logic of Nuclear Terror* (Boston: Allen and Unwin, 1987); "The Rational Deterrence Debate: A Symposium," *World Politics* 41, no. 2 (January 1989): 143–237; Paul C. Stern et al., eds., *Perspectives on Deterrence* (New York: Oxford University Press, 1989); Edward Rhodes, *Power and MADness: The Logic of Nuclear Coercion* (New York: Columbia University Press, 1989); and James H. Lebovic, *Deadly Dilemmas: Deterrence in U.S. Nuclear Strategy* (New York: Columbia University Press, 1990).

4. Raoul Naroll, Vern L. Bullough, and Frada Naroll, *Military Deterrence in History: A Pilot Cross-Historical Survey* (Albany: State University of New York Press, 1974); and Michael G. Fry, "Historians and Deterrence," in Paul C. Stern et al., eds., *Perspectives on Deterrence*, (New York: Oxford University Press, 1989), pp. 84–97, are particularly useful.

5. See Bernard Brodie, *Strategy in the Missile Age* (Princeton, NJ: Princeton University Press, 1959), chap. 8; and Colin S. Gray, *Strategic Studies and Public Policy: The American Experience* (Lexington: University Press of Kentucky, 1982), chap. 4.

6. The most sophisticated discussion of this question is Robert Jervis, *The Meaning of the Nuclear Revolution: Statecraft and the Prospect of Armageddon* (Ithaca, NY: Cornell University Press, 1989), chap. 1.

7. The proposition is that all people understand how devastating a nuclear war most likely would prove to be. Belief in cheap and fairly painless victory may have been sustainable, if frequently erroneous, in prenuclear times, but no longer. Joseph S. Nye, Jr., "Old Wars and Future Wars: Causation and Prevention," in Robert I. Rotberg and Theodore K. Rabb, eds., *The Origin and Prevention of Major Wars* (Cambridge: Cambridge University Press, 1989), p. 11.

8. After the fashion of Jomini's "immutable principles of strategy." See his *The Art of War* (London: Greenhill Books, 1992; first pub. 1862), p. 331.

9. For example, Sir John Slessor, *The Great Deterrent* (London: Cassell, 1957).

10. Quoted in Keith B. Payne, "Deterrence: What Can We Learn from the Past?" (presentation at "Counter-Proliferation: Deterring Emerging Nuclear Actors," a strategic options assessment conference, Strategic Command, Offutt Air Force Base, Washington, DC, National Institute for Public Policy, 7 July 1993).

11. See Glenn Snyder, *Deterrence and Defense* (Princeton, NJ: Princeton University Press, 1961).

12. The idea persists, especially in British publications, that there is or was a "war-fighting" theory of nuclear strategy advocated by distinctive nuclear "war fighters." See my article, "War Fighting for Deterrence," *Journal of Strategic Studies* 7, no.

1 (March 1984): 5–28. For the strange British view that there have been nuclear "war fighters," see Ken Booth, "Strategy," in A. J. R. Groom and Margot Light, eds., *Contemporary International Relations: A Guide to Theory* (London: Pinter Publishers, 1994), p. 114.

13. Godfried van Benthem van den Bergh, *The Nuclear Revolution and the End of the Cold War: Forced Restraint* (London: Macmillan, 1992), pp. 186–90, is especially clear on "common deterrence."

14. See Robert Jervis, "Cooperation under the Security Dilemma," *World Politics* 30, no. 2 (January 1978): 167–214; and Nicholas J. Wheeler and Ken Booth, "The Security Dilemma," in John Baylis and N. J. Rengger, eds., *Dilemmas of World Politics: International Issues in a Changing World* (Oxford: Clarendon Press, 1992), pp. 29–60.

15. I advance this argument in my *Villains, Victims and Sheriffs: Strategic Studies and Security for an Inter-War Period, An Inaugural Lecture* (Hull, England: University of Hull Press, 1994), pp. 25–26.

16. Patrick Morgan, *Deterrence: A Conceptual Enquiry* (Beverly Hills, CA: Sage Publications, 1977), chap. 2.

17. McGeorge Bundy, "Existential Deterrence and Its Consequences," in Douglas MacLean, ed., *The Security Gamble: Deterrence Dilemmas in the Nuclear Age* (Totowa, NJ: Rowman and Allanheld, 1984), pp. 3–13; and Lawrence Freedman, "Whither Nuclear Strategy?" in Ken Booth, ed., *New Thinking about Strategy and International Security* (London: HarperCollins Academic, 1991), pp. 81–85.

18. See Raymond Aron, *Clausewitz: Philosopher of War* (London: Routledge and Kegan Paul, 1983; first pub. 1976), part V.

19. See Ken Booth, "War, Security and Strategy: Towards a Doctrine for Stable Peace," in Ken Booth, ed., *New Thinking about Strategy and International Security* (London: HarperCollins Academic, 1991), particularly pp. 356–58.

20. For reasons detailed in Bruce G. Blair, *The Logic of Accidental Nuclear War* (Washington, DC: Brookings Institution, 1993); and Scott D. Sagan, *The Limits of Safety: Organizations, Accidents, and Nuclear Weapons* (Princeton, NJ: Princeton University Press, 1993).

21. Jonathan Schell, *The Abolition* (London: Picador, 1984).

22. Schelling, *Arms and Influence*, pp. 69–91.

23. Herman Kahn, *On Thermonuclear War* (Princeton, NJ: Princeton University Press, 1960), chap. 4.

24. See Stephen J. Cimbala, *Extended Deterrence: The United States and NATO Europe* (Lexington, MA: Lexington Books, 1987); and Paul K. Huth, *Extended Deterrence and the Prevention of War* (New Haven, CT: Yale University Press, 1988).

25. Edward N. Luttwak, *On the Meaning of Victory: Essays on Strategy* (New York: Simon and Schuster, 1986), p. 290.

26. This disturbing thought is inspired especially by Jervis, *Meaning of the Nuclear Revolution*, pp. 69–70.

27. See J. Michael Legge, *Theater Nuclear Weapons and the NATO Strategy of Flexible Response*, R-2964-FF (Santa Monica, CA: RAND, April 1983); and David N. Schwartz, *NATO's Nuclear Dilemmas* (Washington, DC: Brookings Institution, 1983).

28. The concept is outlined in Herman Kahn, *On Escalation: Metaphors and Scenarios* (New York: Praeger, 1965), pp. 23, 290. For a highly skeptical view see Robert Jervis, *The Illogic of American Nuclear Strategy* (Ithaca, NY: Cornell University Press, 1984), chap. 5. The importance of escalation dominance, if attainable, is emphasized in Colin S. Gray, *Nuclear Strategy and National Style* (Lanham, MD: Hamilton Press, 1986), chap. 8.

29. Ken Booth has gone so far as to say that "those who put war outside the distinctive core [of strategic studies] are not really strategists. They are semi-strategists or they are simply deterrence theorists. They do not deal with war because of their twin obsessions with nuclear weapons and the theory of deterrence. They rarely ask what if deterrence fails? They throw up their hands at that point." In Gerald Segal, ed., *New Directions in Strategic Studies: A Chatham House Debate*, RIIA Discussion Papers, no. 17 (London: Royal Institute of International Affairs, 1989), pp. 7–8.

30. Carl von Clausewitz, *On War*, ed. and trans. Michael Howard and Peter Paret (Princeton, NJ: Princeton University Press, 1976; first pub. 1832), p. 605.

31. For reasons I outline in detail in my *House of Cards: Why Arms Control Must Fail* (Ithaca, NY: Cornell University Press, 1992).

32. When instrument and object are confused, it is open season for the abuse of language and the confusion of the public. Because there is no truly objective deterrent, virtually any favored military system, threat, or even course of action can be touted as having value for deterrence. There is no analytical policeman. For clarity, let me distinguish among (1) a general theory of deterrence; (2) theories for deterrence; (3) theories for deterrence tailored to specific circumstances; and (4) the words, capabilities, and deeds intended to have deterrent effect (i.e., the would-be deterrent).

33. For a classic negative example, in 1939 Adolf Hitler could not understand the genuineness and depth of the British and French distress over his sequential destruction of the former Czechoslovakia. Similarly, he could not even begin to understand why foreign statesmen should be upset over his breaking of his apparently solemn word. When you do not care about small countries and when you view words (promises) merely as diplomatic weapons, it is all but impossible to empathize with people who approach matters differently. For the other side of the coin, it is understandable that British and French leaders in 1938 and 1939 failed to realize that they were endeavoring to cope with a German statesman who actually wanted war. Hitler did not want to have to wage a two-front war, but he was determined to secure his objectives by force. The Munich agreement came as a bitter disappointment to him when he found himself negotiated out of a short, limited, and victorious war. This is not to say that Hitler could not have been deterred in 1939, only that Western statesmen failed to appreciate just how strong was Germany's political velocity toward war. Gerhard L. Weinberg, *A World at Arms: A Global History of World War II* (Cambridge: Cambridge University Press, 1994), chap. 1, is outstanding.

34. But consider the prudential logic in McGeorge Bundy, *Danger and Survival: Choices about the Bomb in the First Fifty Years* (New York: Random House, 1988), chap. 13; Scott D. Sagan, *Moving Targets: Nuclear Strategy and National Security* (Princeton, NJ: Princeton University Press, 1989); and Colin S. Gray, "Strategy in the Nuclear Age: The United States, 1945–91," in Williamson Murray, MacGregor Knox, and

Alvin Bernstein, eds., *The Making of Strategy: Rulers, States, and War* (Cambridge: Cambridge University Press, 1994), pp. 579–613.

35. Linton F. Brooks, "Conflict Termination Through Maritime Leverage," in Stephen J. Cimbala and Keith A. Dunn, eds., *Conflict Termination and Military Strategy: Coercion, Persuasion, and War* (Boulder, CO: Westview Press, 1987), chap. 10, is very much to the point.

36. See Clausewitz, *On War*, pp. 595–97.

37. But see the contrary view in Albert J. Wohlstetter, "Bishops, Statesmen, and Other Strategists on the Bombing of Innocents," *Commentary* 75, no. 6 (June 1983): 15–35.

38. Winston S. Churchill, *The World Crisis, 1911–1918*, vol. 1 (London: Odhams Press, 1938), p. 35.

39. Personal memory of discussion with Herman Kahn sometime in 1979 or 1980.

40. For example, see Glenn A. Kent, Randall J. DeValk, and David E. Thaler, *A Calculus of First-Strike Stability: A Criterion for Evaluating Strategic Forces*, N-2526-AF (Santa Monica, CA: RAND, June 1988). A brief, strongly worded critique of "systems analysis" is Bernard Brodie, *War and Politics* (New York: Macmillan, 1973), pp. 473–79. Gray, "The Holistic Strategist," *Global Affairs* 7, no. 4 (winter 1992): 171–82, also is pertinent.

41. By analogy, the very existence of a competent and respected police force helps encourage civility in civil society.

42. Clausewitz, *On War*, p. 75 (emphasis in original).

43. Michael Howard, "The Forgotten Dimensions of Strategy," *Foreign Affairs* 57, no. 5 (summer 1979): 975–86, is indispensable. Neither world war was decided either by a collapse on the home front or by a social disintegration of armies in the field. In 1918, the German home front collapsed into anarchy after the unexpected revelation of gathering military defeat at the front. France in May–June 1940 is a serious candidate for the historical column of national defeats triggered by social weaknesses, but even in that case, operational errors are at least as impressive as social failings. See Robert Allan Doughty, *The Breaking Point: Sedan and the Fall of France, 1940* (Hamden, CT: Archon Books, 1990).

44. See Sagan, *Limits of Safety*.

45. Hitler was in a hurry for war in 1938–39 for two principal reasons. The first reason was that he understood, accurately, Germany's rearmament lead to be a wasting asset. The second reason was that he believed, again accurately, that the course of expansion upon which he was set required both his personal leadership and his leadership while he was still in the prime of life. Appreciation of Hitler's fear of his own mortality, even debility, is vital for a balanced understanding of why the Third Reich was in such a hurry to fight.

46. Brodie, *War and Politics*, p. 452.

47. As in John Mueller, "The Essential Irrelevance of Nuclear Weapons: Stability in the Postwar World," *International Security* 13, no. 2 (fall 1988): 55–79.

48. Edward N. Luttwak, "Where Are the Great Powers? At Home with the Kids," *Foreign Affairs* 73, no. 4 (July/August 1994): 23–28.

49. Quoted in Payne, "Deterrence."

50. See the discussion in Chapter 10. See also Colin S. Gray with Steven J. Lambakis, *Space Power and the Transformation of War* (Fairfax, VA: National Security Research, 1994). For a controlled overstatement try Alvin Toffler and Heidi Toffler, *War and Anti-War: Survival at the Dawn of the 21st Century* (Boston: Little, Brown, 1993).

51. See Russell F. Weigley, *The American Way of War: A History of United States Military Strategy and Policy* (New York: Macmillan, 1973), p. 416.

52. Clausewitz, *On War*, pp. 119–21; Yehezkel Dror, *Crazy States: A Counterconventional Strategic Problem* (Lexington, MA: Heath Lexington Books, 1971).

Part II
Strategy and Air Power

pendence for the a...
technological-ta...
The air force...
elementar...
Wheth...
besi...

The Adv
and Limitation:

Most countries have some air power, but the United States alone is preeminently an air power. The logic behind, and the implications of, this claim comprise the centerpiece of the analysis in this chapter and two succeeding ones.

It is fascinating to speculate with historian Richard P. Hallion that "[a]s dominant land power characterized a *Pax Romana*, and dominant sea power a *Pax Britannica*, dominant air power is the characteristic of modern America."[1] The problem with this simple, essentialist characterization is that some absent qualifications are important. Continentalist Rome sustained for centuries the finest navy in antiquity,[2] while maritime Britain often was critically dependent upon the armies of land power allies.[3] Properly viewed, the strategic analogy of the United States with Rome and Britain would look for a superior U.S. system of war for which air power typically has become the leading edge. It is not necessary to register exclusive claims. History teaches that Rome used its potency on land to acquire an unequaled and indeed unchallengeable sea power. Britain, in its turn, used superiority at sea to generate leverage for success on land. The United States uses its preponderance in the air and in space to secure advantage on land and at sea, either as a multifaceted contribution to land and sea conflict or as license to wage an operationally all but independent campaign of bombardment from the overhead flank of terrestrial warfare.

Debates over the past and future of air power more often than not address both ancient and irrelevant questions. The great men of air power theory and practice tended to be practical people with an overpowering sense of mission; they were not philosophers of war to be confused with Niccolo Machiavelli or Carl von Clausewitz.[4] The case for institutional and some operational inde-

arm rests unarguably upon the geographical and hence
tical and operational distinctiveness of the air environment.
has to be independent of army and navy service cultures for the
reason that fighting in, for, and from the sky is a unique activity.
or or not air forces can win wars by their own largely unaided action is
the point. This is not to say that air power cannot win wars; in some
circumstances it can and has. It would be agreeable simply to bury the
"independent decision" argument and proceed to more productive realms. A
good deal of post–Gulf War speculation about the future of U.S. military
strategy, defense plans, and force structure was permeated with ill-conceived,
though sincerely held, claims about which, if any, military element really is
dominant.

This book does not seek protective shelter in comfortable generalities about
deterrence and war being team efforts (though they are), or in wise-sounding
but possibly analytically cowardly caveats to the effect that policy, strategy, and
doctrine should not be rewritten on the basis of just one passage of arms,
particularly when that passage of arms is outstandingly successful. The myriad
of small changes in all aspects of air power over the course of nine decades now
have produced an air weapon with an unprecedented lethality which, as a direct
consequence, has political, strategic, and operational implications that did not
hold for most conflicts prior to the 1990s. War is war and strategy is strategy,
regardless of historical period, state players, or technology.[5] But operations,
tactics, and logistics vary radically over time. Judgments about air power that
reflect deep understanding of its historical performance from first military
application in Libya in 1911 until only, say, 1968 in Southeast Asia are almost
certain to be unsound.

In modern times, professional navies changed from short-range coastal
instruments to weapons with truly transoceanic, even global, reach. Similarly,
several times in recent centuries armies have acquired, then lost, then reacq-
uired the ability to achieve rapid operational-level decision in continental war.
It is scarcely surprising that in a century wherein scientific invention and
improved engineering application have been routinized, and wherein the
strategy demands of a series of great balance-of-power wars (World Wars I and
II and the Cold War) have driven military innovation, the newest element in
the military universe should register dramatic relative advances vis-à-vis other,
older elements.

The historical context for this discussion is a ninety-year period anchored
at each end by monumentally contrasting events. In 1918, fifteen years after
the Wright brothers demonstrated that airplanes could fly, U.S. air power acted
as a useful, but not essential, adjunct to the American Expeditionary Force in
its great offensive against the St. Mihiel salient in France. Seventy-three years
later, the U.S. and Allied air weapon was the "key force" in a theory and practice

of war which restricted land and sea forces to adjunct roles of much-argued significance. That Desert Storm 1991 was offensive air power's finest hour is not in question. What must be explored, however, is the extent to which the circumstances of the 1991 Gulf War may have flattered the performance of air power. By way of a hazardous analogy, the German system of air-land war— Blitzkrieg, so called—was flattered mightily by the appalling errors in doctrine and operational art committed by the French and the British in 1940.[6] Until they succumbed to the familiar, transcultural "victory disease" of believing what their own propaganda said about their military invincibility, the Germans adhered to the healthy practice of self-criticism.[7] It is possible that atavistic claims and counterclaims over whether or not air power delivered victory in the Gulf could crowd out discussion of the real questions. Gresham's Law is no respecter of subject.[8]

A set of beliefs and prior judgments informs Part II of the book. At some risk of appearing to offer conclusions ahead of evidence and argument, I present these core beliefs and judgments at this early juncture. They should be regarded as working hypotheses. Bold and sweeping though these points may seem, I deem them relatively noncontroversial. What is controversial, however, are their meaning and implications. In the interest of exploring in depth the more interesting rather than the more settled matters, these beliefs and judgments are offered as a beginning for, rather than as the end to, enquiry.

1. The United States is more genuinely an aerospace, or air and space, power than it is a sea or land power.

2. Air power has matured to the point where (a) it must always be significant in conflict of all kinds (to help deter or in actual use), (b) frequently it will be the key element in the military team, and (c) infrequently it can deter or win wars in the absence of much supporting action by land or sea.

3. The trend in relative advantage favoring air over (nonair) land and (nonair) naval forces is mature but not irreversible.

4. Distinctions among land, sea, air, and space power are not as clear as one would like for analytical confidence.

This analysis explores the validity in the claims that many theorists of air power have imposed unreasonable and unnecessary standards for judging the success of air power in war. If air power visionaries have dreamed of the achievement of decision from the air independent of action by land and sea forces, generic critics of air power have been more than content to hold air forces to that absolute standard. The discussion begins with the question of the appropriate test of success for air power and proceeds to suggest the critical significance of true basic questions. What does it mean to be an air, indeed to be *the* air, power? By what method or approach can one best determine how much and what kinds of air power the country should acquire?

SELF-INFLICTED WOUNDS

The largest cloud by far on the horizon for air and space power is muddled thinking about the history and promise of airplanes and spacecraft in war. Notwithstanding ninety years of multinational experience in conflicts of all kinds with heavier-than-air flight, disciplined discussion of air power and closely related topics is harassed at every turn by unhelpful definitions, institutional vested interests in certain orthodoxies, and plain incompetence in strategic reasoning.

The development of aerospace power and air power (one of several key distinctions tackled below)[9] is imperiled by its more zealous advocates as well as by skeptics. Indeed, ever since 1918 the more doctrinaire of the proponents of air power have given a good impression of seeking to snatch defeat from the jaws of victory. For understandable reasons the leading theorists of air power in Britain, Italy, and the United States confused air power theory with a theory of war and, as a consequence, set standards of expected strategic performance for air forces that were as unnecessary as for many decades they were unrealistic. In important respects, the admittedly varied teachings and writings of Hugh Trenchard, "Billy" Mitchell, Giulio Douhet, and Alexander de Seversky reiterated for the air environment the vices in Alfred Thayer Mahan's theory of sea power.[10] To be strategically valuable beyond reasonable argument, a great navy does not have to be the "key force" for victory. By logical and practical extension, to be recognized as an essential player in conflict air power does not have to demonstrate that it is able to win wars independently.

For the better part of seventy years some air power theorists and air forces have waged doctrinal-political wars that should not have been fought. This is not to deny the historical fact of often deeply prejudiced and self-interested opposition to the growth of "independent" air power on the part of earthbound and sea-girt minds. Nonetheless, real and influential though the institutional and hence political opposition to air forces frequently has been, a proper understanding of what air power could accomplish in particular conditions persistently has been impeded by air power theorists who have overreached themselves. Inadvertently, those advocates have all but invited government and the public to ask the wrong questions and hold air force performance to irrelevant standards of superheroic strategic effectiveness.

As a general rule, navies do not expect to be the sole executive agency delivering success in deterrence or the actual conduct of war.[11] Even ardent navalists have tended to appreciate that command of the sea helps threats to be deterred or wars to be won. To the degree to which sea power doctrine has strayed into the realm of claims for an allegedly independent decisive effect on the course of history, it has hurt its excellent case for strategic utility. Much, indeed most, of sea power doctrine and the theory of maritime strategy is sensible and relatively noncontroversial. It is ironic that the leading theorists of air power, who had in hand an excellent case that was easy to make, chose to commit a fallacy similar to Mahan's by claiming too much for their strategic instrument.

There is a burden of history upon this analysis which renders cool consideration of the future of air and space power needlessly difficult. Specifically, some theorists of and commentators upon air power continue in the 1990s to pursue the elusive and dubious goal of "dominant weapon" status for the air arm. For example, the ghosts of Trenchard, Mitchell, and Douhet will have approved of Richard P. Hallion's judgment that "[a]ir power execution caught up with air power theory, as evidenced by the conduct and results of the Gulf war, over sixty years later [than when Mitchell wrote *Skyways* in 1930]."[12] The point is not that Hallion is wrong. In fact Hallion is resoundingly correct about the essential fit between U.S. air power performance in the Gulf in 1991 and the central thrust of classical air power theory. The point, rather, is that classical air power theory often, though not invariably, postulated the wrong requirement of the air weapon—that it be capable of winning wars on its own—and that glorification of the apparent vindication in 1991 of that absurd standard is not useful.

FIND THE RIGHT QUESTIONS

Because the primary focus of this analysis is upon air and space forces and upon ideas for their employment, it may seem that undue criticism is leveled here at the community of air power theorists past and present (as yet, there are no space or aerospace theorists worthy of particular note).[13] Such an impression would be false. I am well aware of the historical circumstances of air force experience and am sensitive to the actual and potential errors of those who proclaim as eternal truths what, in fact, were but temporary terms in military relationships. Strategic utility should follow military effectiveness, other things being tolerably equal.[14] The value of air forces in relation to other kinds of forces must alter over time, as well as from conflict to conflict. For example, the relations among infantry, cavalry, and artillery shifted cumulatively and dramatically from the mid-sixteenth century to 1900, even though each was modernized. The relations among ground, sea, and air forces from 1914 to today have altered more noticeably than did those among the ground trinity just cited over a two-hundred-and-fifty-year period. Nonetheless, many people still have failed mentally to come to grips with the political, strategic, operational, and tactical meaning of modern air and space forces.

The problem is not so much parochial theorists who seek willfully to direct debate with terms inherently favorable to their preferred strategic worldview. Rather, the problem is both air power theorists who inadvertently are waging yesterday's battles and theorists generically hostile to air power who are only too happy to join some of the air power advocates in intellectual combat over what amounts to the wrong issues and questions. The post–Desert Storm literature is shot through with foolish arguments about who, or what, really won the war and what kind of armed force truly proved itself decisive or dominant. Arguments thus framed are inherently silly and lead to a blind alley for defense planning: everybody loses.

The time is long overdue for the U.S. body politic to engage the question of what it means to be the leading air power. If that is the first of the right questions to pose, the second such question has to probe for the methodology for determining how much, and what kinds of, air power the country needs to provide for a prudent defense. The conduct of detailed force planning is a military-professional specialty with which this book will not seek to compete.[15] Rather than attempt to pick the right number of wings and the right mix of weapon systems, this analysis identifies the right, or at least a good enough, way to guide defense and force planning. It is not useful to ask such questions as Has air power finally come of age? (in some respects air power came of age in 1916 over Verdun); Is Giulio Douhet vindicated at last? (which is to pretend that Douhet was a careful theorist instead of a romantic visionary, albeit a visionary who sometimes wrote wisely);[16] and the like. The right questions to pose are, What does it mean for the United States to be the leading air power? How can U.S. defense planners best determine how much, and what kinds of, air power to acquire?

In a deceptively simple manner these questions point the way forward. The first question is about the strategic utility of air forces in different kinds of conflicts. Also, this question is about the probable fit of air activity with American strategic culture.[17] Air power thus has both a foreign and a domestic context for consideration by U.S. policymakers who must address the second question. Although national grand and military strategy has to "work" abroad, in the first instance it has to "work" at home.

CONCEPTS

Conceptual confusion can be costly. In particular, lack of clarity about distinctions within two sets of related concepts continues to wreak gratuitous damage upon national defense. The first set of concepts are the linked notions of strategy, operations, and tactics; the second are the concepts of aerospace power, air power, and space power. The analysis and the judgments provided here are offered without apology to historical usage, current doctrinal authority, or indeed to anything except common sense and experience.

Strategy and Tactics

It is distracting enough to have to cope with the realities of an air power that is land based or sea based and that may be operated by any one of four armed services (to distinguish the Marine Corps from the U.S. Navy but to disregard the Coast Guard), without attempting to grapple with falsely drawn distinctions. As explained at some length in Chapter 1, there is no such beast as "strategic" air power and there are no such things as "strategic" targets. Military strategy is the art of employing armed force for the political purposes set by and as policy. Weapons, broadly understood, will vary in range, lethality, and other effects, and even in relative significance, but they do not divide into strategic as contrasted with tactical types. By way of a healthy conceptual cleansing, most of the sundry and varied meanings of strategic should be discarded. Specifically, the adjective *strategic* should not be taken to imply any of the following: long-range; off-battlefield (narrowly interpreted as the area of engagement between armed forces); nuclear; important; or earmarked for, or regularly commanded by, a military organization that is labeled strategic. Current discourse on air power is confused by the undisciplined use of all of the above purported meanings of strategic.

As suggested already, there is only one simple distinction that makes sense and is readily understandable. Namely, whereas tactics is the realm of the actual employment of armed forces, strategy refers to the intended or real consequences of the use of forces for the course and outcome of a war. It follows that all weapons are tactical in their immediate effect, and all weapons are strategic in the consequences of their actions. Similarly, in principle all weapons can have operational consequences when they are threatened or employed in order to attempt to achieve campaign-wide objectives.

This commonsense distinction between tactics and strategy should have contributed to the liberation of the air force from the tyranny of unhelpful concepts. It was not really ironical that most of the "strategic" bombing in Korea, Southeast Asia, and the Gulf War of 1991 was conducted by "tactical" aviation, while "strategic" bombers (with the exception of Linebacker II in December 1972) in those conflicts typically were confined to "tactical" missions. With the creation of Air Combat Command and the inauguration of the composite wing, the U.S. Air Force in the 1990s effected what should prove to be a historic breakout from the tactical/strategic straitjacket. Nonetheless, the mental habits of a professional lifetime or two are not so easily cleansed and transformed. It is useful to highlight some of the costs of the old thinking on tactics and strategy.

- The relationship between tactics and strategy was fundamentally confused. If there are inherently tactical and inherently strategic (and, in some speculation, even inherently operational) forces, what does that imply for the utility and value of each? Indeed, this absurd distinction implies that somehow there are separate tactical, operational, and strategic wars![18]

- Strategic planning and reasoning are hindered, because the source of strategic effect (tactical and operational behavior) is not clear.

- The defense community as a whole, military and civilian, is encouraged to focus on what weapons or forces do, rather than on the consequences of what they do. If a weapon is called strategic, by implication at least the performance of that weapon and the effect of that performance are conflated.

Many defense professionals have succeeded in thinking clearly despite the conceptual confusion under discussion here. The time is long overdue, however, to render the key concepts and their interrelationship much more user-friendly. To repeat: tactical refers to the threat or use of any kind of armed force, while *strategic* points to the consequences of that threat or use. Therefore, in variable degree from context to context, all weapons and forces can be called strategic, which is precisely why no weapons or forces should be so designated.

Air Power and Aerospace Power

Air power is a younger conceptual relative of sea power and it shares some of the same problems that have beset the older term. Just as many states have had some sea power, few such have warranted plausible description as sea powers. Virtually all states today have some air power, but only the United States can lay convincing claim to being an air power. But what is air power (sea power, land power, or space power)? Plainly it is more, much more, than the first-line air fighting strength of the armed services (let alone of the air force specifically). In fact, a satisfactory definition of air power has proved elusive. Since sea power too has evaded a firm definition, it is probably the case that the difficulty is a systemic one. One of the reasons is suggested by the claim advanced in a superior study of the future of sea power: "Sea power and air power are indivisible."[19] The sense in that aphorism was signed in Norway and at Taranto in 1940, sealed at Pearl Harbor a year later, and delivered in May and June 1942 at the Coral Sea and Midway. Similarly viewed, sea power and land power also are indivisible. Without the power developed by the national territory, where could the country's sea power come from and what strategic meaning or purpose could it have?

For the United States at least, land power, sea power, air power, and now space power cannot be mutually exclusive categories of environmentally specialized military strength. The interdependencies among these categories are pervasive and significant, albeit to a degree elusive to specify. When in doubt it is a good idea to resort to common sense and to remember that definitions are arbitrary and more or less useful; they are not in any positivist sense true. On that relaxed note, it is necessary to identify the components of (U.S.) air power:

- the first-line fighting strength of military aviation and its essential immediate support services
- the second-line, or reserve, fighting strength of military aviation and its immediate support services
- the military infrastructure of organized activities (education, training) which ultimately produces air fighting strength
- the industrial and scientific base which produces the machines of all kinds necessary to generate and support aircraft in action
- the civil aviation industry that shares some skills, some technologies, and potentially some people and aircraft with military aviation

In his path-breaking discussion of the "principal conditions affecting the sea power of nations," Mahan wisely included a discussion of the "character of the government."[20] U.S. government policy will be critical to the future of the components of air power, even the future of civil aviation. Governments have been known to try to acquire first-class naval power without investing suitably in dockyards, naval stores, and the training of seamen.[21] More recently, Germany and Japan demonstrated what can happen to air power that has virtually all of its wares in the window and little in reserve to replace expended or obsolete items. To be adequate, a characterization or definition of air power must accommodate, end to end, the total process that produces a stream of combat and combat support aircraft.

The development and sustenance of first-class military aviation is a story of uncompromising personnel standards, technological frontiersmanship (e.g., stealthy design and precision guidance for vehicles and munitions), and an intelligent procurement system and acquisition strategy. In addition and more important still, there are the realms of high policy and grand and military strategy which provide the demand for military aviation. Recognition of or hope for tactical prowess can shape strategy and even trigger particular strategic choices, but the tactical world of forces as threat or in action is meaningless without the sanction and guidance of policy and strategy. Over the next several decades, choices in policy and strategy will have far more to say about the future of U.S. air power than will exciting technological possibilities, a military tradition of success, or skilled and dedicated people. What will be asked of U.S. air power cannot be independent of expectations of air prowess, but likely tactical or even operational merit is not a self-validating quality in the struggle for scarce resources during a long peace.

The conflation of air and space into aerospace has the authority of three and a half decades and points, accurately enough, to the leading role of the air force in developing, acquiring, launching, and maintaining space systems. On 3 February 1959, Air Force Chief of Staff Thomas D. White explained that

> The Air Force has operated throughout its relatively short history in the sensible atmosphere around the earth. Recent developments have allowed us to extend our operations further away from the earth, approaching the environment popularly referred to as space. Since there is no dividing line, no natural barrier separating these two areas, there can be no operational boundary between them. Thus air and space comprise a single continuous operational field in which the Air Force must continue to function. This area is aerospace.[22]

Understood simply as air and space, or as the environmental domains for which the air force has or should have primary responsibility, aerospace is unobjectionable. Unfortunately, however, the concept of aerospace has some potential to mislead the unwary. It is true that there is no visible, sharply edged natural barrier separating the atmosphere from space, but it is manifestly not true to suggest that there is no natural barrier at all. The concept of aerospace refers to forces in two environments allegedly with "no operational boundary between them." Since aircraft cannot function in the vacuum of space and spacecraft can operate only in space, General White's reasoning is hard to follow.

What has happened is that a good case for air force preponderance in space has been and remains endangered by claims that no operational boundary exists. General White's argument that technology has allowed the air force to reach higher and higher is a valid claim. The foolish implication that there is no operational boundary between air and space, however, needs to be replaced. It is more accurate to say that space systems are force multipliers for air power (*inter alia*) and that the air force is best situated to take the lead, indeed to continue to take the lead, in space power development for the benefit of all the armed forces. Aerospace is an unfortunate term because it denies the laws of physics and implies an operational continuum which technology and its dependent tactics thus far flatly deny (pending realization of an aerospace plane).

The least developed of environmentally specialized forces, space systems, have a notable way to go before their strategic, operational, and tactical integration with land, sea, and air forces could be considered mature.[23] Desert Storm illustrated in the least arguable of fashions just how valuable assistance from space can be for land, sea, and air forces.[24] Space systems are not uniquely useful to air forces, though such utility may be of extraordinary military significance if air power is the leading element of military power, a status more likely to be achieved with assistance from maturing space capabilities. Space forces have in common with air forces activity in the "overhead flank" of terrestrial operations, and space systems function "next" to the air envelope (rather than to the sea or the land). But the space environment is geophysically and hence technologically, tactically, and operationally as distinctive from the air as it is from the land and the sea.

Because the air environment is the primary focus of attention of the air force, there is always the danger that the concept of aerospace will conceal that which should not be concealed: the operational distinctiveness of the space environment. The air force, at the highest level, is not confused about the reality behind this discussion. Former chief of staff General Merrill A. McPeak has said that "[o]ur mission . . . is to defend the United States through control and exploitation of air and space."[25] In any unequal marriage, for example as between air and space forces today, there is peril for the interests of the weaker partner. A concept such as aerospace that effects a linguistic fusion of physically and operationally distinctive elements needs to be treated with caution.

ON UNDERSTANDING AIR POWER

Even in this joint "purple" era ushered in by the Goldwater-Nichols Defense Reorganization Act of 1986, in-depth understanding of the strengths, limitations, and particular characteristics and requirements of air, sea, land, or space forces by people focused upon another geographical environment is not widespread. Douhet made a point for the ages when he wrote in February 1928: "There are army experts but there are not war experts. And war is indivisible, and so is its purpose."[26]

The problem has several levels. At the most fundamental level, people who are not air professionals can have genuine difficulty understanding the nature of the air environment and the constraints and opportunities unique to it. Next, there are always ample grounds to dispute just how useful a particular country's air assets will be in a particular conflict. Finally, rarely is it abundantly plain how the treasured generalities of theory and doctrine should be applied in practice.

Historically considered, the relative operational and strategic utility of air power (or sea power or space power) has not always been self-evident. Beliefs abound, but actual knowledge of what historically specific air power could achieve today or in the near future typically has been as arguable as have been the alleged implications of the conclusion to that analysis for other contexts. Military historians are right, for example, to emphasize the innate difficulty of understanding what a rapidly developing air power could achieve in 1914–18.[27] But it is worth noting that the historians of military aviation tend to be so focused upon the skies that they neglect to notice the technical-tactical, and hence operational and strategic, novelty of the industrial-age mass armies and the steel and steam navies of that period. Military aviation was the least mature of the players in 1914–18, but war on land and war at sea in practice were experimental also.[28]

By their natures, theory and doctrine are abstract and yield only general explanations and generalized guidance for behavior. In practice, the world is always concrete, never abstract. Air power, in its relationship to land power, for example, always has national historical, geographical, and strategic-cultural particulars. Theory and doctrine crafted on the basis of past experience, especially if that experience is distinctive in character, are unlikely to provide sound guidance for different circumstances. For no branch of the armed forces has this been more true than for air power. The liberation of force projection from the surface of the earth understandably effected a like liberation of the strategic imagination and strategic controversy. Doctrine needs constantly to be revisited as theory interacts with practice. Every air force has learnt some faulty lessons from historical experience and has neglected to note lessons of enduring merit. Examples abound. Most clearly of all perhaps, the U.S. Army Air Forces (USAAF) and then the U.S. Air Force were obliged to rediscover the feasibility and importance of close air support (from the lessons of 1918) no fewer than three times (1941–45, 1950–53, 1965–72).[29]

Sweeping generalizations about air power, though enlightening across many cases and many years, are always liable to refutation in particular cases. Air power is stronger on the offense than the defense,[30] but in a particular war that may not be true. The Luftwaffe was defeated in the Battle of Britain in 1940, while the Royal Air Force (RAF) similarly lacked offensive potency over the continent in 1940–41, and both the RAF and the USAAF were defeated, for a while, in the Combined Bomber Offensive as it was conducted in 1943 and the winter of 1943–44.[31] The strategic and operational effectiveness of an air force depends upon such factors as strategy, technology, numbers, political constraints, *and the enemy*, and cannot be deduced in any particular case from general principles which purportedly govern the universal utility of air power.

While it is true that historical circumstances must always be unique, still there are environmentally specific factors that influence the character of military operations. It is commonplace, but important, to claim that speed, range, flexibility, precision, and lethality are characteristic of the air force. It is not quite true to claim, as did an air force white paper, that those qualities are "unique characteristics of the Air Force."[32] Is one talking strategically, operationally, or tactically? With good reason the army would claim precision and lethality for its multiple launch rocket system, its laser-guided Copperhead artillery shells, and its special operations forces (*inter alia*), while the navy would argue that its Gulf-demonstrated precision in shore bombardment by gun and missile was lethal enough. Blanket claims to the effect that the air force, uniquely, operates at high speed and with useful range, flexibility, precision, and lethality are so obviously wrong as stated that they hurt the credibility of the story the air force should tell. This is another case of the self-inflicted wound. Obviously false or exaggerated claims impair credibility. Whether or not this too is an exaggeration, the view remains popular that

> The ultimate determinant in war is the man on the scene with the gun. This man is the final power in war. He determines who wins. There are those who would dispute this as an absolute, but it is my belief that while other means may critically influence war today [1967], after whatever devastation and destruction may be inflicted on an enemy, if the strategist is forced to strive for final and ultimate control, he must establish, or must present as an inevitable prospect, a man on the scene with a gun. This is the soldier.[33]

The author of that judgment, Rear Admiral J. C. Wylie, risks confusing causes with precipitating events and is perilously general in his argument. Nonetheless, there is sufficient merit in his point as to remind air power theorists of the need to think holistically about conflict, if only for the purpose of providing plausible refutation of others' claims.

THE ADVANTAGES OF AIR POWER

Each geographical environment is an operating medium with distinctive characteristics for geographically "tailored" forces. Those forces function with distinctive advantages and disadvantages that vary from situation to situation. Air power as threat or in action is not an abstraction. But to understand what a unique air force in a unique conflict might be able to achieve, and hence might be tasked to attempt, the general advantages and limitations of the air environment have to be appreciated. Seven claimed advantages of air power now are presented and discussed briefly.

Ubiquity. Sailors are fond of remarking that nearly 70 percent of the world's surface is water; they are less willing to advertise the fact that 100 percent of the world's surface is "surrounded" by air. It is true that the better maritime theorists think globally because "all the seas of the world are one."[34] But it is also true that the world's landforms impose noticeable physical restrictions upon ease of marine movement. (Consider the difficulty that Russia/the

U.S.S.R. traditionally has had in implementing a coherent naval policy and strategy with major fleets distributed among the Black Sea, the Baltic Sea, the Barents Sea, and the Pacific. Or consider the problems for fleet size and U.S. naval deployment that were resolved by the opening of the Panama Canal in 1914.)

The overhead flank. Command of the air flank has long been a necessary, if not always sufficient, precondition for success in mid- and high-intensity conflict. The permanent, if variable, significance of freedom to use, and deny use of, the third geographical dimension means that all overt military operations must have an air story of one kind or another. As threat or as support, operations in and from the air flank to terrestrial operations generally assume the importance of literally vital enabler or disabler. The air story is not restricted to the tale of a flank to operations on land and sea. Land and sea operations may assume flanking status vis-à-vis principal military operations which take the form of an air offensive. Ground and maritime forces can have as their primary mission the securing of bases for the projection of air power and the forward delivery and protection of fuel, ordnance, and other bulky stores necessary for the conduct of an air campaign. Admiral Chester Nimitz's central Pacific drive in 1943–45 toward the Philippines and then the Japanese home islands, though in one sense a triumph for sea power, also can be interpreted as the securing of the maritime flank from which long-range, land-based aircraft could wage the concluding campaign of air bombardment.

Range and reach. Because of the nature of the air environment, late-model military aviation today literally has the range to reach anywhere on the globe. Operating from Whiteman Air Force Base in the continental United States and with continuing access to bases on Diego Garcia and Guam, the B-2 bomber, for example, can reach anywhere on earth within twenty-three hours and perform "silver bullet" duty with smart ordnance. Whether or not range truly grants reach depends on the penetrability of the air assets. The weight, and hence potentially the strategic effectiveness, of the reach must depend upon the quantity and lethality of the sting that can be projected by air. In principle, at least, air power grants an access to distant targets that does not have to be earned by the prior defeat of terrestrial forces. Contrary to the beliefs of some early air power theorists, as well as of the RAF and the USAAF prior to the winter of 1943–44, however, reliable access by air to an enemy's center of gravity does have to be earned by prior victory in and for the air.[35] The range, reach, and defining focus of operational attention are uniquely global for air and space forces. Ground and sea forces have their distinctive mobility stories and their individual merits with continental and maritime reach, but the adjectives *continental* and *maritime* define major limits that do not apply to air power.

Speed of passage. The mechanics of flight and the lack of geographical barriers in the air, as contrasted with the friction that impedes rapid progress on land

and sea, allow for an expedition in military air operations that can be a quality of unique worth. Speed is time and time is an invaluable asset, or an implacable foe, in war.[36] Air power may not arrive with the largest punch, a qualification of diminishing merit even without nuclear considerations in mind, but as a general rule air power will be able to get there first. Speed of response is not always critical, but when it is, the potential strategic effectiveness of air power all but speaks for itself. Air power may well more than pull its weight if by early intervention in a regional conflict it can limit the rate of gain on the ground by an aggressor. U.S. air power alone did not defeat the North Korean invasion of South Korea in the summer of 1950, but it did, albeit barely, enable that invasion to be halted.[37] In the Korean War, as so often in twentieth-century military history, a search for the independently decisive employment of air power risks undervaluing the actual record of achievement.

Geographically unrestricted routing. This is an exaggeration, but it is an exaggeration licensed by the importance of the point highlighted. In practice, aircraft routing can be restricted by political, operational, tactical, technical, and meteorological considerations. In principle, however, and generally in practice to a notable degree, there is a natural freedom of choice in the movement of airplanes that is physically impossible for land, sea, and space vehicles. Geographical barriers do not hinder movement by air. However, the all-vector menace posed by an enemy in the air is somewhat alleviated by the fact that whatever his choices of routes, he has to arrive over or close to targets whose value is well known. In other words, we may not know how a foe is coming, but we should be able to anticipate his destination.

Superior observation. The air and space environments truly comprise the "high ground" for terrestrial conflict. The first and in some ways still the most valuable military quality of air and space vehicles is their ability to see over the continental or maritime horizon.[38] This superiority in observation is both a vital contributor to the potency of air power itself and a critical force multiplier for land and sea forces. The implications of early detection and observation of the enemy have varied with technology. In 1914, aerial observation of the German retreat from the Marne encouraged the Franco-British armies to advance cautiously on the ground to the Aisne River. In 1991 in the Gulf, the detection by airborne radar of large-scale troop and vehicle movement led inexorably to devastating air strikes which decided the course and outcome of the battle. Of the battle of Khafji, which began on 29 January 1991, for example, Richard Hallion notes justly that "Khafji was not a totally clearcut case of a victory through air power, but it came very close—close enough for the point to be argued with vigor."[39] Whether or not air power itself does the lion's share of the damage to enemy forces is a subject only of secondary significance; what matters profoundly is that the superior power of observation granted by air (and space) vehicles enables the enemy to be located, tracked, gripped, bombarded, or evaded. The theory and practice of air and space forces in deterrence and in war are about the deterrence or defeat of the enemy, not necessarily about his deterrence or defeat by those forces alone.

Flexibility in concentration. The revolution in war triggered most noticeably by the marriage of information-age systems to airplanes and cruise missiles requires consideration of the validity, or perhaps interpretation for application, of the revered principle of mass for concentration of force in war. Carl von Clausewitz, writing of Napoleonic continental warfare, advised that "there is no higher and simpler law of strategy than that of *keeping one's forces concentrated.*"[40] Readers had just been told that "[t]he best strategy is always *to be very strong*: first in general, and then at the decisive point." In other words, do not dissipate strength which should be applied in a concentrated fashion at the point or points of decision. Mass, and concentration to achieve mass, were not ends in themselves to Clausewitz; they were means to the end of the ability to win. To adapt Marshall McLuhan, in military affairs the medium is the message, with a caveat for the impact of evolving technologies.

Concentration and mass have meanings quite distinctive for land, sea, and air warfare. British naval theorist Julian S. Corbett, writing in 1911, observed that "[w]ell as this terminology [three senses of concentration: assembling an army; moving an army; readying an army to strike] appears to serve on land . . . something more exact is required if we try to extend it to the sea. Such extension magnifies the error at every step, and clear thinking becomes difficult."[41] Corbett distinguished between mass and concentration, a distinction that demands further refinement for this era of mature air forces. Mass traditionally has offered essential benefits both for defensive and for offensive strength. Notwithstanding their commitment to precision bombing, the leaders of the USAAF in World War II would have agreed with Vice Admiral Lord Nelson's aphorism that "numbers only can annihilate."[42] Traditionally, numbers (mass) have been essential in order to apply the weight of firepower essential for offensive or defensive success. The logic is unaltered from the 1940s to the 1990s (or, in Nelson's case, from the 1790s and 1800s to the 1900s), but the numbers now necessary to secure a concentration of force for decisive tactical, operational, and ultimately strategic effect can be very small relative to the numbers required in past decades. The revolution just described flows from the following comparison: the circular error probable (CEP)[43] of a two-thousand-pound bomb dropped by a B-17 or B-24 over Europe in World War II was 3,300 feet; the CEP of a precision-guided munition (PGM) delivered in the Gulf War of 1991 was 10 feet, which is in the asymptotic range of effectively zero CEP.[44] This is not to say that all aerial munitions in Desert Storm were that precise; in fact, only 7 percent were PGMs. Nonetheless, courtesy of improved aircraft navigation and much improved bomb design even the "dumb" bombs of today are rendered precise by 1944 standards. It should be noted that there are no lethal munitions, precision guided or other, if target intelligence is absent or poor. There is nothing inherently uniquely precise about aerial bombardment. Indeed, given the motion of the weapon delivery platform quite the reverse is true. But there is a unique quantity and quality of lethality from the sky which flows synergistically from all of the attributes of modern aircraft and their support systems. The speed, range and reach, and agility of airplanes allow them to concentrate with a flexibility unmatchable by vehicles specialized for operation in the land and sea environments and to achieve a potentially decisive concentration of force at the critical point.

KEY VALUES

Unity, flexibility, and concentration are the three values which, properly interpreted, penetrate to the heart of the distinctive strategic utility of air power. These are the key values which should guide proposals for the roles of air forces in the future. The unity of the air environment is an invitation to the shapers of air forces to forge doctrine, organization, and force structure capable of exploiting that geographical fact to the full. Notwithstanding the undeniable needs of land and naval forces for closely adjunct aviation support, air forces should seek to offset and sidestep (literally overfly), as well as to overcome, the distinctive limitations of terrestrially bound military power.

Wars, like political causes and would-be warriors, come in a wide variety of shapes and sizes. Air power has the flexibility to be influential, if not always decisively so, in all of them. Key to clarity of thought is recognition of the essential unity of the effectiveness of air power. In its many specialized variants air power has different roles and missions, but there is a common currency in strategic consequences. Douhet was wrong to advocate an all-purpose "battleplane,"[45] but he was resoundingly correct to see a unified air power influencing the course and outcome of war as a whole. Air power may be nuclear or conventionally armed, loaded with "dumb" or smart ordnance, short or long in range, and so forth. Similarly, air power may be applied in an attempt to coerce society or to overthrow a state's military power. But air power cannot be divided into strategic or tactical elements. The importance, even the feasibility, of different kinds of missions will vary from conflict to conflict. Air power has to be guided in its development by a comprehensive theory of success in deterrence and war. The plain meaning of this logic is that all of the country's air power assets comprise an instrument that generates strategic influence.

The flexibility in behavior that the air environment allows to aircraft finds ample parallels in the operational purposes to which air power profitably can be applied. This point serves to warn against rigid notions of the allegedly proper employment of air power and against a view of the value of aircraft that assigns strategic merit to some roles but not to others. The nature of the air environment, as exploited by modern technology that allows "air power" to embrace rotary-wing gunships and stealthy intercontinental bombers, allows a flexibility in concentration of projected force from a local battlefield to the enemy's capital city. Whether or not air power actually will achieve an independent or decisively enabling concentration of force is a question that can be answered only in specific cases.

The seven identified sources of strategic advantage amount to a potent promise of political-military effectiveness. Considered and applied in their order of presentation the seven advantages can operate as follows. Air power (1) has a truly *global* domain; (2) necessarily takes and exploits the *overhead* flank, the "high ground"; (3) enjoys, with some forward-basing support and with aerial refueling, a practically unlimited *range and reach*; (4) can have a *speed* of passage in mission execution that is unrivaled (except by ballistic missiles or spacecraft); (5) because of geographically *unrestricted routing* can menace an enemy from all directions; (6) is granted the benefit over terrestrially bound elements of *superior observation* of objects and activities of interest; and (7) can project power with an *unparalleled flexibility* for the purpose of achieving what could be a *decisive concentration of force*.

As noted already, a theory of air power for deterrence and war is not synonymous with a theory of war. Speaking in 1953, General Hoyt S. Vandenberg, then air force chief of staff, said, "Let us keep our eye on the goal of air power, which is to knock out the ability of a nation to fight."[46] The general was wrong. He was not wrong in pointing to the potential utility of air power, especially nuclear-armed air power, to knock out the ability of a nation to fight. But he was wrong to assert that goal as the sole purpose of air power. Even Giulio Douhet was not so single-tracked in his logic, though admittedly the Italian general did not envisage nuclear weapons or fleets of B-36s, B-47s, and B-52s.

Douhet wrote, correctly, that "[t]he conquest of the command of the air will be a necessary condition of future wars, even if it will not insure victory by itself."[47] He proceeded to argue that "[i]f the Air force is not left with enough strength ['to crush the material and moral resistance of the enemy" after winning air superiority], the conflict will be decided by the land and sea forces, whose task will be greatly facilitated by having the command of the air on their side." In other words, air power can play critically either as an independent agent of victory or as an enabling agent for other elements of the armed forces. In seeking sensibly to avoid the misuse of air power, theorists should not confuse the proper use of air power with a single vision of future conflict. It is worth recalling that even in Desert Storm the goal of the war was formally neither the overthrow of Saddam Hussein's regime nor the utter ruin of Iraq as a functioning state and society.

Peril lies in inappropriate historical analogies which capture the strategic imagination. For example, just because U.S. air power failed for nearly three years to coerce North Korea and China to a tolerable peace,[48] and because Operation Rolling Thunder was a failure for more than three years against North Vietnam,[49] most emphatically it does not follow that air power should not be used as a coercive instrument.[50] Air power can serve well the logic of policy that should govern the conduct of many conflicts, provided the "grammar" of air warfare is respected by politicians and adhered to by military professionals.[51] Air power cannot be judged to have failed or succeeded in the abstract, but only in relation to specific tasks assigned in unique political-military contexts.

THE LIMITATIONS OF AIR POWER

> [S]uch background factors as topography, vegetative cover, the availability of airfields and ports, human settlement patterns, the ratio of troops to space, and the run of weather will continue to affect the fortunes of air war.[52]

Following the format established above, the discussion here invites respect for the limitations of air power. The factors so identified are gravity, the cost of sophistication in dollars and low numbers, weather, brevity of presence in a combat zone, the distance from terrestrial conflict provided by altitude, and the political boundaries of sovereign air space. In particular cases, these generic limitations are not always such, and often they can be alleviated by technology, tactics, operational design, and strategy and policy choices. The analysis concludes with a set of qualifications to the potential significance of the limitations upon air power.

To cite and discuss a list of air power's limitations, as though the items specified were permanent in value, is not to be blind to the reality of choices that diminish or strengthen their potency. Governments can choose to buy more or less air power; to buy more or less of different kinds of air power; to weaponize and procure in large numbers technologies at a certain time rather than later; and to employ their chosen mix of air power in a variety of ways. The limitations of air power must therefore have specific historical reference to particular strategic and policy demands. To discuss the advantages and the limitations of air power in a general way will not point to conclusions applicable to any real individual case. The strengths and weaknesses of the RAF and the Luftwaffe over France and England in 1940, for example, were unique and traceable to policy and program choices made several years previously. But, as with the taxonomy of air power's advantages, the purpose here is to explore the nature of air power in all periods so that the points are independent of policy, time, and technology. To understand the bounds of the possible and probable and to perceive the structure of the subject, it is essential to achieve liberation from the tyranny of the historically particular. The following items are the principal persisting structural limitations of air power.

Gravity. To fly is briefly to defeat gravity. The machinery necessary to defeat gravity and achieve desirable combat qualities (e.g., range and speed) in flying vehicles is expensive both financially and in the useful payload that it consumes. Prior to the outbreak of World War I there was a prevailing belief that aerial combat was a physical impossibility. The Fokker Eindecker laid that temporary orthodoxy to rest in 1915,[53] while a new orthodoxy maintained that aircraft would not be able to carry a payload, for example, a bomb load, sufficiently significant as to render the bomber an important independent, or perhaps semi-independent, agent in war. Those passing fallacies rested upon overestimation of the physical constraints upon aircraft. The air power visionaries were correct. The much and unduly maligned Giulio Douhet offered the following apparently absurd judgment in his 1921 book: "The day will come when no one will think of crossing the ocean by steamer, just as no one today thinks of doing it by sailboat."[54] The air and space environments, however, provide geographical constraints of considerable operational importance. More than ninety years after Kitty Hawk, air power (let alone space power) is not competitive with sea or land power for the long-haul carriage of bulky or (most) heavy cargoes. This is not to demean air and space vehicles; it is simply to recognize enduring, geographically attributable economic facts. Experience has shown that there are practicable limits in each period to the performance requirements that can be placed upon aircraft design. One can be optimistic over the advantages likely to be yielded by future air and space technologies, yet still believe that the very nature of the air environment will continue to impose significant constraints upon the practicable design and purposes of air-breathing vehicles.

Sophistication, expense, low numbers. Only rarely has a lack of numbers failed to be a significant limitation upon the utility of air power. The Gulf War of 1991 was just such an exception, while in Southeast Asia two decades and more earlier the limitations of most import were political constraints, poor intelligence, and distinctly suboptimal technologies (e.g., a lack of air superiority fighters and the unavailability until late of "smart" bombs). It has always been expensive to put men in state-of-the-art combat machines that defy gravity. That expense can be assessed fairly only in the context of the relative military effectiveness that is purchased. Many air forces have found a workable compromise solution to the high cost of late-model aircraft in some variant of a high-low (cost/capability) mix. There is an old saying that "quantity has a quality all its own." If only 20, rather than the original 132, B-2 bombers are acquired, each aircraft has to be treated as a precious resource. The situation is not quite analogous to the operational care that the navy takes with its twelve or so aircraft carriers, but the comparison is not wholly misleading. There is a flexibility in large numbers and an inflexibility in lack of numbers. It is true that each late-model aircraft can be so militarily effective that functionally it replaces tens and even hundreds of its predecessors. But still, that F-15E, F-117, or B-2, no matter how elusive, is only one target on the ground or in the air and can be in only one place at one time. The technological sophistication that enables handfuls of modern aircraft to perform missions previously assigned to whole air fleets therefore comes at the cost of small numbers, high unit prices, and necessarily a distribution of military value over few vehicles. First-line air power typically, though not invariably, has been a scarce resource with high opportunity costs for its faulty employment. The case against a genuinely low side of a high-low mix is well nigh overwhelming.[55] (The U.S. "low" is the distinctly "high" F-16 and F-18, as contrasted with the F-15 and F-14.) The experience of Desert Storm notwithstanding, it is only prudent to assume that in the future air power is likely to be short in supply relative to strategic demand, and hence in need of the most careful prioritization for its use.

Weather. Just as technology can more than offset a reduction in aircraft numbers, so also can it defeat many adverse weather conditions. Air power is becoming less and less constrained by weather, but it is not, and is unlikely ever to be, truly independent of weather. Such geophysical effects as snow, sand storms, high winds, high sea states, volcanic ash, solar flares, and even low clouds, to cite but a few, will all have a negative impact upon the feasibility or tempo of air operations. Not only do flying combat platforms have to be all-weather and day-night capable, but so also does their ordnance.

Brevity of presence. In the form of near continuous attack an air force as a whole may secure a grip upon an enemy on the ground or at sea. The physics and logistics of flight, however, require that each individual aircraft can be present in a combat area only relatively briefly; relative, that is, to the local endurance of troops on the ground or to ships at sea. The plainest historical example of the problem posed by brevity of air presence was in the Battle of Britain. In that case, the short reach of the German fighter force relative to the reach of German bombers and the endurance of British fighters (equally short-legged, but fighting at home) was a fact that shaped the campaign. As Alfred Price has written, "Dominating all tactical considerations on the German side, during the Battle of Britain, was the short range and endurance of the Messerschmidt 109."[56] A similar judgment was to apply in 1943 to the short-legged fighter assets of the RAF and the USAAF vis-à-vis their inability to escort Eighth Air Force B-17s and B-24s deep into Germany. The endurance of aircraft and aircrew in a combat zone is limited severely by the nature of the air environment and by the technical requirements of flight. Sustained local presence in the air typically is physically impracticable. Indeed, pending the achievement of air superiority, the operational demands of the counterair campaign must dominate other considerations. An ever present (defensive) air power is achievable for the navy with aircraft carriers, albeit at a heavy price in offensive punch eschewed (i.e., at the cost of a heavy "virtual attrition" in potential offensive punch). As a general rule, which does admit of exceptions, it is of the nature of air power to be present in concentrated form over a combat zone only intermittently. Of course, helicopters, short takeoff and landing aircraft, and gun ships can approximate continuous presence *in a permissive air environment.*

Altitude. The very height that is to the comparative advantage of air (and space) power also limits air power's utility. Aircraft can observe, bomb, strafe, drop supplies, and perform all manner of useful services for ground and naval forces, as well, as a first priority, as prosecute the necessary campaign for supremacy in the air. But aircraft cannot come physically to sustained grip with the enemy. Of necessity aircraft are apart from conflict on the ground or on and under the surface of the sea. It is no criticism of air power to note that although it can bombard and observe the results (bomb damage assessment, or BDA), assessment of the military effectiveness of such action often is difficult from the air. Forces specialized for combat in each environment tend naturally enough to acquire a culture, a mindset, adapted to maximize their proficiency in that environment.[57] In practice, as history shows all too clearly, armies, navies, and more recently air forces have been known to prepare and wage their own environmentally specific wars with scant regard for the perspectives and operational needs of other kinds of forces. This phenomenon has plagued the history of air power both in reality and even more often in perception. The all-encompassing nature of a geographically unified air environment that in principle grants comprehensive access to an enemy's assets, regardless of his armed forces, has long fueled bitter arguments over whether air power is an adjunct or a strategically independent force, or both, in war. The distinctive character of air power (as of land power and of sea power) encourages a no less distinctive perspective on defense preparation, deterrence, and the conduct of war that needs to be reconciled within a total coherent structure of national defense.

Political boundaries in the air. In common with armies and navies, but unlike space forces, air forces are constrained by the political exigencies of sovereign air space. Examples abound, but particularly painful illustration was provided by the extracontinental routing mandated for British-based U.S. F-111s in the 1986 raid on Libya or, further back, by the absence of much NATO-European tolerance of overflights for the resupply of Israel in October 1973. Great powers have been known to treat the sovereign air space of small neutral countries with some disdain for legality, but most countries have provided themselves at least with a token "aerial coast guard" capability. In common with the other limitations of air power discussed in this chapter, political boundaries in the air are both an enduring general problem and a condition that can be alleviated more or less satisfactorily in specific cases.

CAVEATS

Analysis of the limitations upon air power demands overall qualification in four respects. First, many advantages also have some disadvantages (i.e., a price is paid for the benefit). Second, air and space forces have general characters that are geographically determined and specific, but advances in technology alter the particular force of particular advantages and limitations at particular times. Third, historical experience is always unique in its details and hence in the ways in which general factors bearing upon the utility of air power will apply. Fourth, if the true strategic worth of air and space forces is to be determined, both strengths and limitations need to be considered fairly. Air power is not alone in the relevance of this logic. Armies, navies, and air forces all have their limitations.

In and of itself none of the analysis in this chapter demonstrates the utility of air power, because such utility exists only in the context of national need. The discussion thus far has focused upon air power rather than upon the national need for air power. The succeeding chapters in Part II proceed into the murky and contentious waters of strategic culture, international security conditions, and guidance for U.S. defense planning.

NOTES

1. Richard P. Hallion, *Storm over Iraq: Air Power and the Gulf War* (Washington, DC: Smithsonian Institution Press, 1992), p. 267.

2. See Chester G. Starr, Jr., *The Roman Imperial Navy, 31 B.C.–A.D. 324* (Westport, CT: Greenwood Press, 1975; first pub. 1941).

3. Superior discussions include Paul Kennedy, *The Rise and Fall of British Naval Mastery* (New York: Charles Scribner's Sons, 1976); and David French, *The British Way in Warfare, 1688–2000* (London: Unwin Hyman, 1990).

4. Air power historian David MacIsaac judges that "[d]espite the efforts of Douhet and Mitchell, neither proved to be a Mahan or a Jomini from whom the air power enthusiasts could draw the secrets of the third dimension in warfare." "Voices from the Central Blue: The Air Power Theorists," in Peter Paret, ed., *Makers of Modern Strategy: From Machiavelli to the Nuclear Age* (Princeton, NJ: Princeton University Press, 1986), p. 635.

5. In his major study of technology and war, Martin van Creveld concludes that "the logic of conflict, that logic which in turn dictates the principles of its conduct, is likewise immutable and immune to any amount of technology that is applied to or

used for it." *Technology and War: From 2000 B.C. to the Present* (New York: Free Press, 1989), p. 314.

6. See Robert Allan Doughty: *The Seeds of Disaster: The Development of French Army Doctrine, 1919–1939* (Hamden, CT: Archon Books, 1985); and *The Breaking Point: Sedan and the Fall of France, 1940* (Hamden, CT: Archon Books, 1990).

7. The classic examination is Williamson Murray, "The German Response to Victory in Poland: A Case Study in Professionalism," in his *German Military Effectiveness* (Baltimore, MD: The Nautical and Aviation Publishing Company of America, 1992), pp. 229–43.

8. Gresham's Law: The theory that when two or more kinds of money of equal denomination but unequal intrinsic value are in circulation, the one with the greater value will tend to be hoarded and exported; popularly the principle that bad money will drive good money out of circulation. *Webster's New World Dictionary*.

9. There is much to be said in favor of General Boyd's robust handling of this matter: "I use the term *air power* in its most comprehensive sense of air and space power. Such inclusive air power values every role and mission, as well as all the support services, and—most importantly—all the people the Air Force needs to be a fully capable service." Charles G. Boyd, "Air Power Thinking: 'Request Unrestricted Climb,' " *Airpower Journal* 5, no. 3 (fall 1991): 5 (emphasis in original).

10. See Hugh M. Trenchard, "Air Power and National Security," in Eugene M. Emme, ed., *The Impact of Air Power: National Security and World Politics* (Princeton, NJ: D. Van Nostrand, 1959), pp. 192–200; William Mitchell, *Winged Defense: The Development and Possibilities of Modern Air Power—Economic and Military* (New York: Dover Publications, 1988; first pub. 1925); Giulio Douhet, *The Command of the Air* (New York: Arno Press, 1972; first pub. 1942); and Alexander P. de Seversky, *Victory Through Air Power* (New York: Simon and Schuster, 1942). Alfred T. Mahan's theory of sea power is presented most explicitly in *The Influence of Sea Power upon History, 1660–1783* (London: Methuen, 1965; first pub. 1890), pp. 1–89; and *The Influence of Sea Power upon the French Revolution and Empire, 1793–1812*, vol. II (of 2) (Boston: Little, Brown, 1898; first pub. 1892), pp. 358–411.

11. See Colin S. Gray, *The Leverage of Sea Power: The Strategic Advantage of Navies in War* (New York: Free Press, 1992).

12. Hallion, *Storm over Iraq*, p. 7.

13. A possible exception to this rather harsh judgment would be David E. Lupton, with his useful monograph, *On Space Warfare: A Space Power Doctrine* (Maxwell Air Force Base, AL: Air University Press, June 1988).

14. A point urged persuasively in Robert A. Pape, Jr., "Coercive Air Power in the Vietnam War," *International Security* 15, no. 2 (fall 1990): 103–46; and his "Coercion and Military Strategy: Why Denial Works and Punishment Doesn't," *Journal of Strategic Studies* 15, no. 4 (December 1992): 423–75.

15. Colin S. Gray, "Off the Map: Defense Planning after the Soviet Threat," *Strategic Review* 22, no. 2 (spring 1994): 26–35, emphasizes the importance of political guidance and the limitations of the technical skills of the planner.

16. For recent opposing views of Douhet, both of which are unbalanced in their judgments, see John F. Jones, "Giulio Douhet Vindicated: Desert Storm, 1991," *Naval*

War College Review 45, no. 4 (autumn 1992): 97–101; and Claudio G. Segré, "Giulio Douhet: Strategist, Theorist, Prophet?" *Journal of Strategic Studies* 15, no. 3 (September 1992): 351–66.

17. See Eliot A. Cohen, "The Mystique of U.S. Air Power," *Foreign Affairs* 73, no. 1 (January/February 1994): 109–24.

18. See Colin S. Gray, *War, Peace, and Victory: Strategy and Statecraft for the Next Century* (New York: Simon and Schuster, 1990), chap. 1. Also see Judy M. Graffis, "Strategic: Use with Care," *Airpower Journal* 8, special edition (1994): 4–10.

19. Eric Grove, *The Future of Sea Power* (Annapolis, MD: Naval Institute Press, 1990), p. 138.

20. Mahan, *Influence of Sea Power upon History, 1660–1783*, pp. 58–88.

21. For example, France in the age of the "fighting sail." See N. A. M. Rodger, "The Continental Commitment in the Eighteenth Century," in Lawrence Freedman, Paul Hayes, and Robert T. O'Neill, eds., *War, Strategy, and International Politics: Essays in Honour of Sir Michael Howard* (Oxford: Clarendon Press, 1993), pp. 39–55.

22. General Thomas D. White, quoted in Robert Frank Futrell, *Ideas, Concepts, Doctrine: Basic Thinking in the United States Air Force*, vol. 1, *1907–1960* (Maxwell Air Force Base, AL: Air University Press, 1989), p. 554.

23. For a brief but authoritative status report, see Thomas S. Moorman, Jr., "Space: A New Strategic Frontier," *Airpower Journal* 6, no. 1 (spring 1992): 14–23. Merrill A. McPeak, "Making Tomorrow's Realities: USAF Investment in Space," address to the Thirtieth Space Congress, 27 April 1993, also is relevant.

24. Three articles which convey the correct flavor are Peter Anson and Dennis Cummings, "The First Space War: The Contribution of Satellites to the Gulf War," *RUSI Journal* 136, no. 4 (winter 1991): 45–53; William A. Dougherty, "Storm from Space," U.S. Naval Institute, *Proceedings* 118, no. 8 (August 1992): 48–52; and Steven Lambakis, "Space Control in Desert Storm and Beyond," *Orbis* 39, no. 3 (summer 1995): 417–33.

25. Merrill A. McPeak, "Does the Air Force Have a Mission?" Address at Maxwell Air Force Base, AL, 19 June 1992, p. 5 (emphasis added).

26. Douhet, *Command of the Air*, p. 291.

27. See Lee Kennett, *The First Air War, 1914–1918* (New York: Free Press, 1991), pp. 21, 90, 224. A sharply contrasting view of the strategic utility of air power in World War I can be found in Richard P. Hallion, *Rise of the Fighter Aircraft, 1914–1918* (Baltimore, MD: Nautical and Aviation Publishing Company of America, 1984), p. 149.

28. See John Terraine, *White Heat: The New Warfare, 1914–18* (London: Sidgwick and Jackson, 1982).

29. An excellent recent history of air power in World War I advises that from 1914 to 1918, "[t]he airplane established its real significance in support of the army on the battlefield. . . . Theory and wishful thinking after the Great War, however, focused on strategic aviation and actually threatened to drive the lessons on tactical success from the minds of observers." John H. Morrow, Jr., *The Great War in the Air: Military Aviation from 1909 to 1921* (Washington, DC: Smithsonian Institution Press, 1993), pp. 365, 376. Useful historical studies also include Richard P. Hallion, *Strike from the*

Sky: The History of Battlefield Air Attack, 1911–1945 (Washington, DC: Smithsonian Institution Press, 1989); Robert Frank Futrell, *The United States Air Force in Korea, 1950–1953,* rev. ed. (Washington, DC: U.S. Air Force, Office of Air Force History, 1983); James T. Stewart, ed., *Airpower: The Decisive Force in Korea* (Princeton, NJ: D. Van Nostrand, 1957); Mark Clodfelter, *The Limits of Air Power: The American Bombing of North Vietnam* (New York: Free Press, 1989); and Earl H. Tilford, Jr., *Crosswinds: The Air Force's Setup in Vietnam* (College Station: Texas A and M University Press, 1993). In the light of this history, it is particularly encouraging to find an air force chief of staff say that, "for me, it is a central truth that the Air Force will often make its most valued contribution by helping our brothers on the ground or at sea achieve *their* operational objectives." McPeak, "Does the Air Force Have a Mission?" p. 8 (emphasis in original).

30. This is a central tenet of Douhet, *Command of the Air,* e.g., pp. 15, 17, 18, 52–55. The alleged superiority of offense over defense also is vital for Mahan's credo on sea power.

31. See Wesley Frank Craven and James Lea Cate, eds., *The Army Air Forces in World War II,* 7 vols. (Chicago: University of Chicago Press, 1948–58), especially vols. II–III; and Charles Webster and Noble Frankland, *The Strategic Air Offensive Against Germany, 1939–1945,* 4 vols. (London: HMSO, 1961), especially vols. II–III. Stephen L. McFarland and Wesley Phillips Newton, *To Command the Sky: The Battle for Air Superiority over Germany, 1942–1944* (Washington, DC: Smithsonian Institution Press, 1991), provides a well-focused analysis.

32. Donald B. Rice, *The Air Force and U.S. National Security: Global Reach—Global Power,* white paper (Washington, DC: Department of the Air Force, June 1990), p. 1.

33. J. C. Wylie, *Military Strategy: A General Theory of Power Control* (Annapolis, MD: Naval Institute Press, 1989; first pub. 1967), p. 72 (emphasis in original).

34. J. H. Parry, *The Discovery of the Sea* (Berkeley: University of California Press, 1981; first pub. 1976), p. xi.

35. See John Terraine, *A Time for Courage: The Royal Air Force in the European War, 1939–1945* (New York: Macmillan, 1985), especially p. 509; and McFarland and Newton, *To Command the Sky.*

36. The time dimension is emphasized boldly in McPeak, "Does the Air Force Have a Mission?" pp. 6–7.

37. Futrell, *United States Air Force in Korea, 1950–1953,* chaps. 3–4.

38. As Morrow has written of World War I, "Aircraft reconnaissance made it difficult for armies to achieve surprise and forced the movement of men and materiel behind the lines at night." *Great War in the Air,* p. 365.

39. Hallion, *Storm over Iraq,* p. 223. Also see Cohen, "Mystique of U.S. Air Power," p. 111.

40. Carl von Clausewitz, *On War,* ed. and trans. Michael Howard and Peter Paret (Princeton, NJ: Princeton University Press, 1976; first pub. 1832), p. 204 (emphasis in original).

41. Julian S. Corbett, *Some Principles of Maritime Strategy* (Annapolis, MD: Naval Institute Press, 1988; first pub. 1911), p. 129.

42. Actually, Nelson wrote (on 6 October 1805) that "[n]umbers can only annihilate." Quoted in Julian S. Corbett, *The Campaign of Trafalgar* (London: Longmans, Green, 1910), pp. 327–28. The full text makes it quite plain that Nelson was arguing the point that the country and he wanted to annihilate the enemy, an immoderate goal that would require a large number of ships.

43. CEP means circular error probable, a measure of weapons delivery accuracy, the radius of a circle around the target within which half of the weapons delivered should be expected to fall. Useful works on accuracy include Stephen L. McFarland, *America's Pursuit of Precision Bombing, 1910–1945* (Washington, D.C.: Smithsonian Institution Press, 1995); and Donald MacKenzie, *Inventing Accuracy: A Historical Sociology of Nuclear Missile Guidance* (Cambridge, MA: MIT Press, 1990).

44. Hallion, *Storm over Iraq*, p. 10.

45. Douhet, *Command of the Air*, pp. 117–18.

46. General Hoyt S. Vandenberg, quoted in Clodfelter, *Limits of Air Power*, p. 35.

47. Douhet, *Command of the Air*, p. 193.

48. See Futrell, *United States Air Force in Korea, 1950–1953*; and Michael A. Kirtland, "Planning Air Operations: Lessons from Operation Strangle in the Korean War," *Airpower Journal* 6, no. 2 (summer 1992): 37–46.

49. See Clodfelter, *Limits of Air Power*; and Tilford, *Crosswinds*.

50. For valuable overviews, see William W. Momyer, *Air Power in Three Wars* (Washington, DC: U.S. Government Printing Office, 1978); Pape, "Coercive Air Power in the Vietnam War"; and Richard H. Shultz, Jr., "Compellence and the Role of Air Power as a Political Instrument," in Richard H. Shultz, Jr., and Robert L. Pfaltzgraff, Jr., eds., *The Future of Air Power in the Aftermath of the Gulf War* (Maxwell Air Force Base, AL: Air University Press, July 1992), pp. 171–91.

51. On the "grammar," as contrasted with the policy logic, of war, see Clausewitz, *On War*, p. 605.

52. Neville Brown, *The Future of Air Power* (New York: Holmes and Meier, 1986), p. 276.

53. See Hallion, *Rise of the Fighter Aircraft, 1914–1918*, chap. 2.

54. Douhet, *Command of the Air*, p. 68. Bernard Brodie wrought considerable damage to Douhet's reputation when he wrote: "The several essays usually gathered together under the name of the most famous of them—*Command of the Air*—are brilliant, but they are also narrow in outlook, dogmatic, and, as the Second World War proved, in all their specific prescriptions altogether wrong." One need not be an apologist for Douhet to note the arrogance and the error in Brodie's concluding shot at *Command of the Air*: "As with Foch's book we again have a body of work that has no utility today [1976]." Brodie, "The Continuing Relevance of *On War*," in Carl von Clausewitz, *On War*, ed. and trans. Michael Howard and Peter Paret (Princeton, NJ: Princeton University Press, 1976; first pub. 1832), p. 51. Bernard Brodie's chapter on "The Heritage of Douhet" in his *Strategy in the Missile Age*, (Princeton, NJ: Princeton University Press, 1959), chap. 3, is not his finest work, but it is more balanced than were his observations on Douhet in the 1976 essay on the relevance of *On War*.

55. For a fascinating historical perspective on the high-low mix question, see Hallion, *Rise of the Fighter Aircraft, 1914–1918*, pp. 151–53. Hallion enunciates the

general principle that "*[s]ophistication should not be sacrificed to numbers*" (emphasis in original), p. 151. His conclusion is that "[a]s a rule, the First World War experience (and subsequent ones as well) indicates that a high-low balance is desirable, but that quality is overall more significant than quantity," p. 152. Also see I. B. Holley, Jr., *Ideas and Weapons: Exploitation of the Aerial Weapon by the United States During World War I: A Study in the Relationship of Technological Advance, Military Doctrine, and the Development of Weapons* (Hamden, CT: Archon Books, 1971; first pub. 1953), especially pp. 150–51.

56. Alfred Price, *The Hardest Day: The Battle of Britain, 18 August 1940* (London: Arrow Books, 1990; first pub. 1979), p. 15. See also Terraine, *A Time for Courage*, pp. 181–85; and, for the whole story, Richard Hough and Denis Richards, *The Battle of Britain: The Greatest Air Battle of World War II* (New York: W. W. Norton, 1989); and John Ray, *The Battle of Britain, New Perspectives: Behind the Scenes of the Great Air War* (London: Arms and Armour Press, 1994).

57. Carl H. Builder, *The Masks of War: American Military Styles in Strategy and Analysis* (Baltimore, MD: Johns Hopkins University Press, 1989), is relevant on this point, though his tone and argument tend to imply that service cultures on balance are pathological conditions.

Chapter 5

The United States as an Air Power

What does it mean to observe that the United States is an air power? Why is the United States an air power to a degree that no other nation in history could claim? What do the answers to these questions imply for the way the United States structures its armed forces? This chapter proceeds holistically to explain the geostrategic features of the United States. That geostrategic discussion is succeeded by treatment of the relevant complexities of grand strategy and military strategy. The air power theme is pursued in the context of rival and complementary instruments of grand strategy and instruments of military power. The chapter then advances into the important but often indistinct realm of the roots and characteristics of U.S. strategic culture and national style. Each of the characteristics of that culture and style is considered for its implications for the future of air power. The argument proceeds with a design for under-standing better the strategic utility of air power. A four-category classification is adopted to help distinguish among those tasks that air forces are relatively better or relatively worse (than other kinds of forces) at performing. Finally, Chapter 5 provides a historical overview of the strategic utility of air power to the United States. Two quotations, respectively from the writings of John Warden and Eliot Cohen, set the scene usefully for the subject of this chapter.

Air power then [with modern weapons and accuracy as used in the Gulf War] becomes quintessentially an American form of war; it uses our advantages of mobility and high technology to overwhelm the enemy without spilling too much blood, especially American blood.[1]

Reliance on air power has set the American way of war apart from all others for well over half a century. . . . Only the United States . . . has engaged in a single-minded and successful quest for air superiority in every conflict it has fought since World War I. Air warfare remains distinctively American-high-tech, cheap in lives and (at least in theory) quick. To America's enemies—past, current and potential—it is the distinctively American form of military intimidation.[2]

ON CULTURE AND STYLE

There is an American "way of war" and a preferred American way in defense preparation.[3] The United States is no exception to the rule that a country's traditional "way" in matters military is the unique product of its geography and historical experience (or, more accurately, its dominant interpretation of that historical experience). The concepts that capture this subject are strategic culture and national style.[4] Strategic culture can be defined as the socially transmitted habits of mind, traditions, and preferred methods of operation that are more or less specific to a particular geographically based security community. Strategic culture incorporates the more restricted concept of a national style. National culture and style are the products and expression of strategically adaptive reasoning behavior; they are not casual or eccentric phenomena.[5] If, for example, Stephen B. Jones was correct when he wrote in 1955 that "[a] number of American habits of mind favor acceptance of 'the airman's view' [of the world],"[6] he pointed to a relatively enduring cultural context favorable to air power.

National strategic culture and style should represent a tolerable fusion of what a society prefers and of what tends to succeed for that society. A strategic culture that is persistently maladaptive or that is grossly so even for a brief time could promote a style in behavior that would threaten the survival of the polity in question. Strategic culture and style tend to be adaptive because when they are not, the consequences can be dire and unmistakable; in the last resort wars are lost. National style and the strategic culture with which it interacts and whence it derives necessarily look Janus-like in different directions. On the one hand, American style has to be adequate to cope with the field test of non-American phenomena upon which it must seek to act. On the other hand, American style in action must be domestically acceptable and sustainable over time.

Although the subject of culture and style may appear at first glance abstruse, in practice it has a deep and pervasive influence over policy, strategy, defense organization, military doctrine, and force planning. In addition, Carl H. Builder of the RAND Corporation has shown persuasively how the concepts of culture and style apply at the level of the individual armed services,[7] an analysis that could be extended profitably to different military functions within the services. Service or military function-specific advocacy has a way of abusing the U.S. cultural and stylistic inheritance in military matters. In a universe peopled near exclusively by careful and honest defense analysts, the propagation of strategic cultural half-truths would be self-defeating, as foolish claims would attract an instant and deadly ridicule. As it is, however, claims of an essentialist kind (the United States is *really* . . .) lean upon strategic cultural assertions that typically escape disciplined evaluation. All too often, an extreme claim for one kind of military power simply triggers extreme countervailing claims from competing services or functions.

GEOSTRATEGIC COMPLEXITIES AND GRAND STRATEGY

The United States is an air power. In strategic fact today the United States probably is more an air power than it is a land power, sea power, space power, or even a nuclear power (to risk changing the currency of account). Moreover, the United States is more truly an air power than it is a maritime or continental power in that its air power is as "natural" as its naval power is not.[8] The United States is an air-minded, air-using society with a huge and longstanding scientific-industrial base for commercial and military air power. The United States is not a sea-minded, sea-using society (by many individuals, that is), and its nationally flagged commercial sea power is almost trivial in comparison with its naval strength. This is not to deny that the United States is by far the world's greatest naval power, and depends critically upon maritime communications for the flow of its trade.

Geostrategically viewed, the United States is

- a continental power
- rendered geopolitically insular by the persisting, and even structural military weakness of its northern and southern neighbors
- centrally located between the western and eastern littorals of Eurasia—a geostrategic condition aided vastly by the Panama Canal and rendered more significant still by the emergence of transoceanic air power
- the world's leading naval power whose navy, from the closing of the internal frontier until the advent of nuclear-armed air and missile forces, was the country's first line of defense[9]
- an air, or aerospace, power in senses in which it has never really been a great "natural" land power or sea power
- a country whose last line of defense for its homeland remains the deterrent and possibly defensive value of the long-range and nuclear-armed forces which transcend geographical specialization

In the quotation provided above, John Warden did not claim that air power becomes quintessentially *the* American form of war; he claimed judiciously only that airpower "becomes quintessentially an American form of war." By implication at least, properly American forms of war should serve the country better than would un-American forms. As a caveat, there is the possibility that the American content of a form of war may reside less in its broad and general character (e.g., air power) and more in the way in which it is used (e.g., an American style in air war). Placing that tendentious qualification to one side, it is necessary to ask with what air power is competing to be an, or the leading, American form of war. Two levels of analysis usefully can be combined or closely associated if this discussion is to have the appropriate domain: the grand-strategic and the military-strategic. Warden's judgment on air power pertains only to forms of war, but it is useful to think of competition and complementarity both within and without the military realm.

As an instrument of policy air power can compete not only with sea power and special operations, but also with diplomacy and economic aid. President Johnson believed that North Vietnam could be bribed as well as, or instead of being, coerced by aerial bombardment. Typically, several instruments of grand strategy will play in more or less well harmonized combinations, just as the several elements of military power can function synergistically for the common purpose of bringing influence to bear on the foe. Two taxonomies (Tables 5.1 and 5.2) together express the context within which one can debate the meaning and implications of the United States as an air power.

Table 5.1 says that exploration of the meaning of the United States as an air power or, in Billy Mitchell's phrase, as an "air-going people,"[10] has to take account of the other broad qualities of the country. In addition to being an air power, the United States is a trading nation and a culturally somewhat missionary nation. The table is a somewhat diverse, even disparate, taxonomy, but each item is a candidate "prime" instrument of policy. The bulleted items are not tightly exclusive; they are employed in clusters. Table 5.2 poses the same kind of question as does Table 5.1, only in this case it identifies the possible "prime" or "key force" categories of U.S. military power in particular crises and wars. Strategically considered, the taxonomy represented in Table 5.2 has integrity. Each of the instruments listed could serve as an identifiable "key force" for, and certainly as the "prime" to, military support of policy. The instruments are not wholly exclusive (land, sea, and special operations forces all employ, indeed incorporate, air power). Also, some nuclear-capable forces are dual-capable (conventional as well as nuclear).

Grand-strategic and military-strategic analyses interpenetrate. For example, the United States as an air power in the 1990s may have an aerial instrument for strategic effect so potent yet precise that the choice of policy means can be driven by military argument. When, acting grand-strategically,

Table 5.1
Grand Strategy: Instruments of Statecraft

• Diplomacy	• Military assistance and arms sales
• Trade and investment	• Military power (threat or use of force)
• Economic and financial assistance	• Arms control
• Propaganda, information, education	• Peacekeeping
• Cultural influence	• Humanitarian assistance
• Espionage, covert action/political warfare	

policymakers select the mix of instruments they will employ, that selection must be influenced critically by the plausibility of the competing promises of net strategic effectiveness. Arguments over the putative effectiveness of air power to help resolve a problem will include not only partially competing claims advanced on behalf of other instruments of military power, but also possibly by claims for the merit in allowing a prime role to multilateral diplomacy or economic sanctions.[11] The U.S./U.N. confrontation with Iraq in 1990–91 certainly witnessed debate over the proposition that "air power can do it." Also, there was debate at the level of grand strategy over the proposition that "economic sanctions can do it"; while at the level of policy there has been retrospective debate over the proposition that, allegedly, "deterrence could have done it, had it been tried seriously."

Exploration of the strategic utility of air power thus has to be attentive to the time-phasing of an issue, which is to say to deterrence as well as to defense. Also, such exploration needs to appreciate that whether or not air power is the principal executor for the direct chastisement of an enemy—as in Desert Storm—the contribution of air power to military operations of all kinds has become so pervasive as to call into question traditionally distinctive notions of land power and sea power.

AMERICAN STRATEGIC CULTURE: ROOTS AND CHARACTERISTICS

Culture unites a nation's present with its past and its future. The literature on air power is studded with passing assertions about this or that alleged characteristic of American political and strategic culture. Given the breadth and depth of this analysis, it is essential that the threads of argument about air power take full account of strategic cultural habits and preferences. This section discusses the more important and enduring of the influences upon U.S. defense policy.[12]

Table 5.2
Military Strategy: Instruments of Power

• Air power	• Sea power
• Space power	• Special operations forces
• Land power	• Nuclear forces

Cultural characteristics are not etched in stone; they evolve gradually. Even a social, political, economic, and military event as immense as World War II had, in the American case, the net effect of reinforcing existing tendencies. The experience of the seventeenth, eighteenth, and nineteenth centuries formed an American strategic culture with roots in five interdependent factors.

First, as Denis Brogan noticed, "[s]pace [meaning extensive terrain on the frontier] determined the American way in war, space and the means to conquer space." Brogan points out: "Into empty land the pioneers moved, feeling their way slowly, carefully, timidly if you like. The reckless lost their scalps; the careful, the prudent, the rationally courageous survived and by logistics, by superiority in resources, in tenacity, in numbers. Americans who did not learn these lessons were not much use in the conquest of the West."[13]

The U.S. military forces have not always been well directed strategically or operationally; sometimes their tactical skills have left much to be desired and their weapons have not always been state of the art.[14] But that military establishment always has shown a mastery of logistics. The insouciance with which German staff officers approached planning and execution of the supply of great campaigns in two world wars stands in significant contrast to the twentieth-century logistic triumphs of the United States. U.S. soldiers have not always capitalized on their superior supply services; indeed, a fine line runs between the prudent exploitation of logistical excellence and dependence on logistic systems at the expense of operational initiative. Nevertheless, the national experience of coping with a continental scale of geography bred a respect for physical distance that has improved U.S. military performance.

Second, the experience of a moving frontier had a lasting influence upon what might be called the American strategic personality. The American fascination with technology, particularly with mechanical means of transportation, resulted from the conquest of a wilderness. The relative absence of societal support on the frontier bred a pragmatism that translated into an engineering, problem-solving approach to life; an approach that at times has foolishly sought to dismiss conditions as merely problems. American society responded sensibly to its shortage of labor, particularly highly skilled labor, by embracing machines and taking the lead in producing machine tools. The U.S. preference for the use of machines in war lies rooted in the sparse people-to-space ratio of frontier

America and in an acute shortage of skilled artisans that lasted well into the nineteenth century.

Third, contemporary American strategic culture is the product of a society that has embraced the myth of well-merited national success. Notwithstanding some blemishes,[15] the pages of world history generally read well for Americans. It is therefore understandable that many Americans have confused success with virtue. In the national experience, thirteen squabbling colonies evolved into a world power which succeeded in most important national endeavors up to the Vietnam War, and that subsequently succeeded in the heroic historic mission of peacefully seeing off the evil empire of the heirs of Lenin. Such a record has fostered an optimism that inevitably influences and sometimes shapes the discussion of, and decision making on, national security issues.

Fourth, the country which emerged from its geostrategically tenuous colonial origins resulted in a nation of unusual size in all of the standard measures of power.[16] The scale of resources influenced both the national security enterprises undertaken and the manner in which Americans approached them. For example, from 1941 to 1945 the United States waged two geostrategically distinct wars half a world apart, outproduced friends and enemies alike, developed the atomic bomb, and created in the fabulously expensive B-29 Superfortress the instrument for its delivery. The United States was able to wage a rich man's war.[17]

Fifth, American society is deeply convinced that the world is destined to be governed by the precepts of American liberal democracy. Influential Americans took Soviet collapse as proof of the superiority of American ideas on good governance and enlightened economics over the ideas of the forces of darkness and evil.[18]

Culture, whatever the forces that have shaped it, is by definition slow to change. But culture is neither immutable nor unitary. American society accommodates subcultures; each geographically focused armed service has an institutional personality that speaks to the unique features of different missions; many countries share some cultural characteristics; and policymakers do exercise choices outside the traditions of their strategic culture. For example, Britain decided in World War I to field a continental-size army and after August 1915 to wage as much land combat as should prove necessary to defeat the enemy. For other examples, the United States elected in 1917 to intervene massively in a European war and in 1965 decided to wage war in Southeast Asia but not according to some theory of victory via decisive battle. In all three cases, British and American societies eventually punished the policymakers who had affronted the strategic norms, even though the first two enterprises were successful.

Eight characteristics of American strategic culture are readily discernible. Each of these is discussed with explicit reference to its implications for air power.

Indifference to History

In myth as well as to some practical effect, the United States is still the New World. The study of history is not popular in the United States. America is the land of new beginnings, apparently endless horizons, and infinite possibilities. When an American politician says of his country's achievements that "the best is yet to come," his words are not banal to American ears. History and historical experience suffer an equal lack of respect from Americans. The United States is not only indifferent to historical experience; its culture is actively antihistorical. With a minimum of baggage from the past, each new policy review tackles the future boldly and rediscovers the obvious, often committing old errors in new ways.

Implications for air power. This indifference to history does not translate into an unwillingness to ransack historical experience for purported "lessons." Current debate over the future of air power is harassed persistently by the deployment in argument of half- or quarter-truths about air power in World War II, Korea, Vietnam, and even the Gulf.[19] There is a cult of modernity in American culture which makes it difficult for Americans to learn from the past, even their own past. The good news of the bad news, as it were, is that American society and institutions are not the captives of the past. The U.S. defense community would never need to be reminded of the problem highlighted for Italians by Giulio Douhet in 1928: "But woe to him who tries to fight the war of the future with the theories and systems of 1914!"[20]

The Engineering Style and the Technical Fix

The true parent of American thinking on national security is Jomini, not Clausewitz. Jomini wrote of war as an art, but his quest for certainty and his obsession with reducing the complex and ambiguous to a few apparently simple principles have also characterized American military thought and practice. The domestic historical experience yielded the belief that American know-how will find a solution—generally technical—to every problem. The RAND school of strategic analysis, with its "fixes" for an arguably vulnerable strategic air command, has epitomized this engineering approach to security.[21]

The same national security community which believed in 1941 that it could calculate precisely the number of heavy bomber sorties needed to defeat Germany and Japan was just as capable of believing calculations of nuclear damage in a World War III.[22] In a classic study, Russell F. Weigley discerned a national tendency "to seek refuge in technology from hard problems of strategy and policy, . . . [a tendency] fostered by the pragmatic qualities of the American character and by the complexity of nuclear-age technology."[23]

Weigley was careful to distinguish this resort to the technical from the sensible quest for better weapons and for technical answers to genuinely technical issues. The American way in defense preparation as well as war has emphasized the technical and logistic rather than the politically well informed and operationally agile.[24] Mobility, particularly at the strategic and operational levels, has been the long suit of U.S. military power. But full exploitation of transportation technologies represents a necessary but insufficient ingredient of military effectiveness. Operation Desert Storm appeared to illustrate that the art of war had attained new heights in the United States. But it stands as an exception to the usual ponderousness of U.S. military forces. That ponderousness has been the product of the marriage of an initial unpreparedness for war (1861, 1898, 1917, 1941, and even 1965) with an abundance of military potential for mobilization.

Implications for air power. The obvious easy fit between the promise of precise military effectiveness through the employment of air power and an American strategic culture attracted to the problem-solving technical fix gives rise to a paradoxical peril. Air power may be abused as a would-be all-purpose "Mr. Goodwrench." Military professionals and some careful civilian scholars know better, but in the friction-free video-game world of many amateur strategists, weapons always hit their targets and the destruction of the intended targets always solves, or ought to solve, the political issues in contention. In practice, zero-CEP on the right targets is a worthy goal in a distinctly friction-filled world, while the connection between the military effect of (tactical) action and the achievement of strategic objectives can be frustratingly non-linear. As noted already, some air-minded Americans are prone falsely to equate a theory of air power with a theory of war or of statecraft.

Impatience

For better or worse, the United States is a society with a low tolerance for lengthy investment with distant payoffs. Policymakers at home and abroad should take seriously the affirmation in the Declaration of Independence that the United States of America is, *inter alia*, about the pursuit of happiness. It is not the American way to live with problems and worry about them until they become more tractable. American society confronts problems or conditions in the engineering spirit of the resolute problem-solver. Whether the problem is poverty at home, nation building in South Vietnam, teaching respect for multiparty democracy in El Salvador, Nicaragua, and Panama, or reducing the risks of war through arms control, American policymakers seek near-term results. Since major weapon systems may take ten or more years from conception to initial operational capability, a lack of foresight ingrained in culture and institutions renders even the idea of long-range planning mildly humorous.

Implications for air power. A principal implication of American impatience is that the strongly desirable becomes confused with the achievable, and society will not readily pay for a healthy amount of defense insurance. Powerful, indeed possibly irresistible, domestic political forces have been impatient at the pace of defense budgetary decline for this post–Cold War era. The politics of the air power budget will not wait patiently for world events to shake down into some new and more settled pattern of disorder and insecurity before they command an imprudent slackening in technology investment and cuts in force structure (if they have not already done so). The costs of overarmament by the major guardian of order are trivial in comparison to the costs of underarmament, but this kind of reasoning does not appeal in a period that few yet recognize to be one of an interwar kind.

Indifference to Cultural Distinctions

The continental isolation of American society and its success against weaker adversaries bred a lack of awareness of strategic-cultural diversity which has major consequences for choices in national military strategy. Notwithstanding the heritage of immigration, Americans generally have failed to study the strategic cultures of other societies. In the most serious of America's wars—the Revolutionary War and the Civil War—the strategic cultures of the two sides were too similar to make much difference.[25] U.S. involvement in both world wars was vital for victory, but fortunately U.S. armed forces did not have to win either war on their own. In neither world war were American soldiers obliged to purge their strategic culture of habits that undermine military effectiveness and which might prove fatal even to the best armies of the day.

Global victory in 1945 provided apparent confirmation of cultural superiority and a heady sense of being a superpower. Pride in recent military achievements and in the potency of new and largely American weapon technologies did nothing to encourage strategic empathy with others in the postwar world. For many years, American officials and theorists believed that they could enlighten backward Russians with the gospel of strategic stability.[26] But one cannot admire or criticize a national strategic culture like a Byzantine mosaic, according to an aesthetic logic and compatibility with its setting. Although a society will not function effectively for long in a manner that offends its cultural preferences, forces from without ultimately determine the measure of a strategic culture's worth. By definition strategy is a comparative subject.

Implications for air power. Part of the appeal of air power to American society is that it is literally above the messiness of conflict on the ground where alien cultures contend. Sailors and airmen function in an American environment at sea or in the air and by the very nature of their military behavior provide their country with a high measure of political control of involvement in foreign wars. Even forward and land-based aircraft will operate from within a more or less well sealed U.S. military compound. This typical distance from foreign cultures has strong cultural roots in continental insularity, in the national experience of rejection of the "Old World," and in an abundant self-confidence ("what do we have to learn from them?"). A challenge to U.S. air power is to try and overcome this pervasive sense of cultural superiority and attempt to understand friends and foes on their own terms. Whatever the culturally fed U.S. policy errors that may have been committed prior to 2 August 1990, the endeavor after that date by the air force to understand the Iraqi state and Iraqi society as a culturally distinctive object of a carefully tailored air campaign stands as a fine example of what needs to be done. The sensitivity to Iraqi distinctiveness, to identifying Iraq's center of strategic gravity, stands in marked and healthy contrast to much of the planning conducted for the air wars in World War II, Korea, and Vietnam.[27]

Continental Outlook, Maritime Situation, Air Power Preference

The United States is the world's greatest naval power. The U.S. Navy has inherited many of the former duties of the Royal Navy, but the United States cannot wage war beyond North America—with the exception of long-range bombardment—unless it enjoys a working control of the relevant sea lines of communication. Despite those facts, the United States is not a natural sea power, nor do maritime perspectives and precepts dominate its strategic culture. Because of its size, its historical experience of success, and the impatient temper of its people, the American way of war has been quintessentially continentalist. Americans have favored the quest for swift victory through the hazards of decisive battle rather than the slower approach of maritime encirclement. This preference long antedated the impact of nuclear weapons upon American assumptions about the likely duration of major wars.

The spirit of the American way is captured in the exhortations "On to Richmond!" and "On to Berlin!" The American eagerness to come to grips with the still-formidable Wehrmacht of 1942–43, as revealed in the Anglo-American strategy disputes of those years,[28] suggests a country inclined to believe that the shortest distance between friendly bases and the enemy's center of gravity is the highroad to victory.

The mixed continental and maritime heritage of the United States has intriguing consequences. For many purposes, air power offers capabilities for the projection of force superior to those provided by sea power (admittedly, to the limited degree to which the two can be distinguished one from the other). Air power long has enjoyed the transoceanic reach which for centuries was the exclusive domain of sea power. The emergence of air forces over the past ninety years has been both a curse and a blessing for American security. Hostile air (and missile) power has posed the most fearsome of dangers to American society, but the maturing of friendly air power now allows for swift and in some cases decisively effective intervention by the United States worldwide.

Implications for air power. U.S. air power is the cultural beneficiary of the continentalist, direct-approach mindset mentioned above. Brute geography, if one may call it that, commanded the United States to develop a first-class navy if the country was to protect itself in the Americas and be able to wield a sword overseas. Notwithstanding brief periods of enthusiasm, however, American society never entered into a love affair with the sea at all comparable to its emotional commitment to the world of flight. The continental dimensions of the country both spurred the growth of aviation and eventually accorded Americans above all people personal awareness of and experience with aircraft. Because of its size, military potential, and historically relatively brief involvement in the politics of international security, the United States has never had to adopt a classical maritime strategy on the British model.[29] It is the preferred American way in war to proceed rapidly with overwhelming force against an enemy's center of gravity. This thoroughly continentalist approach finds a near perfect fit with the promise of victory through air power.

Indifference to Strategy

Nuclear weapons appear to many Americans to have made strategy obsolete for major, that is, nuclear, conflict.[30] All too often, tactics have masqueraded as strategy. For example, plans for using weapons according to explicit measures of effectiveness are described as "targeting strategy," while in fact plans to lay down force in particular ways may or may not warrant description as strategic. The strategic utility of the threat or actual use of force has tended to attract little interest. Until the unpleasant and confusing experience in Korea in the early 1950s, American society and its military experts had little experience dealing with conflicts that required strategic skills of a high order. American society might have performed more effectively and more economically had it functioned more strategically, but until the 1960s the country did well enough without benefit of excellence in that department.

Indifference to strategy is not simply the natural consequence of U.S. material abundance. Reinforcing factors have been the ideological dimension to most U.S. conflicts: the insulating strategic advantages conferred by oceanic distance from the sources of major potential threat; weak continental neighbors; a partial European surrogate in the form of Britain and its navy; and the careless confidence bred by success.[31] Strategically, it is much less stressful to wage a materially profligate war and defeat an enemy decisively than it is to use military power to prop up uncertain allies in enterprises whose outcomes are often questionable. It has been the American way to reduce war and strategy to narrow military undertakings in the service of broad, ideologically expressed purposes.

But powers neglect the key characteristics of strategy at their peril. The United States was fortunate in that its day of reckoning occurred in Southeast Asia rather than in a World War III. The weaknesses in much of U.S. limited war theory and strategy manifested themselves in a war waged without benefit of a theory of victory, much less clear goals. The weaknesses in NATO's Cold War "strategy" of flexible response could have had similar consequences on a much grander and more dangerous scale.

But strategy is not a magical elixir that a properly fortified society can use with total reliability to accomplish its ends. It is not a panacea. That U.S. strategic performance in Vietnam was so lamentable does not mean that a better strategy assuredly would have produced success. Unsuitable policy choice will frustrate strategy just as much as will operational incompetence or tactical ineptitude.

Implications for air power. In Douhet's words, "[t]he choice of enemy targets . . . is the most delicate operation of aerial warfare."[32] More delicate still is the question of how aerial warfare is to be employed to affect the course and outcome of a conflict. The acme of American strategic skill was demonstrated in the War of Independence. The reason is not hard to discover. General George Washington lacked the material means to rely upon brute force for success. He could not simply pile tactical victory upon tactical victory and assume that the end result would be victory in the war as a whole. Strategic agility had to compensate for missing quantity. Apart from the "bookend" high points of American strategic prowess in the War of Independence and the Gulf War of 1991, brighter episodes include General Winfield Scott's march on Mexico City in 1847 and much of the campaigning against Japan in World War II. When brute force pays off well enough and reliably, finesse in strategy usually is at a discount. Traditionally, it has not been the American way to probe much beyond tactics and operations into the speculative realm of strategic effect. It is always easier to focus upon actions rather than consequences. If the air force has a dramatic story to tell on behalf of the strategic effectiveness for policy satisfaction of new air power capabilities, it will have to develop that story itself. The American defense community does not live and breathe strategic argument. Indeed, facility in genuinely strategic reasoning is so rare that it tends to attract an awed respect that in particular cases it often will not merit.[33]

The Resort to Force, Belated but Massive

As a popular democracy whose system of government is very heavily influenced by societal pressures, the United States is not ideally suited to an

agile use of armed force for limited political purposes. The United States is a
large country that tends to perform extremely well on large tasks when its
citizenry accepts their necessity.[34] But attempts to wage war without the
blessings of American society are certain to fail.[35] For any enterprise lacking
obvious life-or-death implications, the government of the United States can
expect public support only if the military operation is brief, successful, and
attended by few casualties. A quarter century after General George C. Marshall
said that "a democracy cannot fight a Seven-Years War," Presidents Johnson
and Nixon proved him correct.[36] The traditional American mindset has viewed
peace as the normal and self-evidently desirable condition of humankind. It
follows then to most Americans that only evil men or evil causes promote wars
(for aggressive reasons). Americans do not resort to force quickly, but when
they do, as the exceptional polity, they expect a thumping triumph. With few
exceptions, American forces have been inept relative to their foes at the start
of wars,[37] but as John Shy has observed, the experience of the Revolutionary
War taught Americans to expect as much.[38]

Americans do not expect their armed forces to be committed to morally
dubious battle. In the late 1950s and early 1960s influential civilian defense
intellectuals constructed a theory which promised success in just such a
commitment to morally dubious enterprises; purportedly, the Korean experience had shown that American society must learn how to wage limited war in
the nuclear shadow.[39] Then Lyndon Johnson discovered that this theory did
not fit the real American polity. The public would not tolerate sacrifice without
the likelihood of a favorable decision.

Implications for air power. In part because of the strategic context of the
Cold War, the United States waged war in Korea and later in Vietnam
without benefit of suitable doctrine or appropriate forces. Those reasons did
not exhaust the list of U.S. difficulties, but they were important. In the
1990s, however, the U.S. air instrument is vastly more potent and flexible
than were its predecessors in Korea and Vietnam. Notwithstanding the
example in 1991 of what can be done from the air, in some circumstances
at least, it is not obvious that American strategic culture has registered the
necessary adjustment. It is un-American to wage war half-heartedly. Aside
from the domestic political reasons why that should be so, history suggests
strongly that countries should expect to have to fight hard to win. The air
power, supported by space power and special operations, which ruined Iraq
as a military power (effectively in one night) now has the ability to operate
surgically to strategic effect worthy of the description. That is a radical claim,
albeit not a particularly controversial one. Air power today and in the future
can satisfy the American cultural preference for large-scale military action by
providing, with only tens or hundreds of aircraft, the effects previously
generated by massive numbers. Moreover, U.S. policy need not always resort

to force belatedly if the action in question is precisely focused and small in the scale of forces to be committed.

The Evasion of Politics

The enforcement of continental Manifest Destiny and the belated yet vital participation in crusades against kaiserism and Nazism have not encouraged Clausewitzian approaches to the use of force by the United States. The United States transformed into military problems—and inelegantly but definitively solved through machine warfare—the political challenges that American Indians and menacing empires in Europe and Asia had posed.

American strategic studies in the Cold War—with the three central theoretical pillars of deterrence, limited war, and arms control—were deeply respectful of Clausewitz. Defense theorists tended to parrot the arguable proposition that "war is simply a continuation of political intercourse, with the addition of other means."[40] Those same theorists, however, proceeded to design and elaborate ideas on stable deterrence, crisis management, the conduct of limited war, and approaches to arms control that were pervasively apolitical. Studies specified the requirements of stable deterrence with scant acknowledgment of the political motives for crisis and war. The U.S. defense community found comfortable certainty in the application of a few elementary apolitical principles for the determination of strategic sufficiency. Such advice manifested faith in defense planning as a science. The United States has a strategic culture that is more comfortable with administration than with politics and that is centered upon the quaint belief that the country can purchase the right weapons in the right numbers to serve both as a deterrent in peacetime and as an adequate arsenal in crisis or war. The American literature on force planning resolutely declines to recognize that its subject is an art and not a science.[41]

Implications for air power. A society that honors, or at least rewards most handsomely, the practice of law and of business management is unlikely to be a society prone to reason and plan strategically on the use of force. Physicists, historians, and political scientists are used to dealing with contexts wherein the rules or principles that govern behavior are either deeply uncertain or essentially contestable. American strategic culture, reflecting and expressing its dominant domestic roots, is prone to an uncritical reductionism. A few rules of thumb, guiding principles, magic numbers, and the like, all suitably supported by analytical studies which demonstrate the necessary truth in the fashionable nostrums, supposedly indicate the right force levels via administrative processing. Unfortunately, nonlinear possibilities do not compute by extrapolation. Also, the flexibility that is the central strategic glory of air power is not easy to prove by analysis that seeks a quantitative demonstration of truth. Strategic effect, which is to say the consequences of (tactical) actions for the course of a conflict, is calculable only in a qualitative way, albeit with quantitative measures of effectiveness as helpful indicators of progress. The theory and practice of air campaigning are about the application of force for the purposes of policy. Those purposes are not necessarily advanced by an arithmetic progression in damage threatened or attempted and achieved. It may be recalled that two key questions were identified earlier: What does it mean to be an air power? How should one go about discovering how much air power is enough? Temptations abound to have resort to some elementary formula for cranking out purportedly "correct" numbers. Such temptations should be resisted.

THE STRATEGIC UTILITY OF AIR POWER

Although there can be no simple, general answer to the question of the strategic utility of air power, the way in which a suitably complex answer is framed demonstrates historical evolution, even revolution. In any decade from the 1920s to the 1990s it could be claimed correctly that air power had the contemporary capability to win some wars independently or all but so and to enable some other wars to be won, while there were a few conflicts wherein it could exercise little strategic influence. There is a stark difference between the claim in the 1920s and the claim in the 1990s, however. In the 1920s, the wars that air power acting effectively alone could decide were limited to colonial conflicts in desert terrain. In the 1990s, air power with critical space-system assistance has shown itself able to defeat an exceptionally strong regional rogue state, although again in desert terrain.

A significant uncertainty about the strategic lethality of air power in Desert Storm pertains to the difficulty of weighing the contributions which the desert terrain, the large-scale conventional character of the conflict, and the particular tactical and operational errors committed by Iraq made to the victory achieved (largely) through air power. As Edward Luttwak has noted, superior air power always has shown up to great advantage by employment over a desert.[42] Notwithstanding the open question about the transferability of air power prowess from Desert Storm to campaigns in very different geographical, strategic, and political contexts, it is necessary to record a potential utility for air power that stretches across the full range of possibilities. It is important to grasp the whole subject of U.S. air power and what it may be able to accomplish. Table 5.3 is an aid to disciplined thought in the form of a four-way classification of air power's instrumental utility.

Some caveats or qualifications to Table 5.3 beg for prompt recognition. First, although four clear categories are identified for clarity of argument and as an aid to focused thought, it is more true to practice to think of the utility of air power as a continuum without sharp breakpoints. For example, the table

Table 5.3
Utility of Air Power

1. *What, uniquely, can air power do?*
   - Directly assault centers of gravity, attack enemy inside > outside (from his center to his periphery)
   - Project force rapidly and globally
   - Observe "over the hill" from altitude
   - Transport people, modest equipment, and supplies rapidly and globally
   - Sustain and support small, isolated expeditions/garrisons

2. *What can air power do well?*
   - Protect friendly forces and other assets from enemy air power
   - Deter high-level and mid-level conflicts
   - Compensate for (some) deficiencies in ground and sea forces
   - Deny or seriously impede enemy access to particular land and sea areas
   - Deny enemy ability to seize, hold, and exploit objectives

3. *What does air power tend to do poorly?*
   - "Occupy" territory (from the air)
   - Send precise diplomatic messages
   - Grip the enemy continuously
   - Apply heavy pressure in low-intensity conflicts
   - Discriminate friend from foe and guilty from innocent

4. *What is air power unable to do?*
   - Cost-effectively transport very heavy or bulky cargoes
   - Seize and hold territorial objectives
   - Accept an enemy's surrender

specifies protection against enemy air power only as a task that friendly air power can do well. The reason that this task is not in the "unique" category is that surface-to-air missiles can play important roles, while friendly ground forces might seize the enemy's airfields.

Second, the many judgments expressed in Table 5.3 will not fit each and every actual case. As Clausewitz wrote of theory, "It is meant to educate the mind of the future commander, or, more accurately, to guide him in his self-education, not to accompany him to the battlefield."[43] For example, desert terrain or a sea area can be "occupied" from the air far more meaningfully than can urban or densely wooded environments. The utility of air power varies from case to case.

Third, although technological change improves the capabilities of land, sea, and air forces, the most recent of the three, air forces, has enjoyed the greatest growth potential of recent decades. Table 5.3 implies qualitative figures of merit that are fixed neither from case to case nor over time. Nonetheless, each of the judgments in this table points to a structural feature about air power that is unlikely to be transformed at all rapidly by technological or other change.

Fourth, with only partial exceptions Table 5.3 seeks to evade passing overall strategic judgment upon the value of air power. Important exceptions include the claims that air power tends to perform well at deterring high- and mid-level conflicts, but relatively poorly at deterring or, in important respects, actually waging low-intensity conflicts. In the latter class of events, the enemy rarely makes himself accessible to efficient and effective bombardment from the air; he operates virtually at all times in a highly dispersed mode.

Fifth, by definition the second, third, and fourth categories of utility identified in Table 5.3 can be performed more or less well by forces other than, or as well as, air forces. Generally there are alternative ways to perform missions in war, just as there are rival theories of how best to deter war. In particular historical cases, typically preferred methods of accomplishing difficult tasks simply may be infeasible. For example, in World War II the cost-ineffective aerial resupply of Nationalist Chinese forces from India "over the hump" of the Himalayas was mandated by the temporary unavailability of the "Burma road" and the prospectively permanent unavailability of Allied maritime access to China.

Sixth, Table 5.3 is not presented as a would-be definitive accounting of the utility of air power. Its contents certainly could be augmented with additional judgments.

Seventh and finally, Table 5.3, as indeed are all of the arguments in Part II, is developed with the mindset of a first-class air power. The subject of primary interest here is the future utility of superior air power. With good reason, it tends to be assumed that anything less than first-class air power is readily defeated and therefore can have little strategic value to its owner. Such need not always be the case, however. A second-class air force cannot readily change its strategy and force structure after the manner of a second-class navy that decides to wage *guerre de course* (war against trade) after it recognizes that battlefleet command is unattainable. Nevertheless, not all inferior air forces need be as operationally impotent as was the Iraqi in 1991, and not all terms of engagement will be as permissive as were those of the Gulf War for coalition air power. This is not to suggest that circles miraculously can be squared or that lead can become gold. An inferior air force is an inferior air force and as such it certainly ought to lose a contest for air superiority. The point, rather, is that a country or coalition with distinctly inferior military air assets still may be able to craft a scheme of operations likely to extract substantial nuisance value from those inferior assets. Intelligent strategies for irredeemably militarily weaker powers comprise a subject that tends to pass without enough study in the United States.

PAST, PRESENT, AND FUTURE

The United States is a natural air power and not merely a military air power. The quantity and quality of U.S. air forces will vary over time with the shifting political mood of the country, just as the potency and relevance of those forces will fluctuate from conflict to conflict. Viewed overall, however, American status as probably the dominant air power is not fragile.[44] The country's distinctive geography, and hence American geostrategic problems and opportunities, American strategic culture and history, the scope and scale of the high-technology industry in the United States, and the permanent fact of the American people's personal interface with flight all point to an enduring air-mindedness.

From time to time the question has been posed, Why does the United States need a (very large) navy? Immediately after World War II, for example, the U.S. Navy was bereft of a maritime enemy. No matter how foolish, that question of strategic utility does reappear occasionally vis-à-vis the navy and the Marine Corps.[45] It is all but inconceivable that the parallel question would be asked of the air force. The question to the navy and to the marines really is why do we need naval power and the ability to assault a hostile shore. The periodically renewed debate about air power is fundamentally different. The relevant air power debate has been about who should provide it, not about its utility. That point may provide only small consolation to an air force engaged in protecting the integrity of a coherent and unified air power mission, but the distinction is nonetheless significant. It is one thing to have to defend the provision of different kinds of air power by an independent air force; it is quite another to have to defend the strategic utility of air power itself. Indeed, it is precisely the military value of air power that periodically obliges the air force to have to defend air force provision of it against the claims of sundry terrestrial and maritime military clients who want to provide more of it for themselves.

There is room for argument and rival analyses over how U.S. air power should be "balanced," to have resort to the familiar contested concept, as among land-based and short-range, land-based and long-range, and sea-based elements. But there is little scope for sensible contention over the political and strategic meaning of the claim that the United States has become the air power. The United States has, and most likely will sustain, air and space forces sufficiently potent that those forces will be able, albeit infrequently, to deter or win wars without the benefit of much assistance from other branches of military power; frequently will enjoy "key force" status in joint endeavors; and always will have some shaping influence upon the course and conduct of conflict.

Air power is an enabling agent: the scope of what it enables must vary from context to context. Therefore, to claim that the United States, as the air power,

Figure 5.1
Strategic Utility of Air Power

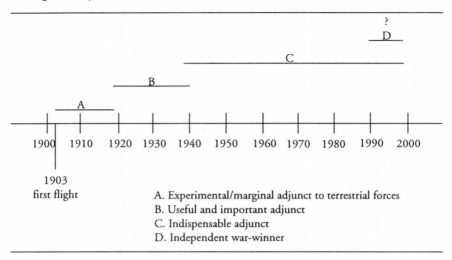

A. Experimental/marginal adjunct to terrestrial forces
B. Useful and important adjunct
C. Indispensable adjunct
D. Independent war-winner

Figure 5.2
Strategic Utility of Space Power

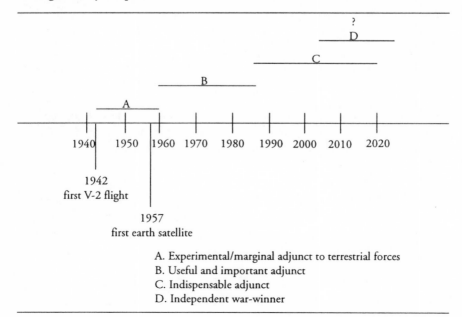

A. Experimental/marginal adjunct to terrestrial forces
B. Useful and important adjunct
C. Indispensable adjunct
D. Independent war-winner

has air and space forces that have war-winning capabilities is an important half-truth. Air and space forces can win, or can play the key roles in, those kinds of conflicts wherein aerospace power is both able and is allowed to play the strategic lead. The apparent circularity in that reasoning should not obscure significant distinctions. Evolving air and space capabilities should become ever more (absolutely) potent—though beware of expectations that do not sufficiently take into account the enemy's ability to resist—but they will not be suitable as the executor for military victory or as the problem solver for all seasons. As air and space forces become more and more capable, the limitations upon their value will more and more often be strategic and political rather than technical-tactical (e.g., enemy assets may be vulnerable, but air forces will be denied the license to strike them).

To illustrate simply and graphically just how far air and space forces have progressed over the course of ninety years, this chapter concludes with two figures which sketch the relevant strategic history (Figures 5.1 and 5.2). On four-category scales the advancing strategic prowess of air power and space power is tracked notionally.

There are historical exceptions to the elementary generalities expressed in Figures 5.1 and 5.2. Nonetheless, the figures are robust overall and they show just how far and fast air power and space power have progressed strategically. In addition, the figures suggest how useful it can be to think in common strategic terms about the utility of these two forms of military power. The figures should not be interpreted as meaning that (superior) air power today and (superior) space power tomorrow will win all the wars in which they are applied. Furthermore, the figures should not be interpreted as implying an inevitable, let alone irreversible, progression from "experimental/marginal" (A) status to the category of "independent war-winner" (D). Space forces may never achieve that strategic distinction, while space-assisted air forces will achieve it only infrequently. Nevertheless, the strategic distance traveled from 1903, or from the first large-scale air battles over Verdun in 1916, has been nothing short of awesome and has made air and space forces the strongest suit of contemporary U.S. war fighting across the widest range of representative scenarios of conflict.

NOTES

1. John A. Warden, III, "Employing Air Power in the Twenty-First Century," in Richard H. Shultz, Jr., and Robert L. Pfaltzgraff, Jr., eds., *The Future of Air Power in the Aftermath of the Gulf War* (Maxwell Air Force Base, AL: Air University Press, July 1992), p. 61.

2. Eliot A. Cohen, "The Mystique of U.S. Air Power," *Foreign Affairs* 73, no. 1 (January/February 1994): 120.

3. See Russell F. Weigley, *The American Way of War: A History of United States Strategy and Policy* (New York: Macmillan, 1973); Colin S. Gray, *Nuclear Strategy and National Style* (Lanham, MD: University Press of America, 1986); Bruno Colson, *La culture stratégique Américaine: L'influence de Jomini* (Paris: FEDN/Economica, 1993); John Shy, "The Cultural Approach to the History of War," *Journal of Military History* 57, no. 5, special issue (October 1993): 13–26.

4. See the editor's introductory essay, "Warfare and Strategic Cultures in History," in Gérard Chaliand, ed., *The Art of War in World History: From Antiquity to the Nuclear Age* (Berkeley: University of California Press, 1994), pp. 1–46.

5. See Yitzhak Klein, "A Theory of Strategic Culture," *Comparative Strategy* 10, no. 1 (1991): 3–23. Two exceptionally profound and historically wide-ranging studies of the cultural roots of political behavior are by Adda B. Bozeman: *Politics and Culture in International History* (Princeton, NJ: Princeton University Press, 1960); and *Strategic Intelligence and Statecraft: Selected Essays* (Washington, DC: Brassey's [US], 1992). Some suitably cautionary notes are struck in Alastair Iain Johnston, "Thinking about Strategic Culture," *International Security* 19, no. 4 (spring 1995): 32–64.

6. Stephen B. Jones, "Global Strategic Views," in Eugene M. Emme, ed., *The Impact of Air Power: National Security and World Politics* (Princeton, NJ: D. Van Nostrand, 1959), p. 125.

7. Carl H. Builder, *The Masks of War: American Military Styles in Strategy and Analysis* (Baltimore, MD: Johns Hopkins University Press, 1989).

8. The naval analogy makes the point. Alfred T. Mahan wrote that "[t]he mutual dependence of commerce and the navy is nowhere more clearly seen than in the naval resources of a nation, the greatness of which depends upon peaceful trade and shipping. Compared with a *merely military navy*, it is the difference between a natural and a forced growth." *Naval Strategy, Compared and Contrasted with the Principles and Practice of Military Operations on Land* (Boston: Little, Brown, 1919; first pub. 1911), p. 163 (emphasis added). Analogously, a "merely military air force" would be an air force maintained in the near absence of American commercial aviation.

9. This is strictly true only with reference to a politically isolated United States. In practice, in the first half of this century the first line of defense for the United States comprised formal or functional allies in Europe and Asia.

10. William Mitchell, *Winged Defense: The Development and Possibilities of Modern Air Power—Economic and Military* (New York: Dover Publications, 1988; first pub. 1925), p. 6.

11. Careful historical study of the record of economic sanctions in action, more broadly of the strategic effectiveness of economic warfare, is extremely rare. As a practical matter it can be close to impossible to pass judgment upon the relative effectiveness of the economic weapon when several other "weapons" of grand strategy were applied simultaneously. The general truth, unsurprisingly, would seem to be that economic pressure is most effective when it is applied in the context of powerful military operations. A superior case study on this question is Avner Offer, *The First World War: An Agrarian Interpretation* (Oxford: Clarendon Press, 1989).

12. This section draws heavily upon a part of my essay, "Strategy in the Nuclear Age: The United States, 1945–1991," in Williamson Murray, MacGregor Knox, and

Alvin Bernstein, eds., *The Making of Strategy: Rulers, States, and War* (Cambridge: Cambridge University Press, 1994), though with substantial additional material addressed directly to the subject of air power.

13. Denis W. Brogan, *The American Character* (New York: Alfred A. Knopf, 1944), p. 150.

14. For example, see the negative judgment on U.S. armor in 1944–45 in Allan R. Millett, "The United States Armed Forces in the Second World War," in Allan R. Millett and Williamson Murray, eds., *Military Effectiveness*, vol. III, *The Second World War* (Boston: Allen and Unwin, 1988), pp. 61, 72–74, 79–80. Consider Correlli Barnett's sweeping judgment: "Yet for all the German misdeployment of technological and industrial resources so shrewdly analysed by Overy [in Richard Overy, *Why the Allies Won* (London: Jonathan Cape, 1995)], the German Army remained virtually to the end [of World War II] equipped with better tanks, better guns, better small arms and better mortars than the Anglo-Americans." "Numbers Do Matter: Why the Axis Powers Failed to Exploit Their Early Successes," *Times Literary Supplement*, 18 August 1995, p. 7.

15. At some risk of appearing ungenerous, one could cite the significant contributions of Bourbon France to American independence (see Jonathan R. Dull, *The French Navy and American Independence: A Study of Arms and Diplomacy, 1774–1787* [Princeton, NJ: Princeton University Press, 1975]); British war-weariness, Royal Navy overconfidence, and limited motivation in 1812–14; the less than first-class character of nineteenth-century opponents; and the prior and simultaneous attrition that U.S. allies imposed upon the Germans twice in this century.

16. See Allan R. Millett and Peter Maslowski, *For the Common Defense: A Military History of the United States of America* (New York: Free Press, 1984), chap. 1.

17. See Millett, "United States Armed Forces in the Second World War," pp. 60–61, 82–83.

18. For what amounts to a self-parody of this pleasing thesis, see Francis Fukuyama's unduly celebrated article, "The End of History?" *National Interest*, no. 16 (summer 1989): 3–18.

19. In one of his less contentious judgments, critical strategic theorist Jeffrey Record observes that "[i]n the wake of Desert Storm, drawing lessons from the Gulf War became a premier growth industry in an otherwise shrinking U.S. defense analytical community. It remains a sport open to all." *Hollow Victory: A Contrary View of the Gulf War* (Washington, DC: Brassey's [US], 1993), p. 134.

20. Giulio Douhet, *The Command of the Air* (New York: Arno Press, 1972; first pub. 1942), p. 206.

21. See Colin S. Gray, *War, Peace, and Victory: Strategy and Statecraft for the Next Century* (New York: Simon and Schuster, 1990), chap. 4. The vulnerability analyses produced in the RAND style and the stability precepts which appear to flow from them showed virtually no recognition of the dominant role of politics in decisions over war or peace. Similarly reductionist in effect were the writings of the 1980s that purported to demonstrate systemic positive connections between offensive strategies and the risks of war.

22. The figures were 66,045 sorties for the nine critical German target systems and 51,480 sorties for Japan. Cited in R. J. Overy, *The Air War, 1939–1945* (New York: Stein and Day, 1985; first pub. 1980), p. 310. For essential background see Wesley Frank Craven and James Lea Cate, eds., *The Army Air Forces in World War II*, vol. I, *Plans and Early Operations, January 1939 to August 1942* (Chicago: University of Chicago Press, 1948), particularly chaps. 4, 7, and 16. To be fair, in 1937 Britain's RAF Bomber Command calculated in its Western Air Plan 5 that "given the right conditions, the command could bring the German war machine to a standstill in a fortnight, with the expenditure of only 3,000 sorties and the loss of only 176 aircraft, by attacking 19 power-stations and 26 coking-plants in the Ruhr." Basil Collier, *A History of Air Power* (New York: Macmillan, 1974), p. 113.

23. Weigley, *American Way of War*, p. 416.

24. Operational agility did, however, receive official blessing in the U.S. Marine Corps and Army in the 1980s. Never ones to do a job by halves, Americans discovered "maneuver" warfare. See Richard D. Hooker, Jr., ed., *Maneuver Warfare: An Anthology* (Novato, CA: Presidio Press, 1993); and H. T. Hayden, *Warfighting: Maneuver Warfare in the U.S. Marine Corps* (Mechanicsburg, PA: Stackpole Books, 1995).

25. See Ira D. Gruber, "The Anglo-American Military Tradition and the War for American Independence," in Kenneth J. Hagan and William R. Roberts, eds., *Against All Enemies: Interpretations of American Military History from Colonial Times to the Present* (Westport, CT: Greenwood Press, 1986), pp. 21–47; and, for a different twist, John Shy, "The Military Conflict Considered as a Revolutionary War," in Shy, *A People Numerous and Armed: Reflections on the Military Struggle for American Independence* (New York: Oxford University Press, 1976), pp. 193–224.

26. Albert J. Wohlstetter, "The Delicate Balance of Terror," *Foreign Affairs* 37, no. 2 (January 1959): 211–34; Thomas C. Schelling, "Surprise Attack and Disarmament," in Klaus Knorr, ed., *NATO and American Security* (Princeton, NJ: Princeton University Press, 1959), chap. 8; and Thomas C. Schelling and Morton H. Halperin, *Strategy and Arms Control* (New York: Twentieth Century Fund, 1961).

27. See Mark Clodfelter, *The Limits of Air Power: The American Bombing of North Vietnam* (New York: Free Press, 1989).

28. See Michael Howard, *Grand Strategy*, vol. 4, *August 1942–September 1943* (London: HMSO, 1970); and Mark Stoler, *The Politics of the Second Front: American Military Planning and Diplomacy in Coalition Warfare, 1941–1943* (Westport, CT: Greenwood Press, 1977).

29. The British model of maritime strategy was the model for a state weak in land power; such weakness has not been characteristic of the U.S. experience, at least not to the degree suffered by Britain. The British model is well presented in David French, *The British Way in Warfare, 1688–2000* (London: Unwin Hyman, 1990). The Anglo-American strategic maritime relationship is explored in depth in the essays in John B. Hattendorf and Robert S. Jordan, eds., *Maritime Strategy and the Balance of Power: Britain and America in the Twentieth Century* (New York: St. Martin's Press, 1989). Hew Strachan begins a recent essay on "The British Way in Warfare" with the challenging claim that "[t]here has never been a British way in warfare." In David

Chandler, ed., *The Oxford Illustrated History of the British Army* (Oxford: Oxford University Press, 1994), p. 417.

30. A negative view of nuclear strategy as strategy pervades McGeorge Bundy, *Danger and Survival: Choices about the Bomb in the First Fifty Years* (New York: Random House, 1988); and Kenneth N. Waltz, "Nuclear Myths and Political Realities," *American Political Science Review* 84, no. 3 (September 1990): 731–45.

31. On the subject of what Americans have learned from their experience, see John Shy's path-breaking essay, "The American Military Experience: History and Learning," in Shy, *A People Numerous and Armed: Reflections on the Military Struggle for American Independence* (London: Oxford University Press, 1976), pp. 224–58.

32. Douhet, *Command of the Air*, p. 59.

33. Although American military literature is immense, American writing on strategy is a rare and endangered species of theory.

34. In the words of Samuel P. Huntington, "the United States is a big country, and we should fight wars in a big way. One of our great advantages is our mass; we should not hesitate to use it." *American Military Strategy*, Policy Papers in International Affairs, no. 28 (Berkeley: University of California, Berkeley, Institute of International Studies, 1986), pp. 15–16.

35. A plausible point hammered home as a major theme in Harry G. Summers, *On Strategy: A Critical Analysis of the Vietnam War* (Novato, CA: Presidio Press, 1982).

36. See Weigley, *American Way of War*, p. 5.

37. See Charles G. Heller and William A. Stofft, eds., *America's First Battles, 1776–1965* (Lawrence: Kansas University Press, 1986). A dissenting view may be found in Geoffrey Perret, *A Country Made by War: From the Revolution to Vietnam—The Story of America's Rise to Power* (New York: Vintage Books, 1990; first pub. 1989). Perret argues that "the American record of military preparedness is not uniform, simple or clear, but for the most part the United States has been better prepared for what actually ensued than its enemies" (p. 561). Given that the United States has won nearly all of its wars, there is a vital sense in which Perret has to be correct. The key to the argument is just what is meant by "better prepared." The United States was "better prepared" to wage the Pacific War than was Japan, but it was not better equipped to do so in 1941–42.

38. Shy, "American Military Experience," p. 239.

39. For period pieces, see William W. Kaufmann, "Limited Warfare," in William W. Kaufmann, ed., *Military Policy and National Security* (Princeton, NJ: Princeton University Press, 1956), chap. 4; Robert E. Osgood, *Limited War: The Challenge to American Strategy* (Chicago: University of Chicago Press, 1957); and Morton H. Halperin, *Limited War in the Nuclear Age* (New York: John Wiley and Sons, 1963).

40. Carl von Clausewitz, *On War*, ed. and trans. Michael Howard and Peter Paret (Princeton, NJ: Princeton University Press, 1976; first pub. 1832), p. 605.

41. See Colin S. Gray, "Off the Map: Defense Planning after the Soviet Threat," *Strategic Review* 22, no. 2 (spring 1994): 26–35, for a brief explanation of why this tends to be so. The root of the problem is the practical political requirement that defense planners have to pretend to know, or at least know how to discover, how much is enough.

42. Edward N. Luttwak, "Air Power in U.S. Military Strategy," in Richard H. Shultz, Jr., and Robert L. Pfaltzgraff, Jr., eds., *The Future of Air Power in the Aftermath of the Gulf War* (Maxwell Air Force Base, AL: Air University Press, July 1992), p. 21. James F. Dunnigan and Austin Bay, *From Shield to Storm: High-Tech Weapons, Military Strategy, and Coalition Warfare in the Persian Gulf* (New York: William Morrow, 1992), p. 493, usefully augments Luttwak's judgment.

43. Clausewitz, *On War*, p. 141.

44. For reasons presented and developed persuasively in Cohen, "The Mystique of U.S. Air Power."

45. An object lesson in how that question should be answered is provided in Samuel P. Huntington, "National Policy and the Transoceanic Navy," *U.S. Naval Institute Proceedings* 80, no. 5 (May 1954): 483–93.

Chapter 6

Air Power and Defense Planning

Policy, strategy, and forces should form a single subject as they each play their distinctive, but interlocking, parts in providing for national security. To assert the complementary connections among the three categories, however, is much easier than to explain how and why those connections function. The first half of this chapter outlines briefly the architecture of logic and process that should bind policy to strategy and forces and identifies national-interest analysis as the key mechanism that can ensure coherence in the vital relationships between means and ends. The second half of the chapter moves into the more contentious zone of substantive analysis and judgment on the strategic value of air power in the future.

The discussion in this chapter registers many familiar approaches to force planning, while emphasizing the fact that no methodological wizardry can compensate for a lack of policy guidance. A defense establishment as a whole or an air force or an airplane certainly has military-technical merit in and of itself, but that merit requires augmentation by an assay of the instrument in question in relation to the goals of strategy and the purposes of policy.

Moving from method toward substance, the analysis finds the source of future policy and strategic demand for aerospace power in U.S. roles in the world. These roles are described as the obligations of primacy. The United States may have to call upon its air forces for deterrent or denial effect over the full range of possible conflicts—a range which extends from a great balance-of-power struggle down through regional, local, and nontraditional conflicts into the realm of emergency responses (international "911" calls) to natural or manmade disasters.

POLICY, STRATEGY, FORCES: 1941 AND TODAY

> A man who wants to make a good instrument must first have a precise
> understanding of what the instrument is to be used for; and he who
> intends to build a good instrument of war must first ask himself what the
> next war will be like.[1]

When, early in August 1941, Lt. Col. Harold L. George, head of the newly
created Air War Plans Division (AWPD) of the U.S. Army Air Forces (USAAF),
was charged with creating the air war plan which would direct the growth of the
USAAF, he had to decide upon the purpose of that USAAF in a European war.
The key choice was between, on the one hand, a USAAF developed to prepare
the way for and subsequently support an invasion of German-held Europe and,
on the other hand, a USAAF constructed to be able independently to defeat
Germany by aerial bombardment. Unsurprisingly, Hal George picked the latter
option, notwithstanding the historical novelty of the concept. AWPD-1 ("Munitions Requirements of the Army Air Forces") of August 1941 identified the
need for a USAAF with 59,727 planes. Ninety-eight bombing groups were to be
the core of the USAAF: they would secure victory by means of an intensive and
unrelenting six-month campaign against 154 specified German strategic targets.
The inspiring story of how Lt. Col. Hal George, Maj. Haywood S. Hansell, Lt.
Col. Kenneth N. Walker, and Maj. Lawrence S. Kuter created the first plausible
war plan in history for victory through air power is cited here because its example
highlights, by sharp contrast, the problems of today.[2]

In August 1941, Hal George knew or thought he knew the identity of the
enemy (Germany, perhaps Japan); the primary air power mission (defeat
Germany via a six-month campaign of "strategic" bombardment); the time
frame to acquire the force (by 1943–45); the capabilities of USAAF aircraft,
current and forthcoming; sufficient facts about the enemy (centers of gravity,
how they were constructed, how they worked as networks or systems); and the
defensive strengths and weaknesses of the identified enemy. The monumental
achievement that was AWPD-1, brilliantly created in only nine days, was orders
of magnitude easier to develop than is its peacetime equivalent today. Hal
George knew his enemy, knew his military instrument, could assume or assert
his dominant mission, and, for some reality testing, could take advice from a
Royal Air Force (RAF) Bomber Command which was attempting what
AWPD-1 intended.

The Hal Georges of the 1990s face problems of daunting complexity and,
with respect to some critical information, even indeterminacy. Much that a
defense planner for air power needs to know today is just not knowable. That
fact does not mean that planners are exonerated from planning; rather, it means
there is a necessity for concepts and a methodology for planning which take

account of irreducible uncertainties. The scope of the challenge to defense planners is to grasp the whole context for the threat or employment of air forces. Air power, whether it enhances all military options or is itself the principal arm of military action, must be directed in the framework of the full array of military options. Those options, in turn, are activated by the grand-strategy choices which implement foreign policy. Those choices are the result of calculations of national interest by a U.S. national leadership reacting within the national domestic climate to the global security environment and to specific "trigger" incidents within that environment.

Figure 6.1 is a calculated exaggeration. It is designed to illustrate the core of the defense planning problem, not to suggest that the problem is beyond useful alleviation (if not comprehensive resolution). This figure is a sketch of the central difficulty addressed in the balance of this chapter: the fact that uncertainty is a condition for defense planning. Figure 6.1 has some degree of merit for any period, but the full force of its implications apply to the 1990s. Needless to add, perhaps, the passage of time will resolve, or at least narrow, many

Figure 6.1
Uncertainty and Defense Planning

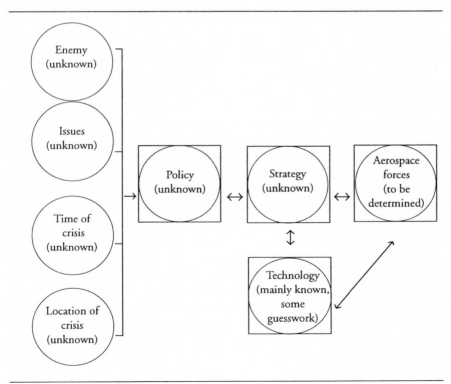

uncertainties, though it will add new uncertainties as the horizon for long-range planning moves ever onward.

It is not unduly cynical, perhaps, to argue that the most basic task for the defense planner is the quest for fault-tolerant assumptions.[3] Given that a uniquely right strategy and force structure are rarely identifiable even in historical retrospect, it is obvious that there can be no demonstrably right strategy and force structure for the future. Instead, the charge has to be a search for strategy and force structure "right enough" that should be tolerant of inevitable errors (in detail). Above all else, history, experience, and some imagination may enable a country's defense planners—if their political masters (e.g., ultimately the public mood) are willing, of course—to answer the big questions as correctly as they need to. That is to say that the answers provided should be both robust against unpleasant surprises and sufficiently flexible as to allow for the exploitation of unexpected opportunities.[4] The key to success in defense planning is to identify the right questions. The most fundamental such question for this topic is the issue of how to determine the character and quality of the air power which should be acquired. It is to that fundamental question that this discussion now turns.

ALCHEMY AND DEFENSE PLANNING

In much the same way that the pseudosciences of alchemy and astrology seek certain knowledge and reliable results by methods that affront physical laws, so many approaches to force planning appear to promise a quality of analytical result that affronts what amount to the "laws" of history. Moreover, the workings of human political and social behavior are a great deal more complicated and less predictable than is the interaction of physical elements and forces. Whether or not lead can be turned into gold, the answer to that challenge would be a correct solution that must hold in all circumstances at all times. By way of contrast, whether or not a twenty-strong B-2 force is the "right" force for the next twenty-five years depends upon a bewildering array of interdependent variables.

Too many of the more popular, simple approaches to force planning lack an ingredient that could render them useful. Specifically, the approaches are not grounded in the political judgments, or in political principles perhaps, which alone could validate them.[5] A force planning design for air power strictly can make sense only if it rests upon guidance from foreign policy. If that guidance itself is to have integrity, it must explain in a general way how national-interest decision rules are applied to event traffic from the global security environment. Since U.S. air power exists solely for the purpose of serving American society, there is no evading specification either of how

American society needs to be served or, more realistically, the method by which American society can proceed to determine the service that it needs.

Figure 6.2 explains the core of the matter. Any approach to force planning has to deal in one way or another with the factors and relationships specified in the figure. For most of the Cold War years, U.S. defense planners could argue and debate over the most cost-effective ways to achieve their tasks, but those tasks by and large were a given, at least at the higher end of the spectrum of peril. Defense planning can display a top-to-bottom, end-to-end rationality (of sorts, at least) if the identity of the enemy and his principal threats are widely agreed upon within the defense community.

If one element is more critical than the others to the functioning of Figure 6.2, it has to be the deceptively innocuous box labeled "interests." It is the identification of interests at stake in the course of international events, by intensity (e.g., vital or major), which fuels the process of decision that can find need for the threat or employment of air forces. Fortunately, many of the more dire potential consequences of the uncertainties of future events can be alleviated by recognition of the merit in prudential, interest-keyed defense planning. To cut through the thickets of political science and defense analysis, the challenge here is first to discover how to conduct the fault-tolerant planning mentioned earlier; in other words, which principles should guide the planning? Second, it is necessary to identify the future roles of air forces in the U.S. force structure.

Two important considerations beg for recognition. They are both obvious, but it is their very obviousness that causes them perennially to be underappreciated. First, Figure 6.2 has an unspecified temporal dimension that is not highlighted. The diagram may suggest an agreeable fit among policy needs and military provision in response to some particular event or trend identified as a threat to a vital U.S. national interest. What the diagram does not highlight is the necessity for the United States to have provided for this call from policy in its force planning many years ahead of the event. The problem is to know what to buy, when, and in what quantities, far ahead of the validation of the need by events. As a minor complication, in its intractably unverifiable deterrent effect, the success of a military capability actually will work politically to invalidate maintenance of that capability, at least in the minds of many people.

Second, although (say) twenty-five years is a long time for people (the duration of a lengthy military career) and modern weapon systems (it is close to the outside limit of the operational lifespan for major weapon platforms), it is almost an eternity in politics. Changes in the global security environment, and policy decisions in response, can move at a speed not remotely approachable by sympathetic alterations in force structure. The moral of this tale is that no matter how it is presented, a prudent defense posture is calculated with

Figure 6.2
Policy Guidance

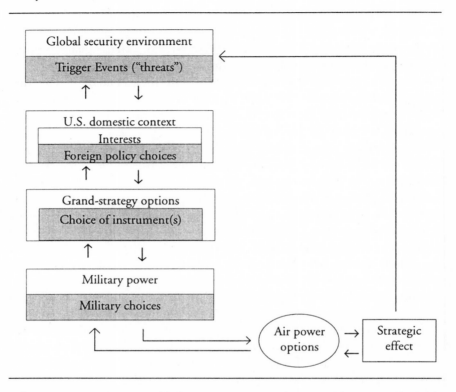

reference to circumstances likely to seem remote from, and hence implausible in terms of, those of today.

The professional force planner does not face the strategic problem that engages this analysis. Specifically, the force planner is given some approximation to policy guidance. Whatever the planner may believe about that guidance, the fact of its provision in tolerably coherent form enables most of the approaches in Table 6.2 to function well enough. Some process has to provide policy assumptions or guiding principles for the force planner.[6] Virtually no matter how heavily qualified with contingencies and broadly framed, policy guidance is essential if the military means to be developed by the force planner are to be anchored on political purpose. To neglect this point for defense preparation in peacetime would be the equivalent in war of conducting conflict after the German manner, which is to say tactically and operationally but not according to firm strategic guidance, let alone according to policy that rested upon sound political-military coordination.[7]

By way of example, the Clinton administration advises that regional conflicts, the proliferation of weapons of mass destruction, the possible failure of democratic reform in the former Soviet Union, and a weak U.S. economy comprise the four "new threats" of most concern to U.S. policy.[8] These four new threats, although a useful indication of significant perils, lack both context and force planning connections. A critic could ask, Why does it matter to the United States if there are regional conflicts, or if weapons of mass destruction proliferate, or if a thousand years of authoritarian political tradition should reassert its authority in Moscow? For the fourth new threat, the point could be made that sensible concerns for the health of the U.S. economy have no particular, let alone necessary, implications for the process of force planning. Deterrence is always cheaper than war. Heavy defense expenditure may damage the economy, but inadequate defense expenditure assuredly will imperil the physical security of the country, as well as the health of the economy. A sound economy is no guarantor of security. On that point history is quite unambiguous.

Although there is no objectively correct approach to force planning and certainly no single correct force structure, one can identify an approach, perhaps more accurately a mixture of approaches, that is both superior to the alternatives and is good enough. To evade the need for alchemy in the analysis, policy guidance must be provided. Given the problem of coping with the deeply uncertain details of the future, the political and strategic basis for deriving policy guidance must be specified. That basis lies in the interpretation of world events by a national-interest "discriminator." The policy demand, through grand-strategic choice, for the services of air power derives from U.S. policymakers deciding that national interests need to be protected or advanced by the threat or application of military power. Table 6.1 portrays a broad design for national-interest analysis.[9]

Naturally, the terse generalities of the architecture in Table 6.1 require specific detailing for the United States over some period in the future. Nonetheless, this national-interest methodology provides the value that has to be added to force planning to avoid heroic efforts in alchemy. If the logic and judgments specified in Table 6.1 are deemed broadly plausible, a basis has been found upon which defense planning in general, and force planning for air power more narrowly, can proceed. One cannot identify exactly where and when the United States will apply its air forces in the course, say, of the next quarter century. But one can discover why the United States should, and hence in broad terms when the United States is likely to decide to, have resort to its military instrument. The three-issue or three-question national-interest intensity "discriminator" in Table 6.1 answers that question.

Table 6.1
National-Interest Analysis

---

1. Survival: unquestionably involves the physical or political survival of the state and society and must be defended by force if need be
2. Vital: generally judged worth fighting to protect
3. Major: difficult to portray as worth fighting to protect
4. Other: virtually never deemed worth fighting to defend or advance

The practical difficulty is not definition but rather political assignment. For example, are the stakes in Bosnia an interest in the "major" or the "other" category for the United States?

High-intensity (survival, vital, vital/major) national interests are likely to be discerned if threats are perceived to

- the balance of power
- U.S. reputation or its "good name"
- American citizens or their property

Notes: These three discriminating "tests" of an issue for its intensity value on the scale of U.S. national interests are not infallible or objective (e.g., degree of "reputation" can be invested purposefully or inadvertently in the outcome to a particular conflict). But they are broadly reliable with reference to U.S. history, political culture, and the enduring character of the politics of international security.

Critical reference has been made in passing to approaches to force planning. Table 6.2, adapted from a primer on force planning,[10] illustrates well the nature of the "alchemical" challenge to transform the unpromising materials for defense analysis into the gold of sound looking recommendations.

Several of the approaches to force planning listed in Table 6.2 plainly have merit, provided the challenge of policy guidance is met suitably. For it to be met suitably for a long stretch of years, it is imperative that the policy challenge be met at the level of principle and method, rather than with guesswork about particulars. In other words, political uncertainty renders it most unwise to key long-term U.S. defense planning to, say, developments internal to Russia. The appropriate referent is not a particular country, but rather to the course of security, or power, relations among countries. As the United States demonstrated in the course of the 1940s, it would wage hot or cold war not against a particular polity, but rather to correct an intolerable adverse drift in the balance of power. Instead of being driven by specific, dominant threats, the United States in the future will continue to be pulled by the commands of prudence to be prepared to cope with a wide range of uncertainty.[11]

Table 6.2
Force Planning Approaches

Approach	Primary Focus
Assumption	Contingent predictions
Top down	Objectives
Bottom up	Current capability
Scenario	Circumstances
Threat	Opponent capability
Mission	Mission area priority
Hedging	Uncertainty
Technology	Technological superiority
Fiscal	Budget

With appropriate humility, the next section of this chapter examines briefly an educated best guess as to the security roles that the United States is likely to wish to play over the course of the next quarter century.

OBLIGATIONS OF PRIMACY

At this juncture the most relevant questions are the following:

- What roles will the United States play in international security affairs over the next quarter century?
- What major trends and developments will shape the course of international events over the next quarter century?
- How could those trends and developments, processed by the kind of national-interest analysis outlined in Table 6.1, translate into strategic demand for U.S. air power?

The entire pattern of logic in the connections among world events, U.S. foreign policy, and U.S. force planning and strategy has to be registered here. Whatever one's personal or institutional preferences over the size and character of air forces, those preferences require legitimization in terms of the strategic demands (for effectiveness) generated by foreign policy decisions which themselves are rooted in national roles as a player in world affairs.

U.S. roles in the world may be summarized as the obligations of primacy and can be encapsulated with reference to four linked functions: keeper of the balance of power; protector of last resort; organizer and leader of collective security; and defender of humane values.[12] The obligations in question pertain to the ethics of consequences rather than to the morality of right conduct in and of itself. The argument reduces to the claims that the United States should do more for an international order (that benefits U.S. national security) than should other polities, because it will be uniquely so enabled. The four roles just identified strictly are all derivatives of the same quantity and quality of international primacy. This is not quite to suggest that foreign policy appetite grows with national capacity, although the aphorism is not wholly without merit. The points, rather, are that a certain kind of world order best serves the national interests of Americans, while the United States in the years ahead will be able to have a larger share in shaping the terms and conditions of world order than will any other single polity. This argument falls far short of claims either that the United States will always be able to shape events abroad or that endeavors to effect such shaping regularly must be strongly (in vital or major ways; see Table 6.1) in the U.S. interest. Even when U.S. policymakers discern a moral imperative to act, a scenario from hell, such as the events in Bosnia, illustrates the limits even of superpower.

There is nothing uniquely American about the U.S. roles cited here, notwithstanding the rhetorical and cultural legacy of Woodrow Wilson's idealism.[13] These roles attach to the United States now because it is a satisfied power and because its relative influence is so much greater than is that of any potential ally or foe. Just as there is nothing uniquely American about these four mutually supporting derivatives of international primacy, so also there is nothing inherently permanent about that primacy. Indeed, competitive strategy, to recall a widely favored notion from the late 1980s, will be required if this temporary era of U.S. preeminence is to be prolonged.

For many years to come, however, the broad and general obligations of U.S. primacy will be as indisputable as will be that primacy itself. The application of those general obligations to specific cases, be they scenarios from heaven or from hell, typically will provide ample fuel for political, strategic, and military controversy. What does all this mean for U.S. air forces? The United States will need to maintain the air forces appropriate to its roles as keeper of the balance of power, protector of last resort, organizer and leader of collective security, and defender of humane values. These obligations of international primacy are unbounded locally, regionally, or globally. The relevant bounds upon U.S. obligation are imposed by U.S. national-interest calculation. Figure 6.3 indicates just how extensive could be the range of demands for U.S. air force effectiveness which derive from international primacy.

Figure 6.3 is not a prediction that over the next quarter century the United States will participate in a global war, in regional wars, in local disorders, in meeting nontraditional threats, and in responding to emergencies. But since the Cold War ended, there have been policy demands for the services of U.S.

Figure 6.3
Strategic Demand for U.S. Air Force Effectiveness

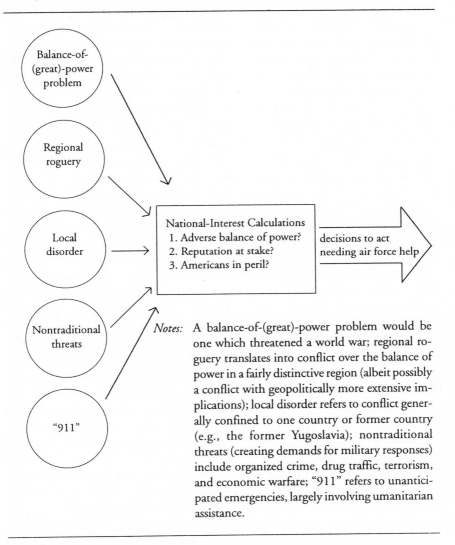

Notes: A balance-of-(great)-power problem would be one which threatened a world war; regional roguery translates into conflict over the balance of power in a fairly distinctive region (albeit possibly a conflict with geopolitically more extensive implications); local disorder refers to conflict generally confined to one country or former country (e.g., the former Yugoslavia); nontraditional threats (creating demands for military responses) include organized crime, drug traffic, terrorism, and economic warfare; "911" refers to unanticipated emergencies, largely involving umanitarian assistance.

armed forces in all of these categories of conflict save for the first, the balance-of-(great)-power problem that has the potential for world war. The qualification is not a very powerful one. On the one hand there is still general, if declining, agreement in the United States that the country must be prepared to play a proactive role in promoting global stability, which translates as roles supportive either of regional balances of power or of balances healthily tilted in favor of status quo polities. On the other hand the balance-of-power struggle that was the Cold War has been concluded so recently that the current absence of a conflict of that magnitude and scale of peril is evidence of nothing at all about the future.

Figure 6.3 simply is descriptive. Four of the conflict classes are extant, while the fifth (the balance-of-[great]-power struggle) is either a strong possibility or a certainty, depending upon how far into the future one elects to peer. The details, however, are as murky as the structure of the strategic context is clear. The United States requires that its air forces be expressive of its primacy with reference to all dimensions of conflict ranging from world war to the provision of emergency relief. So much is not really worth debating. More contentious by far is the defense planning question of lead time to a period of major balance-of-power peril. All of the other conflict categories are with us today in live forms, but the shape, mass, and velocity of a future threat to peace akin to that posed by the Soviet Union cannot be predicted with confidence.

The challenge to defense planning is therefore twofold. First, the United States, the principal protector of order, needs to have air forces constantly ready to intervene in regional and local quarrels and to tackle terrorism and sudden manmade as well as natural disasters. Of course there will be many cases of such conflict and emergency to which the United States should not respond; U.S. policymakers will have to conduct careful (intensity of) national-interest analysis. Second, as *the* keeper of the balance of power, the leading obligation of international primacy, the United States requires air forces suitable to discourage dissatisfied states from mounting major challenges to the balance of power and hence to order; to deter dissatisfied states from taking warlike actions; and if necessary to deny dissatisfied states the military ability to reorder forcefully and favorably the terms of their security. Given that a new, post-Soviet threat to the global balance of power and quite literally to U.S. survival interests does not currently exist, it is no easy matter to prescribe in a rational manner a defense program demonstrably well tailored to the frustration and defeat of such a threat.

The historical record of modern statecraft proves nothing in detail about the likelihood, timing, or players in a future struggle over the balance of power in Europe and Asia. Scientific, in the form of quantified, enquiry into the duration between great wars since, say, 1500 is quite useless. What is not useless is an approach to history which recognizes the general value of experience (all else is theory) as providing some guide to the issues and problems worth thinking about.[14] For a narrow but pertinent example, the history of strategic air campaigns from World War II until the Gulf in 1991 proves nothing about their future efficacy. Technology, terrain, opponent, and political goals and rules assuredly differ from case to case. Nonetheless, the factors and the relationships among them that all together contribute to success or failure in particular campaigns are present in all cases, with only the detailed values being distinctive.

CLOSING THE LOOP

> The conquest of the command of the air will be a necessary condition of future wars, even if it will not insure victory by itself.[15]

> The [1991 Gulf] war suggests that if a "military-technical revolution" is now under way, it is only in its early stages. There were precedents for many of the ways the war was planned, for the technology used, and the organizations that fought it. But there are glimmerings of something very different ahead, in the role played by space-based assets, the unified command and control apparatus, and the routine precision of air attacks. A great deal of organizational and doctrinal preparation would be needed to make the promise of such a revolution a reality.[16]

The analysis here closes the loop that connects foreign policy choices in the face of an evolving global security environment (however characterized), with the decisions made in defense and force planning. The key to prudent decision-making is the posing of educated questions that can be answered. The future is not predictable in detail, but still a great deal of value to the defense planner is known or reasonably can be assumed about the years ahead.

The centerpiece of this discussion comprises the answers to a set of four fundamental questions: (1) Which principles should guide U.S. defense planning? (2) What should be the roles of air power in the U.S. force posture over the next quarter century? (3) Can air power win wars? (4) What is the meaning of the Gulf War for the future of air power? Having answered these central questions in a direct fashion, the argument concludes by revisiting the distinctive advantages of air power and offering a few salient thoughts on weapons and decision in war.

In broad terms, it is possible to delineate with some confidence the strategic utility of air power to the United States over the next quarter century. The boldness of this claim stems not from a disdain for uncertainty, but rather from a willingness to take full account of it. Uncertainty can never be an ally of the defense planner, because it would always be desirable to know exactly what would be demanded of the armed forces by policy and strategy. Nonetheless, it is possible, if not to neutralize fully the perils of unpleasant surprises, at least to mitigate the worst effects of such surprises. It is a favorite tune of this author to urge the merit in fault-tolerant planning. Some people may prefer a more positive approach, but prudence suggests the value in approaching problems in defense and force planning with a view to getting right what can be got right reliably and to ensure that what can be got right is right enough to allow for the inevitable errors in matters of detail. In other words, precise future requirements for U.S. air forces cannot be identified by any methodology, but general requirements suitable to direct detailed planning into the "good enough" range of values certainly can be established. Consider what is known, or at least known well enough, today:

- what air power can and cannot accomplish as a general rule (on the basis of ninety-plus-years' experience and plausible educated guesses about the next twenty-five years).

- the forces and factors, or trends, that are shaping the course of international history in the late 1990s. We can also make reasonable assessments concerning the implications of those trends for the early years of the next century.[17]

- what security roles the United States will be obliged to play. We know this because we have a firm grasp upon the nature of world politics and U.S. political culture and history.

- what kinds of conflicts may attract U.S. participation, a judgment that flows from the prior assessment of roles. In addition, we can guess well enough what kind of foes, in what kind of geographical relationship to us, will be the candidate targets for our strategic leverage.

Scope remains for judgment, even downright guesswork, and the details of future security challenges assuredly will contain many surprises. Two facts, however, serve greatly to diminish uncertainty for U.S. defense planners. First, the United States is, and will for a long time remain, the global superpower. Second, geopolitically and geostrategically U.S. military power is nearly certain to be functioning at least an ocean away from home and just possibly half a world away. The politics, the geography, and by implication even much of the necessary strategy are identifiable in broad terms long in advance. These brief observations help close the loop between choices on force structure and on the threat or actual use of air power and choices of U.S. policy in response to a dynamic global security environment.

The loop connecting policy and forces can be closed defensibly and plausibly, provided the right questions are identified. As an example of a wrong question to pose, today it is impossible to specify exactly which force structure will most closely meet U.S. policy needs in 2006, let alone 2016 or 2021. Similarly, an intelligent answer is difficult, if not impossible, to the question, Will the United States be able to win wars in the next quarter century by the use of air power alone? The correct answer is "yes, but . . . ," and the "but" is very important. Wars might occur that the United States could wage and win solely from the air. Such victories might even possibly be achieved by the use strictly of long-range land-based air power, *or* of short-range land-based air power, *or* of sea-based naval air power. Many things are possible. Nonetheless, answers to questions about the strategic value of air power as an independent war-winner are all but certain to mislead unless they are framed holistically. To provide misleading if technically correct (yes, air power could win some kinds of conflicts—but then so could sea power or land power) answers to this question is to provide no good service to the national security writ large or even to the providers of air power in its several forms. The question of air power's possible independent strategic utility is addressed directly below.

To conclude closing the loop among subjects and arguments raised in Part II of this book, four fundamental questions are posed and answered. Some of these topics have been discussed in passing in the preceding chapters, but it is important that direct answers be provided.

Which Principles Should Guide U.S. Defense Planning?

Chapter 4 discussed in general terms the advantages and limitations of air power. It is important, however, that the distinctive qualities of air power (especially unity, flexibility, and concentration) be considered in the context of the overall needs that the United States has of its defense establishment. Of course, every case of international conflict differs in scale as well as in other critical details. Nonetheless, the United States prudently cannot acquire and maintain military forces carefully tailored to meet only a narrow range of "best guesstimates" of future policy demands for strategic effectiveness. U.S. air (and space) forces, along with land and naval forces, must be capable of deterring and if need be of fighting well enough in a wide range of possible conflicts, for none of which they were specifically designed. U.S. foes in the future may be insular or wholly continental, great powers or small states, nuclear armed or nonnuclear, in need only of discouragement or of massive military defeat, and so forth. The possibilities could be a defense planner's nightmare. As we saw earlier, Figure 6.1 used scale of crisis to illustrate the potential scope of U.S. military effort.

The question remains, What broad guidance can be suggested for U.S. defense planning? By that I mean guidance that is tolerably well proofed against the ebb and flow of fashion in policy debate. Thirteen somewhat overlapping principles are registered here as a basis for such guidance.[18] Needless to say perhaps, these principles (see Table 6.3) are defense-wide and environmentally nonspecific and will require distinctive mixes of military power to give them appropriate expression from conflict case to conflict case.[19]

The variety of possible conflicts denies this listing of principles a single, enduring meaning for air forces. There is no prudent alternative to the preparations of armed forces capable of generating strategic effectiveness by different, if complementary, means. If the enemy wages conventional combat in open country (e.g., the desert or much of northern France beyond the hedgerow area of Normandy), it is more likely than not that he can be defeated by air power. By way of contrast, if the enemy is lodged in urban areas and is interspersed with civilians friendly to us, there is unlikely to be a good alternative to a bloody assault on the ground. In the obvious interest of avoiding the latter, the realm of strategy will seek alternative means to lever the foe out of his urban fortress; a "strategic" air campaign is one such possible means.

Notwithstanding the judgment offered above concerning the distinctive needs of each case of conflict, these thirteen principles suitably emphasize how important it is for the United States to conduct its military affairs in as American a way as is compatible with the requirements of success. The capability to win is cited as the master concept. It is always possible that, Clausewitz's advice notwithstanding, policy will ask of the military instrument more than it can deliver,[20] or more than it can deliver at a cost acceptable on the American home front. Not for nothing did Clausewitz insist that the effective prosecution of war depends upon harmony among the people, the army, and the government.[21]

Because the United States is the leading air power and because air power expresses so many of the comparative advantages of the United States, force

Table 6.3
Principles on Characteristics of Armed Forces for Guidance of Defense Planning

 1. Capable of winning
 2. Sufficient in number
 3. Enjoy and merit acceptability at home
 4. Diverse
 5. Modern
 6. Applicable quickly
 7. Logistically supportable
 8. Adaptable to geography
 9. Able to cope with surprise
10. Focus maximum potential power
11. Able to menace and protect centers of gravity
12. Flexible enough for nonstandard missions
13. Earn respect from foes

Notes: These 13 principles include a "master" desideratum (no. 1) and knowingly provide some analytical offense to logic by including points that other points subsume. Each principle, master and others, is registered for the purpose of highlighting a necessary or at least highly desirable quality in the U.S. armed forces overall.

from the air is more likely to be overused or perhaps misused than underused. The low casualties that attend contemporary (post–World War II) air warfare and the avoidance of ground combat are attractions that policymakers will not be inclined to discount. The emergence of a precise lethality achievable by flexible air instruments leads to a condition wherein the first operational question is What can be done from the air? Nonair operations will be added more or less reluctantly as necessity commands.

What Should Be the Roles of Air Power in the U.S. Force Posture over the Next Quarter Century?

The answer to this question may be found in the direct implications of former chief of staff General Merrill A. McPeak's statement of the air force mission: "Our mission—the job of the forces we bring to the fight—is to defend the United States through control and exploitation of air and space."[22] The question remains, What strategic effectiveness can air (and space) power, particularly the power brought to the fight by the air force, deliver? Substantive judgment by way of explicit answer is provided in response to the next question (Can air power win wars?). In reply to this second question on the roles of air power, a three-part answer is necessary in order to explain what air (and space) forces do in fulfillment of the broad mission claimed by McPeak.

First, air and space forces "achieve national objectives in and through this dimension [aerospace],"[23] including the winning of such conflicts as can be won directly by the actions of air forces. As McPeak has said, "[i]n the aftermath of Desert Storm, we take it for granted that we will be asked to act autonomously, independently of the actions of surface forces."[24] In short, air forces should win whatever can be won by success in and through the air medium. Indeed, the other roles cited immediately below depend for the quality of their performance upon success, up to and including the gaining of command, in the air (and in space).

Second, it is a role of air forces to function as an enabling agent, a force-multiplying facilitator of success for the ground and naval elements of military power. Again in McPeak's words, "we take pride in knowing we will also [as well as acting autonomously] be asked to act in concert with them [surface forces]."[25]

Third, air forces provide tangible, visible, audible, and—if need be—painful (to others) expression of U.S. foreign policy. As well as an instrument of military strategy narrowly, air power can operate directly as an instrument of grand strategy. The purpose in this third role is to have a direct political effect upon the course of events, rather than a military effect for strategic consequences ultimately in support of high policy. Visible overflights, limited nonlethal operations of many kinds, and radar-detectable readiness operations are a few examples of the diplomatic uses of air power.

Can Air Power Win Wars?

The precise phrasing of this question is critical to the value of the answer provided. The question must be asked correctly—correctly not in order to yield a prejudged answer, but to yield a valid answer. Whether or not air power will win such wars as the United States elects to enter over the course of the next quarter century must depend in very large part upon the multidimensional character (e.g., political goals, geography, circumstances of outbreak, and so forth) of those wars and in smaller part upon U.S. choices in strategy and force structure. For example, U.S. air power, though admittedly appallingly misused over Vietnam, almost certainly could not have won that war, given that war's character. The effectiveness of U.S. air power in Vietnam in 1972 was not evidence of what might have been achieved earlier; rather, it was evidence of how command of the air can be exploited in conventional warfare.

The complex answer to the question is that air power can win some wars on its own; will certainly be a key team player in most of the wars that it cannot win by its own autonomous action; and will be a significant factor even for conflicts wherein air forces cannot intervene directly for great effect. In order to provide a more specific answer one would have to know the literally unknowable: the identity and character of future wars.

Naturally, just as the identity and character of future wars (or possible wars that might be deterred) are uncertain, so the potential attainments of air power also are uncertain. Nonetheless, certain trends which bear upon the relative significance of air power in the future are apparent today or are confidently predictable. Specifically, now there is an almost routine lethality about precise and flexible air power; a growing difficulty in offsetting inferiority in the air; and a new unity of air power, a fusion of strategic and tactical.

Although there is a still-growing strategic advantage accruing to the holder of superiority in the air, few trends continue indefinitely. Whether or not one signs on for all of the implications of Edward Luttwak's thesis that processes of conflict at all levels are necessarily and essentially paradoxical, the logic of his argument applies as a caveat to the principal judgment here.[26] Both economics and the logic of competitive net effectiveness in conflict command a diminishing marginal return to increasing effort. Because U.S. air power has advanced in prowess to the zone wherein it can win or be the key to victory in some wars and certainly be a significant influence in virtually all others, it does not follow that air power will become an all-occasion war winner (or war deterrer). Just as some acts will be beyond deterrence, so some conflicts will not lend themselves to definitive resolution by the autonomous operation of air power acting as the executive agent of policy. Both intelligent enemy action reflecting paradoxical logic (e.g., do not confront the United States with a massive conventional military challenge in open terrain), and grand-strategic maneuvers to outflank U.S. military power altogether will occasionally reduce the strategic effectiveness that air superiority could deliver in other circumstances.

As noted earlier, air forces will not have failed if they prove unable either to deter all inimical acts or to inflict decisive defeat by themselves upon all enemies in all conditions of conflict. That is to say, air forces will have "failed" only according to the absurd test of a demonstrated ability to win wars by their own autonomous operation. It is but common sense to recognize that the strategic effectiveness of air power has limits, although it is both ascendant and still growing in relative utility.

What Is the Meaning of the Gulf War for the Future of Air Power?

In common with the German use of air power to seize and hold Norway in 1940, the Allied air rout of the German Seventh Army in Normandy in August 1944, the (air) defense of the Pusan perimeter in Korea in 1950, the Israeli air campaign of 1967, the (air) defense of Khe Sanh in 1968, and Linebacker I and II in 1972, the Gulf War air campaign of 1991 showed that air power, properly applied in propitious circumstances, could either deliver victory or at least ensure the avoidance of defeat. It is possible to argue that the Gulf War provided a valuable marker demonstrating just how potent air power has become, but such a claim would mislead rather than inform.

The air power experience in Desert Storm confirmed what careful historians had always known and what many strategic theorists have long believed. Specifically, as stated in answer to the question Can air power win wars? from time to time wars occur that competent air power either can win by all but autonomous effort or can certainly dominate for a friendly all-arms victory. German air power contributed the vital difference for success in Norway in 1940,[27] as did U.S. and Israeli air power in the other cases just mentioned. Nonetheless, Desert Storm both served usefully to reinforce the authority of some traditional beliefs and functioned powerfully to highlight the continuing trend in favor of the relative advantage of air over other kinds of forces, at least in particular, permissive conditions.

Six broad lessons of Desert Storm are of major relevance to this analysis of strategy and air power. First, the Gulf War showed yet again that modern weapons alone do not make for an effectively modern and efficient military establishment. Allied air power defeated the Iraqi army in the field and severely punished Iraq as a functioning polity, economy, and society. But what really defeated Iraq was the whole U.S. system of war making. Iraq demonstrated, in the latest example in history, that even large numbers of modern weapons and large numbers of people under arms do not necessarily equate to a high capacity for collective military action.

Iraq was beaten by everything about the way that Americans (in particular) made war early in 1991. U.S. air weapons were important; indeed they were important enough in their success to render the enemy's territory virtually a free-transit and use zone. Much better armies than Iraq's in 1991 would have been neutralized by the totally hostile air flank that it had no choice other than to endure. Political, strategic, operational, and tactical conditions for the Allied air campaign might have been better—there is always scope for improvement—but, realistically speaking, air commanders should not expect regularly to function against so hapless and helpless a foe.

Second, Desert Storm, for all of the happily redundant reasons for its military success, served usefully to remind anyone in need of reminding about the proper ways in which to develop, prepare, and employ air power. Desert Storm experience highlighted the necessity for unity of command of air power, the scope for flexibility in efficiently directed air power, and the inherent ability of air power to apply concentrated, and if need be sustained, force upon most key target sets.

Desert Storm also served to emphasize that air power is not just about aircraft, even very modern aircraft. Air power, rather, is about strategic effectiveness—whether the flying vehicles are long- or short-legged and whether they are land- or sea-based. Desert Storm demonstrated that smart airplanes with less-than-smart weapons were, for some missions, a poor idea. The Gulf War underwrote the contemporary trend in the U.S. Air Force to consider all air assets as integral parts of a military instrument with necessarily strategic implications. The events of 1991 also encouraged the focusing of renewed attention (following worthy examples set in 1941, 1951, and 1964) upon the strategy of air power, which is to say upon the means-end nexus that should guide planning for air power development and use.[28]

Third, the Gulf War air campaign reminded generic skeptics of air power of just how effective the air weapon could be when it was properly employed in appropriate conditions. Widespread misassessment of the historical achievements of air power over the first eight and a half decades of its existence, misassessments in part attributable to injudicious claims by air power theorists, ironically "set up" the scale of the surprise to many people of air power's success in 1991. The Desert Storm air campaign effected a healthy correction to a widespread belief that air power was locked into a pattern of overpromise and underperformance. Whether or not such a pattern truly characterized the experience of air warfare in conflict after conflict from the 1940s through the 1970s at least, the events of 1991 settled the issue. Those inclined to criticize or belittle air power thereafter are obliged to focus not upon its alleged inherent limitations, but rather upon the limited relevance of the Gulf War as a model for future conflict. It is right to emphasize the uniqueness of the Gulf War. But it is also right to emphasize the scope and scale of the strategic effectiveness that air power can deliver. The challenge to air forces is to develop the ability to achieve high levels of effectiveness in conditions far less permissive than were those of 1991.

Fourth, as an extension of the third point, the Gulf War demonstrated even to those previously skeptical of the utility of air power that conflicts do occur, and may well occur more frequently in the future, wherein the air instrument is the key force, the dominant element, in the war-fighting team. To proceed further down that logical path, there will be wars wherein balanced forces for the United States will mean an air power cutting edge that effectively decides the contests, with adjunct roles for land, sea, and space forces. There is no standard conflict for the next quarter century, so one cannot predict a steadily dominant, let alone independently decisive, role for the air weapon. But the evident trend toward relatively more and more effective air power suggests a likelihood that key force status for that power will be a more common occurrence in the future than the past.

Fifth, the total military experience of Desert Shield and Desert Storm proved to all acute observers, not to mention participant-observers, that the "space" in air and space forces could yield far more enabling value as an effectiveness multiplier than contemporary equipment, organization, plans, and training permitted. Allied naval and land forces did not "think space" the way they had come to "think air," while even Allied air forces were less than mature in their ability to exploit the facilitating potential of space assets. The Gulf War, overall, did not show the misuse or even so much the underuse of space forces. Instead, the war provided a blinding glimpse of what timely and user-friendly space-derived information could mean for the effectiveness of forces in all geographical environments. An implication of this glance into the future is that all parties to conflicts will have growing incentives to control access to and exploitation of earth orbit. The United States has yet to step up strategically to this predictable trend. General McPeak was very much to the point when he said: "We now exploit space, but do not possess the means to establish space superiority in war. This is a critical mission deficiency."[29]

Sixth and finally, although air power played a critical role, and probably the most critical one, in the coalition's victory over Iraq,[30] the war demonstrated also some persisting problems with the effectiveness of air power. For example, no matter how precisely an airborne weapon platform is navigated or how lethal are its munitions, target intelligence is king. This point has been illustrated by the director of the Gulf War Air Power Survey: "It is depressing to recall that the United States began the war with two known Iraqi nuclear facilities on its target list, that it added six during the conflict and that another dozen were uncovered by U.N. inspectors only after the war."[31] Even when targets were located and struck, it proved difficult to determine functional, as contrasted with brute physical, damage. Bomb damage assessment concerning a complex target system requires a sophisticated understanding of how the several inter-acting parts of that system operate. The Gulf War air campaign in practice proved to be a compromise between the desires of some air power theorists who were determined to conduct a classically strategic, "inside to outside," paralyzing assault upon Iraq's believed centers of gravity, and the desires of those battlefield-oriented clients of air power who wanted the enemy on their front pounded into impotence.[32] In retrospect, it is not obvious that all of the "strategic" elements of the air campaign—not the elements dedicated to gaining and keeping air supremacy or the interdiction or close air support endeavors—were entirely appropriate to the character of war at issue. Overall, the Gulf War air campaign was a triumph for the air instrument, but it did reveal yet again many of the historically familiar limitations of air power, as well as advertise that power's full strategic maturity.

AIR POWER: DISTINCTIVE ADVANTAGES FOR BALANCED EFFECT

Advocacy requires simplification and a political attitude toward truth. The generally admirable strategic record of air achievement has been scarred by what amounts to self-inflicted wounds. Glittering accomplishments by air power are devalued because they fall short of the gold standard of victory through the independent operations of air forces. Whenever the strategic effectiveness of air power approaches or appears to approach an immaculate performance, the foolish claim that "this time" history really has vindicated the theory of victory through air power (alone) inexorably stimulates counter-claims by organizationally threatened parties about the uniqueness of a par-ticular passage of arms.

The truth about the still-growing relative prowess of air power, amply dem-onstrated by historical experience, should be good enough. The United States has yet to extract full strategic value from its air power, let alone from its incomplete and immature space power. After all, even by generous calculation, air power is only about ninety years old, while space power is only in its thirties. Disciplined consideration of how the distinctive advantages of a technologically dynamic air power can yield strategic leverage in conflicts of different kinds remains an urgent task. Indeed, when one thinks of air and space as well as of air power alone, the scope for enhanced strategic influence from exploitation of superiority in the overhead flank expands markedly.

When policymakers consider what they would like the armed forces to be able to accomplish for deterrence or defense across the full spectrum of potential conflict and other emergencies, they would benefit from a reminder of what air power offers. Air power is unique in being global; overhead; all but unlimited in range and reach, when properly supported; exceedingly rapid in mission accomplishment; able to proceed geographically by any routes preferred; capable of superior observation of friend and foe; and able to project power with an unparalleled flexibility for what can be a decisive concentration of force against an enemy's centers of gravity.

Air power with the qualities just registered, which is to say superior air power, often can be the leading edge or key element in military forces "unbalanced" in some crudely arithmetical sense in its favor.[33] Such unbalanced air power would of course be well balanced against policy demands, strategic necessity, and the appropriate adjunct value of other forms of military power. This characterization cannot be an abstract prescription for strategy or force planning in the future, because the reality of strategy and force structure always pertains to concrete and distinctive choices for unique conditions. Air power can play the full gamut of roles identified here, ranging from autonomous executive agent of grand strategy to useful adjunct.

As long as the United States will need to maintain military forces appropriate to its roles as keeper of the balance of power, protector of last resort, organizer and leader of collective security, and defender of humane values, it is accepting obligations of international primacy that are geopolitically unbounded. These obligations correspond to the capabilities and potential of modern air power. For the United States as the world's leading air power, the obligations imply a force structure balanced in external integrity, balanced against national needs and culture, balanced by strategic reasoning, and balanced against a reasonable range of conflict scenarios.

WEAPONS AND DECISION

> But there is no *a priori* reason why the air arm cannot become the predominant power in its relations with surface forces. In examining these relations, we came to the conclusion that the air force is destined to predominate over both land and sea forces; this because their radius of action is limited in comparison to the vastly greater radius of the air force.[34]

More often than not, when the adjectives *decisive* or *dominant* are employed to describe the relative effectiveness of the air weapon, it is less than self-evident what sense the theorist means to convey. Because imprecision in language can damage the quality of public debate over the course of defense policy, it is important that the claims for air power be presented without ambiguity, though with the qualifications that are appropriate. A benefit of greater precision in language is that various schools of thought on the relative effectiveness of air power at least would be obliged to make important choices over the domain of their assertions. It is possible that there might be less to the debate over air power's relative prowess than meets the casual eye.

If air power is claimed to be decisive, what might be meant by that? Possible answers include the following:

- Air power alone decides the outcome of a war (or of wars in general?).
- Air power alone decides the outcome of a battle or campaign.
- Air power plays the most important role in a battle, campaign, or war and would appear to have been the factor which decided the issue.
- Air power is very important.

There is no need to choose among these options; from context to context each of these claims has merit. Strictly speaking, a decisive weapon means a weapon the presence or employment of which decides something. In an obvious sense, air power decided the outcome of the Gulf War of 1991. But it is not the case that the outcome of that war otherwise would have been in serious doubt. Although air power was the cutting edge of coalition military strategy and in fact did decide the outcome of the war, it is implausible to argue that air power decided an issue that could have gone either way.

For a rather more complex example of the ambivalence of decisive status, there is no doubt that, in defiance of Douhet's strictures against aerial defenses,[35] the performance of RAF Fighter Command from July to October 1940 decided the issue of whether or not Britain prudently could be invaded that year. Although RAF Fighter Command and the integrated air defense system of which it was a part were the direct agents of decision, it can be easy to forget that a very important object of the German air campaign was the neutralization of the Royal Navy. In effect, Fighter Command's victory in the Battle of Britain meant that the Luftwaffe would be unable to provide adequate protection against the Royal Navy to an improvised and ramshackle amphibious expedition.[36] The Royal Navy did not decide the outcome of the Battle of Britain, but it provided much of the meaning to the decisiveness of the RAF's success.

What has happened in the history of first-class air power is that it has attained levels of absolute and relative military effectiveness where, except in some conditions of low-intensity conflict, it is always either an agent indispensable to victory or is itself the executive agent of victory. It is not profitable to seek a general truth much more exact than that formulation. Because the various conditions of conflict are so broad in their possibilities, no single and simple claim for the relative prowess of the air weapon can be sustained. Indeed, public assertions that air power now has become the decisive weapon, though not bereft of all merit, invite disdain and contradiction for reason of their obvious exaggeration. On a case-by-case basis, from the Six Day War of 1967, to the October War of 1973, to the Falklands in 1982, through the Gulf War of 1991—to pick but a few instances—the relative significance of air power has fluctuated among the categories of very important enabling agent for victory, most important agent for victory, and all but independent deliverer of victory. There is and can be no single right answer to the question, Has air power now become the decisive force in war? One would need to ask, Which war?

It is appropriate to register extensive claims for the influence of air power. A scholarly study of the Gulf War, for example, offers the impeccable judgment that "[t]he key to victory was complete mastery of the air." That same study also advises that "[w]hat is beyond doubt is that chronic inferiority in airpower is a liability for which it is almost impossible to compensate in regular conventional warfare."[37] Those claims held for the campaign in Normandy and beyond in 1944–45 no less than for the Gulf in 1991. From those points it is a short, but important, step to the argument of Richard P. Hallion. "Today, air power is the dominant form of military power. Does this mean that all future wars will be won solely by air power? Not at all. But what it does mean is that air power has clearly proven its ability not merely to be *decisive* in war—after all, it had demonstrated decisiveness in the First World War—but to be the *determinant of victory* in war."[38] Hallion is right, but his argument invites exaggeration in the hands of people less scrupulous, less knowledgeable, or simply more hurried than he. Some explicit caveats are necessary on the subject of the decisiveness or dominance of air power, if only to protect the integrity of the core claims.

First, genuinely inferior weapons can prove to be a fatal handicap, but typically it is the use made of weapons, particularly of combinations of weapons, that produces victory.

Second, weapons, narrowly technically understood, do not triumph in battle. Rather, success is the product of man-machine weapon systems, their supporting services of all kinds, and the organization, doctrine, and training that launch them into battle.

Third, except for those cases of conflict wherein air power can deliver victory by independent action, the strategic value of an air force must be metered by the prowess of other military arms. The significance of air power as the key to victory has to be influenced greatly, even controlled, by the ability of ground and naval forces to proceed through the door that the air power key has opened.

Fourth, air power, space power, sea power, and land power do not quite have the sharp boundaries that theoretical assertion would suggest to the unwary. The primary missions of armies, navies, and air forces are clear enough, but the multitude of interdependencies can be obscured by unduly tidy argument. With a few highly debatable exceptions (e.g., the naval deep-strike mission), there is no doubt that army and naval aviation is, in Giulio Douhet's word, "auxiliary" to continental and maritime concerns.[39] Nonetheless, forces for air, space, land, and sea combat do, or can, contribute significantly to the quality of each other's performance.

Fifth, decisive or dominant weapons, however defined (i.e., the air weapon as a whole or a particular weapon system), attract assault by the paradoxical logic of conflict.[40] It is a general rule of military affairs that combined arms, broadly interpreted, are stronger than single arms. Among the reasons for that rule are the following: combinations of capabilities allow for a flexibility in employment that a single capability does not; decisive or dominant single weapons act like magnets for the competitive skills of an enemy (who necessarily sees in a decisive or dominant weapon a weapon that will decide a conflict against him); combinations of capabilities (swords and shields, offense and defense, heavy bombers and long-range escort fighters, tanks and panzer grenadiers) should preclude the necessity for heroic near perfect performance by any single weapon.

Sixth, even decisive or dominant weapons are subject to the law of diminishing marginal returns to effort. By its very nature there are tasks for which air power is not particularly well suited. Similarly, there are conflicts (by and large of an irregular kind) to which air power in all its forms is less than ideally suited as the leading edge of friendly effort. Decisive or dominant weapon theory encourages an uneconomical, even flatly infeasible, overextension of air power employment into realms of conflict that beg for a more varied military response.

NOTES

1. Giulio Douhet, *The Command of the Air* (New York: Arno Press, 1972; first pub. 1942), pp. 145–46.

2. The story is told vividly and with a human dimension that typically is lacking in historical accounts of the process of war planning, in James C. Gaston, *Planning the American Air War: Four Men and Nine Days in 1941, An Inside Narrative* (Washington, DC: National Defense University Press, 1982). The standard text is Wesley Frank Craven and James Lea Cate, eds., *The Army Air Forces in World War II*, vol. I (Chicago: University of Chicago Press, 1948), especially pp. 146–50. Also see Jeffrey S. Underwood, *The Wings of Democracy: The Influence of Air Power on the Roosevelt Administration, 1933–1941* (College Station: Texas A and M University Press, 1991), chap. 9.

3. Very much to the point are James A. Dewar et al., *Assumption-Based Planning: A Planning Tool for Very Uncertain Times*, MR-114-A (Santa Monica, CA: RAND, 1993); and Carl H. Builder and James A. Dewar, "A Time for Planning? If Not Now, When?" *Parameters* 24, no. 2 (summer 1994): 4–15.

4. See Colin S. Gray, *Weapons Don't Make War: Policy, Strategy, and Technology* (Lawrence: University Press of Kansas, 1993), chap. 5, "Defense Planning for Uncertainty."

5. A structural problem in, for example, Robert P. Haffa, Jr., *Rational Methods, Prudent Choices: Planning U.S. Forces* (Washington, DC: National Defense University Press, 1988).

6. An argument emphasized in Gray, *Weapons Don't Make War*, chap. 4; and "Off the Map: Defense Planning after the Soviet Threat," *Strategic Review* 22, no. 2 (spring 1994): 26–35.

7. Useful commentaries include Dennis E. Showalter, "Total War for Limited Objectives: An Interpretation of German Grand Strategy," in Paul Kennedy, ed., *Grand Strategies in War and Peace* (New Haven, CT: Yale University Press, 1991), pp. 105–23; and Williamson Murray, "The Problem of German Military Effectiveness, 1900–45," in Murray, *German Military Effectiveness* (Baltimore, MD: Nautical and Aviation Publishing Company of America, 1992), pp. 1–38.

8. Les Aspin (secretary of defense), *Annual Report to the President and the Congress* (Washington, DC: U.S. Government Printing Office, January 1994), p. 3.

9. A more detailed discussion of national-interest analysis is presented in Chapter 9 with reference to the utility of special operations forces.

10. Henry C. Bartlett, "Introductory Essay—Planning Future Forces," in Force Planning Faculty, Naval War College, ed., *Fundamentals of Force Planning*, vol. II, *Defense Planning Cases* (Newport, RI: Naval War College Press, 1991), p. 4. I have added the assumption-based approach to planning from Dewar et al., *Assumption-Based Planning*. The focus in this approach is upon assumptions—which amount to contingent predictions—that may prove vulnerable to invalidation by events. Also useful are the essays in Part II of Paul K. Davis, ed., *New Challenges for Defense Planning: Rethinking How Much Is Enough* (Santa Monica, CA: RAND, 1994).

11. See Colin S. Gray, "Defense Planning for the Mystery Tour: Principles for Guidance in a Period of Nonlinear Change," *Airpower Journal* 5, no. 2 (summer 1991): 18–26.

12. See the essays on primacy and its discontents by Christopher Layne, Robert Jervis, and Samuel P. Huntington in *International Security* 17, no. 4 (spring 1993).

13. See Thomas J. Knock, *To End All Wars: Woodrow Wilson and the Quest for a New World Order* (New York: Oxford University Press, 1992).

14. Readers may derive some value from the following: Jack S. Levy, *War in the Modern Great Power System, 1495–1975* (Lexington: University Press of Kentucky, 1983); Paul Kennedy, *The Rise and Fall of the Great Powers: Economic Change and Military Conflict from 1500 to 2000* (New York: Random House, 1987); Ian Clark, *The Hierarchy of States: Reform and Resistance in the International Order* (Cambridge: Cambridge University Press, 1989); Kalevi J. Holsti, *Peace and War: Armed Conflicts and International Order, 1648–1989* (Cambridge: Cambridge University Press, 1991); and John A. Vasquez, *The War Puzzle* (Cambridge: Cambridge University Press, 1993).

15. Douhet, *Command of the Air*, p. 193.

16. Eliot A. Cohen, "A GWAPS Primer," 19 April 1993.

17. The principal features of the new emerging security environment are developed in Chapter 9.

18. These principles have been designed with the U.S. armed forces in mind, but they are in fact applicable to the armed forces of any country or coalition. As with some other methodological features of this chapter, these principles reappear in Chapter 9 in the context of the strategic value of special operations forces.

19. I am grateful to my colleague at National Security Research, Inc., Col. John Kohout, USAF (ret.), for his fruitful assistance over the years with this and related approaches to defense planning. A close working relationship on many studies leads to a situation wherein literally one cannot reliably recall exactly who invented what.

20. Carl von Clausewitz, *On War*, ed. and trans. Michael Howard and Peter Paret (Princeton, NJ: Princeton University Press, 1976; first pub. 1832), pp. 87–88.

21. Ibid., p. 89.

22. McPeak, "Does the Air Force Have a Mission?" p. 5.

23. Ibid., p. 8.

24. Ibid., p. 10.

25. Ibid.

26. Edward N. Luttwak, *Strategy: The Logic of War and Peace* (Cambridge, MA: Harvard University Press, 1987).

27. In the uncompromising judgment of the official British history: "The campaign in Norway witnessed the first completely conclusive employment of air power [by Germany]." Denis Richards, *Royal Air Force, 1939–1945*, vol. I, *The Fight at Odds* (London: HMSO, 1953), p. 105.

28. Whether or not one agrees with much of the argument in John A. Warden III, *The Air Campaign: Planning for Combat* (Washington, DC: Pergamon-Brassey's, 1989; first pub. 1988), the integrity of his subject was well and truly vindicated by the events of 1991.

29. McPeak, "Does the Air Force Have a Mission?" p. 6.

30. See the judgments in Thomas A. Keaney and Eliot A. Cohen, *Gulf War Air Power Summary Report* (Washington, DC: U.S. Government Printing Office, 1993).

31. Eliot A. Cohen, "The Mystique of U.S. Air Power," *Foreign Affairs* 73, no. 1 (January/February 1994): 119.

32. "The coalition conducted the first true 'inside to outside' war, beginning with the most important central [command] ring in Baghdad and working its way to the outermost ring of fielded forces." John A. Warden III, "Employing Air Power in the Twenty-first Century," in Richard H. Shultz, Jr., and Robert L. Pfaltzgraff, Jr., eds., *The Future of Air Power in the Aftermath of the Gulf War* (Maxwell Air Force Base, AL: Air University Press, July 1992), p. 78.

33. See the discussion of balanced forces in Chapter 2.

34. Douhet, *Command of the Air*, p. 29.

35. Ibid., pp. 52–55.

36. See R. A. C. Parker, *Struggle for Survival: The History of the Second World War* (Oxford: Oxford University Press, 1989), p. 50.

37. Lawrence Freedman and Efraim Karsh, *The Gulf Conflict, 1990–1991: Diplomacy and War in the New World Order* (Princeton, NJ: Princeton University Press, 1993), pp. 3–2, 437.

38. Richard P. Hallion, *Storm over Iraq: Air Power and the Gulf War* (Washington, DC: Smithsonian Institution Press, 1992), p. 264 (emphasis in original).

39. Douhet, *Command of the Air*, pp. 215–34.

40. This argument is central to Luttwak, *Strategy*. Broadly speaking, the paradoxical logic of conflict holds that what works well today will not work so well tomorrow, precisely because enemies noticed how well it worked today.

Part III
Strategy and Special Operations

Chapter 7

The Nature of Special Operations

The central purpose of Part III is to identify the strategic utility of special operations. Most operations have strategic utility only if they succeed. The exceptions to that rule imply more than simply the commonsense point that there is usually more to be learnt from failure than from success. There are times when special operations on balance can be strategically successful in their effect, even though they are tactical failures; for example, Dieppe 1942 (to stretch the point) and Son Tay 1970.[1] Moreover, for reasons of historical context there are even occasions when operations are sufficiently important that they are worth doing badly, for example, the Grenada intervention of 1983, with its substantial special operations component.[2]

The subject here is not special operations or special operations forces per se;[3] rather, it is the utility of special operations in war—including virtually all forms of conflict. Tactical excellence usually is a prerequisite for strategic utility, but it is not the issue. The prime concern is not to explain how to conduct special operations, but instead to explore the difference such operations can make for the course and outcome of a conflict. The challenge and the problems which provide focus for this analysis are illustrated usefully, albeit inadvertently, in the following quotation from the memoirs of a brave and skilled British commando of World War II, Stuart Chant-Sempill:

The attack on St. Nazaire was not just a Commando raid. It was an operation of high strategy, and was an important part of the Battle of the

I am grateful to Professor Williamson Murray of Ohio State University for his expert editorial skills as applied to this chapter and to Chapter 8.

Atlantic. For St. Nazaire boasted the largest dry-dock in the world, the destruction of which was vital if Germany's battleships, pocket battle-ships and heavy cruisers were to be denied the safe refuge it then provided from attack.[4]

Tactically speaking, the bold, indeed all but suicidal, raid on St. Nazaire on 27–28 March 1942 was a great success. The authors of the raid had laudably ambitious operational and strategic goals in mind. The pulse of convoys across the Atlantic truly was "the heartbeat of the war."[5] Tactical success at St. Nazaire would have a direct operational effect in the decisive theater of war, the North Atlantic, and thus a profound impact on the course and outcome of the entire conflict. The problem is that the St. Nazaire raid was operationally and strategically redundant. The British government could not know that the sinking of the *Bismarck* in May 1941 had marked the end of forays by German capital ships into the North Atlantic.[6] With hindsight it is apparent that the commando raid on the *Normandie* lock-gates at St. Nazaire was a heroic example of doing the wrong thing well for the right reason. The raid was a critical blow against the German naval strategy of 1940–41, not of 1942–45.

A historical example of similar vintage which warrants a different judgment is the case of the commando raid on the Lofoten Islands on 4 March 1941. That raid secured German Enigma code materials, enabling British cryptographers to read naval Enigma traffic after a delay of only ten days, and eventually only three to seven, in April and May of that year.[7] Moreover, that traffic revealed the presence of two German weather ships with Enigma coding machines in the North Atlantic, which the British captured on 7 May and 28 June. British reading of much of Germany's naval Enigma traffic in 1941 may have been literally decisive for the course of the whole war. Whether or not that was so, the Lofoten and the St. Nazaire raids both illustrate the point of this discussion.

The three binding themes for this book are no less pervasive in the Part III chapters focused on special operations than they were in Parts I and II. It may be recalled from the Introduction that these themes are the ubiquity of strategy, the joint character of contemporary military preparation and action, and the distinctiveness of the advantages and limitations of each major player in the joint arena. Part III examines special operations and special operations forces strategically; it emphasizes the leverage that special operations forces may secure for other kinds of forces, in addition to the occasionally independently decisive value of special operations forces themselves; and it is explicitly aware of the advantages and disadvantages which uniquely belong to special operations.

KEY IDEAS

In the quest for general wisdom on the strategic utility of special operations, a handful of key ideas command attention. In summary form, the key ideas are the following propositions:

- Special operations have strategic meaning only with reference to war, or other kinds of conflict, as a whole.
- Special operations must be considered in relation to, and as a tool of, national or coalition strategy overall.
- Special operations derive much of their strategic meaning—be it on balance negative or positive—from their historical context.
- Special operations are not, or not only, the expression of a culturally free-floating craft, but rather of particular political and strategic cultures.
- The strategic utility of special operations derives largely from the quality and quantity of performance by conventional forces.
- Tactical excellence in the conduct of special operations is no guarantee of strategic effectiveness.

These ideas overlap and illuminate the same phenomena from somewhat different directions. The fundamental idea here is the importance of considering special operations and special operations forces strategically in relation to a war or conflict as a whole. There is no other way to assess strategic utility.

It may be true that countries whose armed forces (or major elements thereof) are relatively weak are especially in need of the effectiveness which special operations can generate. Indeed, countries which have suffered defeat in regular warfare are likely to turn almost in despair to the often extraordinary promise of special operations. Such, at least, was the British experience in 1940–41. However, although special operations are an expression of transnational tactical skills which can be taught and applied almost anywhere, countries which are not proficient in conventional warfare are not likely to make excellent strategic use even of tactically successful special operations. Nevertheless, well-conducted special operations can yield positive strategic value even for lost causes.

It is tempting to argue that because special operations forces are components in a total national military team, they must reflect the strengths and weaknesses of that team and in some measure of the society behind it. That need not be the case, although there are national ways of approaching the opportunities and problems of special operations forces. In practice, countries frequently have created special operations forces precisely to provide qualities which the national regular forces lack. Moreover, if those special forces grow to a noteworthy size, they can have a self-validating negative impact upon the quality of their nonspecial brethren.

Even if some special operations forces comprise islands of tactical excellence amidst a sea of mediocre or worse military performance, the context will tend to stifle potential strategic effectiveness. On the one hand, the political and military leaders who have overseen the creation of a less-than-excellent military establishment probably lack the qualities needed to make proper use of special forces. On the other hand, and even if the first condition does not obtain, the relatively poor state of the regular forces must limit sharply the potential strategic utility of what special operations forces might achieve. War is a team endeavor. A special operation can open a door, but the regular forces may not be able to follow through.

WHAT ARE SPECIAL OPERATIONS?

It is imperative to define special operations, but there is peril in the exercise. In one sense, the exclusiveness that must characterize any good definition is contrary to the very spirit of special operations. There are dangers in a definition either so vague and inclusive as to provide no meaningful guidance or so rigid and focused as to risk inhibiting the imagination of special operations forces themselves and of their political and military clients.[8] One cannot evade the challenge by the tautological escape route of proclaiming that special operations are whatever special operations forces do (or train to do). That descriptive approach would merely define special operations forces as forces that conduct special operations. The historical range of special operations embraces a set of activities so diverse as to render the catalogue type of definition quite useless.

To be useful a definition must be brief and must capture the essence of the subject defined, yet should not sacrifice user-friendliness for the sake of an arbitrary clarity. The terms *irregular* and *unconventional* warfare have some merit over special operations (and low-intensity warfare). They have the advantage of capturing the ethos of the subject, namely, the unusual character of what is described vis-à-vis the normal activities of the armed forces of the day. Unfortunately, both irregular warfare and unconventional warfare carry unhelpful historical baggage. They suggest a focus upon guerrilla and counter-guerrilla warfare which is inappropriate. On the positive side, however, irregular warfare and unconventional warfare do imply the inclusion of protracted activities, as contrasted with the "raid" focus which can be read into special *operations*. Special operations have as their core identity the overt or covert conduct of a desperately dangerous raid by a relatively few elite fighting men for high operational or strategic stakes.[9] There is value in a heroic characteristic definition. Although these chapters emphasize the close interdependence among different kinds of military power, paradoxically, perhaps, they treat special operations as a quasi-separate factor, after the fashion of land power, sea power, air power, and now space power and the nuclear element. This is not to attribute equal strategic significance to special operations, but it is to indicate a distinctiveness for these operations which warrants the treatment accorded them here.

In terms of tactical and technological details and possibly operational goals, specific types of special operations may appear to be defined by their environments and hence in need of treatment most appropriately as components of or adjuncts to land, sea, air, space, or even strategic nuclear warfare. Such an approach, reasonable though it might appear, would be contrary to the spirit and purpose of this analysis and would help perpetuate an unduly narrow perspective. This enquiry is interested in the strategic utility of special operations, whether that utility be generated by actions bearing upon war at sea, on land, or wherever. Much of the military "grammar," as well as the policy "logic," of special operations is not environmentally specific.[10] The details vary for special operations in different environments, but those operations still have more in common with each other due to their "special" character than they do with other activities with a like environmental focus.

Maurice Tugwell and David Charters have offered the most useful, if still overelaborate, definition of special operations. They advise that special operations are "[s]mall-scale, clandestine, covert or overt operations of an unorthodox and frequently high-risk nature, undertaken to achieve significant political or military objectives in support of foreign policy."[11] The precise verbal formula of a definition is not important. What is important is that the definition capture the key elements. In Tugwell and Charters's definition, the reference to "significant" objectives is unduly subjective, and the explicit connection to foreign policy is perhaps gratuitous and somewhat vague. Nevertheless, the Tugwell and Charters definition is terse yet richly suggestive, while avoiding the worst kind of taxonomic fallacies into which the creeping encyclopedism of official definitions can stumble. Six key features make this a superior definition.

Small scale. In special operations as in nearly everything, quantity and quality are opposed. Relatively few military personnel have the physical and psychological strengths necessary for special operations. Special operations require unusual qualities for success. Elite assault troops, such as airborne and marine units (and even the British Army Commandos of World War II and the U.S. Army Rangers then and since), will provide fertile recruiting ground for special operations forces; but special operations encompass a great deal more than heavy raiding. There is no hard and fast line between special operations and regular warfare, and one can merge into the other, as the U.S. Army Special Forces showed in Vietnam and as the British Special Air Service (SAS) demonstrated in the Falklands. Nevertheless, quantity has a quality all its own. Large forces cannot function stealthily, at least not for long, and as they grow in scale their activities necessarily take on more and more of the features of regular warfare. Many of the tasks that come the way of special operations forces can only be performed by small groups of people.

Clandestine, covert, or overt. A clandestine operation is one which attempts to conceal its very existence. A covert operation is one which attempts to conceal its true authorship. An overt operation does not attempt to conceal either the action or its perpetrators. Citing these three alternatives as part of the definition of special operations encourages a broadly inclusive, rather than narrowly exclusive, view of the subject. At the same time, this reference to secrecy helps direct attention to the historical fact that by their small-scale character, special operations forces often have served most valuably in reconnaissance or other intelligence-gathering missions, rather than in combat roles.

Unorthodox. It is missions rather than methods that are unorthodox, though special operations forces tend to employ unorthodox tactics and weapons. Generically, there are few military skills unique to special forces. It is the quantity and intensity or level of skills required of each man or very small group (four to twelve, most typically) and the uses to which those skills are put that distinguish people and missions as "special." Orthodox military operations extend widely on the spectrum of attritional versus maneuver, and in fact there is no fixed meaning to "orthodox." Special operations forces need not be so designated, but to fit the definition they must perform in ways unusual for their historical context. Hypothetically, if a state were to organize a large fraction of its defense establishment along the lines of special operations forces, then the unorthodox might become orthodox; but this is a practical impossibility.

There have been societies whose traditional ways of war were unorthodox or irregular in the eyes of others. For example, the Arabs whose raiding style of unconventional warfare T. E. Lawrence coopted to harass the Turkish desert flank to Palestine had been employed for similar functions fifteen hundred years earlier by the Roman and Persian empires.[12] Similarly, the Russian and British empires in the nineteenth and twentieth centuries encountered strategic cultures of unorthodox, unconventional, or irregular warfare in the mountains of Caucasia and on India's northwest frontier (including Afghanistan), respectively.[13]

It is not quite accurate to say that special operations are unorthodox warfare conducted in the enemy's rear, although that characterization often applies.[14] There are many historical antecedents to the special operations of World War II, but the systematic organization and training of small elite groups of soldiers for insertion into the deep rear of the enemy is essentially a recent innovation in warfare.

High risk. The typical circumstances of special operations, as well as their purposes, generally involve high risks. The operation of Clausewitz's "friction" factor in war can be uniquely deadly to the participants in special operations.[15] A definition of special operations provided by a study of commando raids highlights why such operations are so high risk in nature: Special operations are "self-contained acts of war mounted by self-sufficient forces operating within hostile territory."[16] This is an inadequate definition of special operations, but its emphasis on self-sufficiency within enemy territory accurately suggests that, as a general rule, special operations forces cannot "call in the cavalry" to effect a timely rescue if plans go awry in action. If special operations forces themselves are unable to tie an emergency knot in a plan that comes apart, they likely face capture or death (or both). To compensate, those forces use cover and deception to achieve surprise as a force multiplier and thus attempt to control the risks of their trade and enhance their prospects for success.

Lt. Gen. William E. Yarborough has noted aptly that "[s]pecial warfare is an esoteric art unto itself,"[17] but in its raiding aspect it follows the same principle that Baron Antoine Henri de Jomini and Carl von Clausewitz derived from Napoleon's practice in the field: to be superior at the decisive spot. Unlike regular operations, however, special operations almost never succeed if they lack surprise or simply have bad luck.

High risk is inherent in the nature of special operations, particularly in cases of operations in the enemy's rear. Special operations sometimes proceed so smoothly that little risk is apparent in retrospect, because of good luck or enemy folly, but the basic nature of this kind of warfare ensures that the potential for awesome danger is always present. Special operations forces seek as much protection from extraordinary risk as tactical excellence can provide. With so much uncertainty and so little margin for error, it is not surprising that special forces plan their operations in excruciating detail, mastery of which can provide a sound basis for emergency improvisation.

Strange as it may seem, planners approach special operations and "strategic" nuclear war in much the same way, for many of the same reasons. The risks are extraordinary at both ends of the conflict spectrum. Outside help will be unavailable should operations go badly, and meticulously detailed planning before the event provides flexibility. Large-scale ground and naval warfare, in sharp contrast, amounts more to the free-form exploitation of opportunity in whatever direction evolving circumstances suggest to be the most expedient path to the mission's objective.

Significant political or military objectives. The no-free-lunch principle, which warrants elevation to the status of a principle of war (albeit in some tension with "economy of force"), holds that in conflict with a competent foe the achievement of great strategic returns will require the expenditure of great effort. Special operations represent an attempt to circumvent this principle. Otherwise orthodox-minded soldiers in trouble sometimes give license to special operations forces in hopes of receiving such a free lunch. A classic example was the founding of the SAS. In 1941 Lt. David Stirling of the Scots Guards, then serving in the Middle East with No. 8 Commando, received permission to raise a deep raiding force of six officers and sixty noncommissioned officers and enlisted men. In the words of one of Stirling's biographers:

> It was not surprising that David Stirling's plan appealed to the High Command. It was wonderfully economical. It promised much and risked practically nothing. The new Commander-in-Chief General Auchinleck, was an efficient, thorough, cautious Scot. His temperament would not allow him to take chances that involved whole divisions, but here was a proposal that required only a handfull of men.[18]

Stirling, along with many people at the time and since, was confused about the difference between matters tactical and strategic. He and others regarded his initial memorandum, outlining a daring plan to destroy the Luftwaffe in North Africa on the ground, as essentially strategic in character. For example, a competent history of the SAS uncritically endorses Stirling's notion that "deep penetration operations behind enemy lines" were "strategic raids."[19] Much of the special operations literature, again like that on long-range and large-scale nuclear operations, confuses tactics with strategy.

Many of the most thoughtful commentators on special operations insist upon a strategic rather than a tactical or operational role for such endeavors. Such authors frequently condemn the allegedly tactical uses of special operations forces, which is to say the uses of those forces as close adjuncts to conventional military efforts,[20] claiming they are an abuse or waste of their unique capabilities.[21] Historically, this view may be well founded. The record of special operations is rife with cases in which the scarce assets of special forces were poorly employed. However, the notion that there is an inherent distinction between strategic and tactical missions is both false and counterproductive. The Tugwell and Charters definition of special operations that provides the basis for this analysis avoids the misconception by requiring that such operations be "undertaken to achieve *significant* political or military objectives."

Tactics concern the actual employment of forces of all kinds—Special Forces "A Teams," intercontinental ballistic missile (ICBM) squadrons, naval task forces, antisatellite interceptors, or whatever. Strategy concerns the effect of tactical activity on the course and outcome of a conflict, with the sometimes useful intermediary analysis of operational or campaign effectiveness in between. The significance of particular special operations depends on the context of war as a whole, whether those operations truly are independent of distinctive battle or campaign designs, or if they contribute to a battle or campaign. In the latter case, the potential significance or strategic utility of special operations in turn corresponds to the significance of the grander-scale military operations that they assist.

It is entirely possible for special operations to support military and political endeavors that are strategically or politically unwise. One cannot blame the special operations forces of the Third Reich, for example, either for Hitler's overall incompetence in the conduct of war or for the lack of strategic sense demonstrated by the army high command and its general staff. Nonetheless, an enquiry such as this into the strategic utility of special operations has to pay careful attention to the military and political context for those operations. With some exceptions—for example, when a special operation itself equates with a conflict, as in a hostage rescue venture or a counterterrorist raid—this enquiry must address not only special operations, but also the general course, character, and direction of war. Consideration of the strategic utility of special operations, the difficult judgment as to their significance, demands assessment of their full context.

Foreign policy. It is useful to define special operations as being conducted "in support of foreign policy." Strictly speaking, this may be redundant; but given the tendency to forget that military activity must have a distinct political purpose in order to be successful, the reminder can only be beneficial. Also, the reminder that special operations should serve foreign policy helps elevate analysis to include the grand-strategic level. Special operations forces are a national grand-strategic asset; they are a tool of statecraft that can be employed quite surgically in support of diplomacy, of foreign assistance (of several kinds), as a vital adjunct to regular military forces, or as an independent weapon.

The strategic utility of special operations forces depends at least as much on the imagination and competence of their political and military masters as it does on their tactical effectiveness. First-class special operations forces have the potential for great strategic utility, but political leaders and strategists must understand how to realize that potential.

THE HEART OF THE MATTER

Special operations are operations that regular forces cannot perform, and special operations forces are selected, equipped, and trained to do what regular forces cannot do. To restate the point from a different perspective, special operations lie beyond the bounds of routine tasks in war. Some may take exception to these three claims. For example, one might argue that good, regular, light infantry units—such as the U.S. Marines—can perform special operations. The boundary line between special operations and regular warfare is not always clear. Pedantry is to be deplored, but strategic understanding mandates careful attention to definitions. In the absence of satisfactory iden-tification of special operations, how can their strategic utility possibly be assessed? Six points demand emphasis at this juncture, to assure a firm intellectual grip on the subject.[22]

First, special operations are qualitatively different from regular warfare, not a subcategory of it. Organizational and tactical historical analysis of special operations has revealed a set of conditions for success which vary considerably from those for success in regular operations,[23] although the scale of difference between regular and special forces varies with national setting and strategic circumstances.

Second, although special operations are tactically sui generis (along with naval and air warfare, for example), they function strategically in ways equivalent to all other kinds of operations. However, different means to identical strategic ends may have distinctive consequences. As a hypothetical and admittedly oversimplified example, suppose that the strategic goal of rendering the Third Reich unable or unwilling to continue World War II could have been secured either by a great bomber offensive or by political subversion (perhaps including the assassination of Adolf Hitler). In that case, the difference between these two choices would have had immense political significance. With good reason, T. E. Lawrence discerned a "false antithesis between strategy, the aim in war, the synoptic regard seeing each part relative to the whole, and tactics, the means towards a strategic end, the particular steps of its staircase."[24] Means can vitiate ends. On the one hand, large-scale combat may impose such a high level of human and material destruction as to cast doubt upon the balance between military means and war aims; on the other, assassination, kidnapping, and other methods of "dirty" warfare also may impose intolerable moral penalties upon a war effort. Thus, the correlation of means and ends in war is a complex problem. Even though military and other means will be tactically distinctive, their effect must be commonly strategic.

Third, although special operations and special operations forces display some of the same organizational and tactical features regardless of time, place, or circumstances, the definition of operations and forces as special varies among political and strategic cultures. The tradecraft of special operations is virtually transcultural, although different cultures place distinctive emphasis upon particular skills (e.g., an ambush is an ambush, regardless of which group of special operators plan and execute it). But the development of particular kinds of special warfare capabilities and the choice of the character of special operations actually to undertake are embedded and shaped by unique national histories. The point is not only strategic-cultural preference, but also circumstances which make certain types of special operations seem most appropriate.[25] Every society will approach choices in a time of severe trial with the benefit and burden of cultural predispositions, and one must examine these carefully, case by case, in order to avoid invalid generalizations.

Fourth, a broad study of special operations seems to indicate a trained incapacity, a *déformation professionelle*,[26] on the part of conventional military minds to grasp the principles of special warfare. Although special operations can be complementary to regular warfare, special warfare also challenges the integrity of a traditional military ethos as well as many standard ideas derived from regular warfare on how to conduct military operations. A detached observer or historian of special operations, particularly a civilian, generally will have difficulty grasping just how alien and even distasteful special operations often appear to those trained and socialized in regular military behavior. This point is important because if superior commanders do not appreciate or do not like what special operations forces might do, the strategic utility of those forces will be strictly moot. In many cases the strategic utility of special operations rests in the hands of military officers who have attitudes, interests, and an understanding of war unfriendly to the potential of special warfare. Thus, among the essential conditions for the success of special operations are (1) a willingness on the part of political and military leaders to allow special operations forces onto the field to play and (2) the ability of all concerned to identify suitable objectives for them.

Fifth, in an important sense, special operations comprise a state of mind, an approach to the challenges of conflict. M. R. D. Foot, the British historian of special operations and a wartime intelligence officer for the SAS, provides the following answer to the question, What are special operations? "They are unorthodox coups, that is, unexpected strokes of violence, usually mounted and executed outside the military establishment of the day, which exercise a startling effect on the enemy; preferably at the highest level."[27] The mental approach required for special operations is not one that "ticks the boxes" of some complex definition or which seeks the right answer from some repertoire in a special operations playbook. Instead, as Foot insists, the approach should be unorthodox, perhaps even for special operations forces; unexpected; and designed to achieve a startling effect on the enemy. This is not a sufficient definition of special operations, but it helps to indicate the philosophy of such endeavors. James Doolittle's carrier-borne B-25 raid on Tokyo in May 1942, the creation by the RAF of special "pathfinder" squadrons, and the two Chindit campaigns in Burma were all examples of the spirit or approach characteristic of special operations.

Sixth and finally, special operations are political-military activities tailored to achieve specific, focused objectives (with occasional exceptions)[28] and conducted by units which adapt with great flexibility to the demands of each challenge. One might define special operations as whatever special operations forces do. It is more useful, however, to think of special operations as an almost infinite realm of missions for which special operations forces provide the capabilities most likely to achieve tactical success for strategic utility. To regard special operations merely as justification for the retention of special operations forces which develop their own rigid doctrine is to place the cart before the horse. Of course some doctrine is necessary for the training and employment of special operations forces. But doctrine must not contradict or stifle the ethos and the heart of the matter: the need to be unorthodox, to do the unexpected, and to startle the enemy.

It is important to recognize the relevance of the spirit as well as the actuality of special operations for all aspects of conflict. Special operations can be conducted in peacetime and time of crisis; in conflicts of low, medium, and high intensity; and proximately to influence the course of events on land, at sea, in the air, in space, and even in the realm of "strategic" nuclear warfare. Fed by the movie industry's version of World War II, the popular British image of special operations is indistinguishable from the commando raid. The American image is more complex, more confused, and more recently forged—largely with Vietnam referents. Studies of the strategic utility of special operations have to be alert to avoid the magnetic or imperial pull of "raiding" phenomena as a would-be hegemonic broad class of special operations activities. Special operations forces can be assigned harassing missions in the enemy's rear and certainly they can be ordered to raid, but their more important tasks tend to require the collection and transmission of timely intelligence.

SPECIAL OPERATIONS—UNDERDISCOVERED COUNTRY

A popular historian of the early twentieth century, Philip Guedalla, had this to say about Alfred Thayer Mahan and his "discovery" of sea power:

> It must be nearly thirty years since the late Captain Mahan stood silent on a peak in Darien in the first shock of the discovery that the waters of the Atlantic and Pacific Oceans were wet. The thoughtful sailor indulged his companions of the United States Naval War College with the wild surmise that a liquid of this character might be expected to sustain the weight of warships and that the operations of such vessels would possess a distinct importance in determining the result of disputes between nations, always provided that they were not (as in the happy cases of Switzerland, Luxemburg, and Liechtenstein) entirely cut off from the sea. The leaping inferences of his discovery were communicated, through his English publisher, to the inhabited world; and the doctrine of Sea Power became (if it ever needed to become) a commonplace. Yet there was real merit in Mahan's work. It is easy to complain of him, as [Oscar] Wilde complained of a contemporary, that he pursued the obvious with the enthusiasm of a short-sighted detective; but it is even easier to forget that he produced an articulate and comprehensible statement of matters which had not, before he wrote, been stated at all.[29]

As Britain's Royal Navy had developed and exercised sea power for nearly three centuries prior to Mahan's discovery of it, so have countries conducted extensive special operations with strategic utility at least since World War II and sporadically throughout history. Guedalla noted that "the British Navy, by reason of certain faults in its upbringing and the difficulties of literary composition on a mobile platform, is not given to self-expression." The lack of pre-Mahanian appreciation of sea power contrasted sharply with the plethora of sea stories, accounts of naval action, and naval biographies. The world of special operations, likewise, is abundantly populated with stirring tales of derring-do—many of them true—and with narrowly focused histories. But the subject of the strategic utility of special operations finds little place in popular accounts of desperate actions and thus remains misunderstood. Aside from scattered comments or a bold sentence at the conclusion of a work of history, there is practically no literature on the subject of the strategic utility of special operations. A typical example of such token treatment of this subject is Sir John Hackett's passing comment in his foreword to the war memoirs of Vladimir Peniakoff: "The most important contribution of PPA [Popski's Private Army] to the allies war effort in Italy, however, was probably what it did for morale."[30] Thus, while the literature on special operations and on special operations forces is vast, the literature on their strategic utility in war is all but nonexistent.[31]

As suggested already, an important condition for the success of special operations is that they pursue only achievable objectives. Of course, that formulation begs the prior question, What objectives are achievable? When considering how special operations forces might contribute to the national team effort for the conduct of war or other kinds of conflict, it is helpful to think in terms of four categories of potential tasks:

- Those that only special operations forces can perform
- Tasks that special operations forces can do well
- Tasks that special operations forces tend to do badly
- Tasks that special operations forces cannot perform at all

Distinguishing which types of tasks fall into each category will help shed light on the problem of strategic utility.[32] At the same time, one must remember that even a task which special operations forces alone can perform will have strategic utility only if that task is well chosen with respect to the total structure of a conflict. As Neville Chamberlain wrote in July 1940 in the founding charter of what was to become the Special Operations Executive, "It will be important that the general plan for irregular offensive operations should be in step with the general strategic conduct of the war."[33] If the general strategic conduct of a conflict is unsound, even tactically successful special operations are unlikely to achieve much in a larger sense. Indeed, sometimes there may even be a "special operations paradox" analogous to the more familiar "arms control paradox" (which states that countries in need of arms control agreements generally cannot achieve them for the very reasons why they need them).[34] Those countries most in need of startling, dramatically successful special operations may be the least able to profit strategically from them. The important point here is to emphasize the close connections between special operations and the total military and political contexts of the conflicts in which they take place.

Although the strategic analysis of special operations is largely untraveled territory to date, other regions of military activity are not exactly richly endowed with strategic appreciation, as previous chapters of this book attest. It is much easier to tell the story of a specific special operation and to assess its tactical success or failure than it is to relate that success or failure to the course of the war as a whole. Although the lack of attention to the strategic utility of special operations is an extreme case, the slighting of genuinely strategic matters is pervasive. Part of the problem has been the appropriation of the term *strategic* to mean forces that are long range and nuclear armed. When one thinks clearly about the distinction between strategy and tactics, however, the need for strategic investigation of the actual or potential value of special operations becomes plain.

The regular military establishments of Britain, Germany, and the United States typically have regarded special operations forces with a mix of amused contempt and active dislike. In those countries strong civilian patronage generally has been needed for special operations forces to prosper.[35] That patronage, however, has been a two-edged sword. The cases of France, the Soviet Union, and Israel differ both among themselves and from the typical British, German, and U.S. experience. The French experience was unique. The regular armed forces of the Third Republic suffered a catastrophic and lasting blow to their dignity and reputation in 1940, while the wars in Indochina and Algeria were both politically unpopular at home and unappealing to the regular military. In the former Soviet Union "special" forces (to be defined with great care for local meaning) enjoyed a prestige and significance distinctively tied to the political security of the Communist Party (or of the state, when Stalin operated largely through the organs of state security). As for Israel, the regular Israeli Defense Forces (IDF) had their roots in the conduct of irregular warfare in the 1930s and 1940s. A special operations ethos continues to pervade the entire IDF.[36]

The military establishments of Britain, Nazi Germany, and the United States, for some similar and some different reasons, have rarely welcomed the development of special operations capabilities. One can speculate as to why special operations forces so frequently have had to cope with an unfriendly bureaucratic environment. Aside from the general problem of vested interests, a simple lack of understanding of how special operations forces can contribute to the team effort in conflict of all kinds has been a major part of the problem.

Analyses such as this one probably can do little to change those attitudes which are unfriendly toward special operations forces and which reflect some mix of envy, distaste, and anxiety. But I can aspire to influence the minds at least of those whose indifference toward, or even dislike of, special operations forces rests upon a lack of strategic appreciation. Writing in 1983, David Thomas concluded that "in the case of the American military establishment . . . the lessons of the history of commando operations have escaped the understanding and the attention of senior commanders and strategists."[37] It is perhaps paradoxical that the army of the United States, the country which in its colonial phase all but invented irregular warfare in modern times, "failed totally to grasp the concept of commando warfare as examples in the war [World War II], distilled no coherent lessons from the history of commando operations, and for long did not establish any useful capability to conduct commando operations in conventional war."[38]

It is a condition for the success of special operations that neither too much nor too little be asked of them. Eliot Cohen has argued that "[e]lite unit prominence occurs only during a politico-military crisis, for it is then that the public searches for heroes and politicians look for panaceas."[39] Neither the heroic nor the panacea role requires that special operations forces actually perform tasks of great strategic utility. Ironically, special operations often appeal to politicians for precisely the same reasons why conventional military professionals are deeply suspicious of them. In praising special operations, M. R. D. Foot inadvertently voiced exactly the claim which excites most skepticism: "A good special operation does also secure economy of force, that familiar tag taught in all the staff colleges and so often forgotten by practitioners. Sometimes a special operation can achieve wholly disproportionate results."[40] Viewed negatively, this is the free-lunch syndrome, of which many regular military minds are rightfully suspicious. They are inclined to dismiss a good deal of the promise of special operations as little more than a magic show with smoke and mirrors. Their point is not that special operations can never be useful, but rather that effort and reward tend to remain proportionate and that large strategic results seldom follow without the expenditure of great amounts of energy. In other words, special warfare does not constitute some higher plane of conflict wherein, miraculously, David always defeats Goliath. The detractors' motto could well be Damon Runyon's famous adaptation of Ecclesiastes 9:11: "The race is not always to the swift, nor the battle to the strong but that's the way to bet."

The willingness of some politicians to believe that handfuls of heroes can accomplish what whole divisions or even armies cannot tends to affront the dignity and sense of self-worth of regular forces and eventually is perilous to the reputation and even survival of the special operations forces themselves. Exaggerated, out-of-context expectations for the performance of special operations forces in effect set those forces up to fail. Special operations should function in ways integral to, if tactically distinctive within, national policy and military strategy. The same small scale of special operations necessary for their success also limits them to a supporting role in large-scale conventional warfare. This is not a criticism, but merely a necessary statement of fact. Patrons who express unreasonably high expectations for the results of special operations inadvertently provide fuel for critics. Indeed, proponents of sea power and air power have encountered the same problem when their operations could not independently deliver the decisive strategic results which some of their more ardent prophet-advocates injudiciously promised. In practice in World War II, the strategic effectiveness of Allied sea power and air power (treated together or separately) manifested itself in the successful land war that they "enabled."[41] Similarly, special operations tended to be adjuncts to the progress of the land war (in Europe and Africa) and the war at sea (in the Pacific).

In order to secure a sufficiently holistic understanding of special operations, it is useful to think of them in terms of three things: a state of mind; forces; and a mission. The scope of the mission depends largely upon the state of mind—the ability to think in an unorthodox way—as well as the tactical prowess of available forces and other factors. Without this dynamic, innovative attitude, special operations may reduce to a narrow, tightly defined set of missions that special operations forces already have trained to perform or to merely what bureaucratic definition and assignments formally allow. In addition, there is the danger that excessive focus on a specific mission or missions may lead to the development of overly specialized special operations forces, which—in their own way—may reflect as rigid and orthodox a mentality as the nominally regular armed forces.

Otherwise conventional missions in war sometimes amount to special operations when they benefit from an unorthodox approach. Thus, this book emphasizes that special operations derive their character from a state of mind, as well as from forces and missions. One will miss much of the potential strategic utility of special operations if one focuses attention exclusively on dedicated capabilities and established missions such as stereotyped commando raids.

Earlier I suggested that special operations are operations that regular forces cannot perform. It is more accurate, however, to refer to operations that regular forces, functioning regularly, cannot perform. It is important that one not be captured here by the circular law of the instrument—that special operations are what special operations forces do. Only an unorthodox state of mind can provide true flexibility in the capabilities of special operations forces, including the raising of new units and temporary dedication of regular units, allowing them to rise in an innovative way to meet extraordinary challenges.

NOTES

1. Obviously this is a principle perilously open to abuse. Largely at the expense of the Canadian Army, the Dieppe raid demonstrated the difficulties which the Allies would need to overcome in order to open a second front. The easy defeat of the raiders at the water's edge helped fuel overconfidence on the German side that, although well founded in 1942 and 1943, had cumulatively harmful consequences by the spring of 1944. The Son Tay prisoner of war rescue attempt of 21–22 November 1970 failed in its immediate objective. But the raid demonstrated a U.S. capability for penetration deep into North Vietnam and caused Hanoi to redeploy significant military forces to protect against the threat which the failed rescue attempt illustrated vividly. Son Tay was a tactical failure in a lost war; but it was an attempt to do the right thing and it had a measurable, albeit brief, strategic value for South Vietnam and the United States. Benjamin F. Schemmer, *The Raid* (New York: Avon Books, 1976), p. 267.

2. The Grenada intervention (Operation Urgent Fury) is unlikely to appear on anyone's short list of military masterpieces. However, both at the time and viewed in retrospect Urgent Fury has to be judged a major political success. Urgent Fury sent a message to friends and foes alike that the United States was willing to use force, was capable of acting decisively, and really did regard itself as a superpower guardian. In 1983 that message probably needed to be sent. Urgent Fury, in common with the Reagan administration's increase in the defense effort, was not an exercise in strategic elegance. But the Grenadian intervention worked as statecraft.

3. In the U.S. military establishment, "special forces" usually refers narrowly to U.S. Army Special Forces, while "special operations forces" embraces all the services. Even though this discussion is not confined to U.S. matters, I will avoid all possibility of misunderstanding by maintaining this distinctive language.

4. Stuart Chant-Sempill, *St. Nazaire Commando* (Novato, CA: Presidio Press, 1987; first pub. 1985), p. xi.

5. See John Terraine, *Business in Great Waters: The U-Boat Wars, 1916-1945* (London: Leo Cooper, 1989), p. 444.

6. See Correlli Barnett, *Engage the Enemy More Closely: The Royal Navy in the Second World War* (New York: W. W. Norton, 1991), pp. 315–16.

7. David Kahn, *Seizing the Enigma: The Race to Break the German U-Boat Codes, 1939–1943* (Boston: Houghton Mifflin, 1991), pp. 135–37; Terraine, *Business in Great Waters*, pp. 325–26. A point soon came when raiders were directed not to seize Enigma materials, because of the risk of alerting the Germans to the need to adopt security countermeasures. Indeed, the security of ULTRA (the code name assigned to intelligence gathered from interception of Enigma radio traffic) intelligence as a whole was at stake.

8. A point made forcefully in D. M. Horner, *SAS, Phantoms of the Jungle: A History of the Australian Special Air Service* (Sydney: Allen and Unwin, 1989), pp. 455–56. Richard Simpkin advises that "[t]oday's worldwide spectrum of activities by irregular

forces suggests that the strategic scope for special forces with capabilities ranging from clandestine hit squads through *coup de main* to powerful raids is limited only by the sponsor's imagination." *Race to the Swift: Thoughts on Twenty-First Century Warfare* (London: Brassey's Defence Publishers, 1985), p. 49.

9. Elite, as a quality, refers strictly to the standard of selection, not to the activity that soldiers are selected to perform. Special operations forces must be elite forces, but elite forces generally are not special operations forces.

10. Carl von Clausewitz, *On War*, ed. and trans. Michael Howard and Peter Paret (Princeton, NJ: Princeton University Press, 1976; first pub. 1832), p. 605.

11. Maurice Tugwell and David Charters, "Special Operations and the Threats to United States Interests in the 1980's," in Frank R. Barnett, B. Hugh Tovar, and Richard H. Shultz, eds., *Special Operations in U.S. Strategy* (Washington, DC: National Defense University Press, 1984), p. 35. Their definition proceeds to state that "[s]pecial operations are characterized by either simplicity or complexity, by subtlety and imagination, by the discriminate use of violence, and by oversight at the highest level. Military and nonmilitary resources, including intelligence assets, may be used in concert." It is not obvious that the definition is much improved by these weighty additions to the sentence quoted in the text.

12. See Benjamin Isaac, *The Limits of Empire: The Roman Army in the East* (Oxford: Clarendon Press, 1990), pp. 235–49. Ifran Shahid, *Byzantium and the Arabs in the Fourth Century* (Washington, DC: Dumbarton Oaks Research Library and Collection, 1984); and *Byzantium and the Arabs in the Fifth Century* (Washington, DC: Dumbarton Oaks Research Library and Collection, 1989), provide rich detail.

13. The classic British analysis remains Charles E. Callwell, *Small Wars: A Tactical Textbook for Imperial Soldiers* (London: Greenhill Books, 1990; first pub. 1896). Also see T. R. Moreman, "The British and Indian Armies and North-West Frontier Warfare, 1849–1914," *Journal of Imperial and Commonwealth History* 20, no. 1 (January 1992): 35–64.

14. For this focus see the excellent study by Otto Heilbrunn, *Warfare in the Enemy's Rear* (London: George Allen and Unwin, 1963).

15. Clausewitz, *On War*, pp. 119–21.

16. Edward N. Luttwak, Steven L. Canby, and David L. Thomas, *A Systematic Review of "Commando" (Special) Operations, 1939–1980* (Potomac, MD: C and L Associates, 24 May 1982), p. I-1.

17. Words attributed to Lt. Gen. William E. Yarborough, in Frank R. Barnett, B. Hugh Tovar, and Richard H. Shultz, eds., *Special Operations in U.S. Strategy* (Washington, DC: National Defense University Press, 1984), p. 299.

18. Virginia Cowles, *The Phantom Major: The Story of David Stirling and the S.A.S. Regiment* (London: Collins, 1958), pp. 21–22.

19. Tony Geraghty, *Who Dares Wins: The Story of the Special Air Service, 1950–1982*, rev. ed. (London: Fontana Books, 1983), p. 5.

20. This is not my preferred understanding of what is tactical, of course. See Chapter 1.

21. On the subject of U.S. special operations forces (SOF) in the mid-1980s James Adams wrote: "Yet, even with the structure in place and the right equipment,

insufficient work has been done on developing a strategy and a doctrine for special forces to ensure that they are used correctly. In recent years, they have either been used as a reactive force to counter a terrorist act that has already been committed, or else in support of conventional forces. Both are essentially tactical purposes and in a real war would have little effect on its overall conduct—a key test for SOF actions." *Secret Armies* (London: Pan Books, 1989; first pub. 1988), p. 287. Adams is struggling toward the light. The effect of what he calls "essentially tactical purposes" on the overall conduct of the war depends upon the quality of direction and general potency of the conventional forces. The proposition that special operations forces are most effective when functioning in an independent manner is only a proposition; it is true in some circumstances, but not as a guiding principle. In his bestseller about the British SAS in the Gulf War, Andy McNab offered the opinion that "[w]e're strategic troops, so what we do behind enemy lines can have serious implications." *Bravo Two Zero* (London: BCA, 1993), p. 8.

22. Field-Marshal Viscount Slim, though highly critical of "private armies," recognized "one kind of special unit which should be retained—that designed to be employed in small parties, usually behind the enemy, on tasks beyond the normal scope of warfare in the field." *Defeat into Victory* (London: Papermac, 1986; first pub. 1956), p. 548.

23. See the excellent study by Luttwak, Canby, and Thomas, *Systematic Review of "Commando" (Special) Operations, 1939–1980.*

24. T. E. Lawrence, *Seven Pillars of Wisdom: A Triumph* (New York: Anchor Books, 1991; first pub. 1935), pp. 191–92.

25. See David Thomas, "The Importance of Commando Operations in Modern Warfare, 1939–82," *Journal of Contemporary History* 18, no. 4 (October 1983): 690–91.

26. I am in debt to Arnold Beichman for this felicitous phrase. See *The Long Pretense: Soviet Treaty Diplomacy from Lenin to Gorbachev* (New Brunswick, NJ: Transaction Publishers, 1991), p. 15. Trained incapacity was a favorite concept of the late Herman Kahn.

27. M. R. D. Foot, "Special Operations/1," in Michael Elliott-Bateman, ed., *The Fourth Dimension of Warfare*, vol. 1, *Intelligence, Subversion, Resistance* (Manchester, England: Manchester University Press, 1970), p. 19. Foot's contribution to the success of the D-Day landings is chronicled in Martin Young and Robbie Stamp, *Trojan Horses: Deception Operations in the Second World War* (London: Mandarin, 1991; first pub. 1989), chap. 5, "The Historian's Tale—M. R. D. Foot."

28. Exceptions would include missions to destabilize the enemy's rear area by the harassment of logistic and other targets of opportunity and missions simply to remind all interested parties that one was still very much in a war. In the latter case the tactical objective can be precisely focused, while the intended strategic effect is diffuse.

29. Philip Guedalla, *Men of War* (London: Hodder and Stoughton, no date [but 1920s]), pp. 45–46.

30. Sir John Hackett, foreword to Vladimir Peniakoff, *Popski's Private Army* (Oxford: Oxford University Press, 1991; first pub. 1950), p. xiii.

31. Thomas, "Importance of Commando Operations in Modern Warfare, 1939–82," is the work closest in spirit and purpose to this analysis. In contrast, William H. McRaven, *SPEC OPS: Case Studies in Special Operations Warfare: Theory and Practice* (Novato, CA: Presidio Press, 1995), is entirely innocent of strategic reasoning.

32. For details see Chapter 8.

33. Quoted in M. R. D. Foot, *SOE: An Outline History of the Special Operations Executive, 1940–46* (London: Mandarin, 1990; first pub. 1984), p. 21.

34. See Colin S. Gray, *House of Cards: Why Arms Control Must Fail* (Ithaca, NY: Cornell University Press, 1992).

35. See Eliot A. Cohen, *Commandos and Politicians: Elite Military Units in Modern Democracies* (Cambridge, MA: Harvard University, Center for International Affairs, 1978). In the German case, Otto Skorzeny's special forces were established at Himmler's urging and with Hitler's blessing to serve as a private army within a private army (i.e., loosely within the framework of the Waffen SS). The army special forces, the Brandenburg units (which rose from company to division size), should have been the private army of Admiral Canaris, Germany's head of counterintelligence in the high command. But in practice Brandenburg units were controlled by the commanders of the army and army groups in their areas of operation. See Otto Skorzeny, *Skorzeny's Secret Missions: War Memoirs of the Most Dangerous Man in Europe* (New York: E. P. Dutton, 1950); Charles Foley, *Commando Extraordinary* (London: Longmans, Green, 1954); and James Lucas, *Kommando: German Special Forces of World War Two* (New York: St. Martin's Press, 1986; first pub. 1985).

36. Cohen makes the important argument that whereas countries such as the United States, Britain, and France, which operate typically with a wide margin of safety in the national security field, can afford to risk the damage which elite forces inadvertently can wreak upon nonelite forces, Israel cannot. Israel's margin of safety has been so slender that it could not afford to have heroically competent small elite units and an indifferent remainder. All branches of the IDF have to fight well for the country to be secure. *Commandos and Politicians*, p. 92.

37. Thomas, "Importance of Commando Operations in Modern Warfare, 1939–82," p. 712. Also see Alfred H. Paddock, Jr., *U.S. Army Special Warfare, Its Origins: Psychological and Unconventional Warfare, 1941–1952* (Washington, DC: National Defense University Press, 1982), pp. 157–58.

38. Thomas, "Importance of Commando Operations in Modern Warfare, 1939–82," p. 703.

39. Cohen, *Commandos and Politicians*, p. 96.

40. Foot, "Special Operations/1," p. 2. Charles Foley quoted Otto Skorzeny to the same effect: "He [Skorzeny] predicted that wide changes on the battlefield would open the way for ventures by which small groups of men might decide great issues." *Commando Extraordinary*, p. 189.

41. It is difficult enough trying to understand how special operations function strategically, without presenting detractors with straw targets. Lt. Gen. Samuel V. Wilson, a former Director of the Defense Intelligence Agency, has observed that "special operations are often supplemental to the main action, a kind of military sideshow. They rarely win the battle, and they never win the war." In Frank R. Barnett,

B. Hugh Tovar, and Richard H. Shultz, eds., *Special Operations in U.S. Strategy* (Washington, DC: National Defense University Press, 1984), p. 192. This risks error on the side of undue modesty. A little earlier the general claimed that special operations "never win wars by themselves" (p. 191). It is important not to encourage the view that special operations can always cut Gordian knots and achieve independent, decisive results. One must recognize that the U.S. (conventional) Army, Navy, and Air Force are not, individually, required or expected to "win wars by themselves" either.

Chapter 8

The Strategic Utility of Special Operations: Lessons of History

What strategic utility does the history of special operations suggest to be the outcome of those operations?

One cannot assess the strategic utility of special operations in a general way. Without the historical context, strategic utility is impossible of assay. But on the basis of a wide range of historical cases one can demonstrate the kinds of effects that special operations have had (e.g., to embarrass or humiliate an enemy) and thereby assess the strategic utility of each case. In order to avoid both context-free generalization and overly specific claims, this chapter provides answers by general categories, within which it identifies a breakdown of major components, specific historical illustrations, and explicit guidance as to the scope of the authority of the finding.[1] The question, How useful are special operations? can have no answer without reference to the type of conflict and mission. Strategic utility, positive or negative, is specific to individual cases. This same point can be made for every other kind of military capability or activity.

The term *strategic utility* as employed here means the contribution of a particular kind of military activity to the course and outcome of an entire conflict. With respect to how strategic utility can flow from action in the field, special operations may generate

- *tactical utility* with reference to their impact upon a particular engagement or battle
- *operational utility* with reference both to their direct impact upon operational-level objectives (e.g., the effect of the damage wrought by the SAS

upon the Luftwaffe in the desert in 1942) and to their indirect impact via the tactical successes which they facilitated

- *strategic utility* with reference both to the consequences of their direct impact upon a war as a whole (e.g., the killing or kidnapping of an irreplaceable enemy war leader or the raid mounted by Britain's Special Operations Executive in 1943 that destroyed 350 kgs. of "heavy water" from Norway which was vital for Germany's atomic program), and to their indirect impact via the operational-level military successes which they facilitate (or accomplish unaided)

There are different ways to express the ideas of strategic utility or strategic effectiveness.[2] What is important is not the detail of the formulation, but rather the heart of the matter. The range of activities plausibly identifiable as special operations are so wide, so different in national authorship and execution, and generally nested in conflicts of such complexity that conceptual clarity in analysis is unusually important. In Vietnam, for example, virtually by political default U.S. special operations came to assume a leading-edge role in lieu of a proper comprehensive strategy for the conduct of the war. In contrast, French special operations forces in Indochina and Algeria were accorded a hammer role against the anvil of more regular (and largely conscript) troops who tended to be lacking in military prowess.

An enquiry such as this must capture the relevant consequences of special operations at whatever level of war they occur, with reference to some common currency—strategic utility. The answers provided to questions of strategic utility cannot be other than qualitative and judgmental. The same point applies to answers to questions about the strategic utility of sea power or air power, for example. Sea power and air power, however, do not lack for institutional and doctrinal defenses against those who would discount their value in national military strategy. Special operations and special operations forces are probably uniquely vulnerable to misunderstanding and misapplication.

GENERAL POINTS

Before plunging into detailed argument, one must specify some important general points. These points frame and help interpret the argument presented below.

First, it is a military virtue to achieve maximum results with minimum effort. The principles of war define the virtue as economy of force. One must, however, interpret and apply this principle in the context of the need for reliable action in the friction-beset context of conflict and war. Special operations are expressions of agility, maneuver, and finesse. They are also high-risk endeavors. There are occasions when finesse can and should substitute for brute force;

indeed there are cases where brute force is not applicable (i.e., there are missions that only special operations forces can perform). But there are many cases, particularly in mid- and high-intensity conflicts, where special operations have utility as precise and agile door-openers for brute force.[3] The finesse of special operations and the brute force of large-scale regular military activity are not opposite approaches to war or to the generation of strategic effectiveness. Instead, special operations function as force multipliers. This point highlights the value of different yet synergistic styles of war.

Second, special operations may have strategic value whether they are intended to have immediate effects on a battle, on a campaign, or on a war as a whole. In other words, special operations at the tactical, operational, and strategic levels of war all have strategic utility. Moreover, special operations have strategic value whether one uses them on independent missions or whether they coordinate their action with regular forces.

Third, special operations can have positive strategic utility whether or not their side is victorious. Similarly, the conditions for success of special operations do not include a requirement to be on the winning side. The historical context always places limits on the ability of special operations to influence the course and outcome of a war, but that need not mean that the value of those operations has to be trivial. For example, Otto Skorzeny's rescue of Mussolini in 1943 and his ouster of Admiral Horthy—head of Germany's less-than-loyal Hungarian ally—in 1944 and the French conduct of generally successful special operations in Algeria in the mid to late 1950s, were all strategically futile exercises in the sense that the political causes they served ultimately were beyond effective support. But the German and French operations did have substantial positive impacts upon the war efforts they served. A losing cause will tend to be unable to derive as much strategic utility from the competent conduct of special operations (or any other type of operations) as will a winning cause, but still that utility for a lost cause can be noteworthy. Also, special operations, particularly in the form of unconventional warfare, may create a stalemate which might alter the political climate and terms of a negotiated settlement.

It is a common error to condemn as ineffective the military actions of a losing cause. Obviously, the total strategic utility of all the grand-strategy instruments of the losing side was by definition inadequate. But the value of the contribution of the various unsuccessful military instruments to the overall team effort will vary. For example, to note that the United States lost the war in Vietnam says nothing about the strategic utility of U.S. special operations forces in that struggle—nothing, that is, beyond the self-evident point that the military effort did not suffice, viewed independently and as a force multiplier, to deliver victory. U.S. air power, to make a parallel point, also could not generate the strategic utility necessary to enable the war to be won.

Fourth, this chapter will avoid the trap of immoderate and unrealistic tests of strategic value. More specifically, the test of independent decisive effect on the course of a war is a criterion that special operations would fail in most instances. Since navies, armies, and air forces also fail the "test" of independent decisive effect, one should not hold the special operations community to a higher standard. In many cases of low-intensity conflict, however, the quality of the performance of special operations forces will be critical to victory or defeat.

Fifth, any findings on strategic utility must be judgmental. There is no quantifiable method for assessing the strategic utility of special operations. This does not excuse unsubstantiated assertions or a disappointing vagueness in claims, but it does mean that one can only test the logic of the argument here on its own terms and not with reference to some objective mathematical process. When rendering overall judgment on the value of raiding in World War II, Kenneth Macksey noted that "[t]he raiders' closing balance sheet, to be acceptable, had to show a clear profit, but the main trouble in that sort of exercise lies in the fact that nearly all the assets are unquantifiable." A little later he observed also that "[i]ntangibles, such as the eternal interaction of one activity upon another, have also to be entered into the tally of strategic, tactical and technical benefits and expenses. Inescapably each raid, no matter its size, overlapped elsewhere and called for overheads."[4] Just as one should not require the impossible of special operations, so one should not seek an impracticable precision in strategic analysis.

Sixth, the linkage between strategic utility and conditions for success emphasizes the need for strategic perspective. The strategic significance of a special operation is not contained within that operation. Two questions demand answers: How important were special operations to the solving of particular problems? How important was the solving of those particular problems to the course and outcome of a war? Fallacies menace sound analysis on all sides. For example, people tend to praise special operations which accomplish campaignwide or warwide goals, at the expense of operations which multiply the effectiveness of regular forces.

Seventh, there is something to the claim that special operations forces as elite forces can so skim the better soldiers from regular units as to impair the effectiveness of those units. In his memoirs, Field-Marshal Slim advised that "[a]rmies do not win wars by means of a few bodies of super-soldiers but by the average quality of their standard units."[5] There can be an overall entropic synergism between the raising of would-be special units on a large scale and their ultimate strategic utility. Specifically, if one raises special operations forces to compensate for weaknesses in the regular forces, and if the special operations forces do succeed in accomplishing missions beyond reasonable assignment to regular forces, the debility of those regular forces limits the strategic significance of special unit activity. In other words, war is a team game.

Also, just because decision makers can make errors in the raising of special operations forces in the context of the general needs of the armed forces, that is not an argument against the raising of special operations forces. Indeed, the problem historically has not been one between special and regular forces, but rather between regular and elite troops. In practice, this concern is appropriate with respect to the British Army Commandos and airborne divisions in World War II, but not to the SAS or the Special Boat Service (SBS). In the U.S. case, the concern does not apply to the Green Berets and the SEALS, but rather—albeit arguably—to the Rangers, the airborne/air cavalry divisions, and the Marine Corps. This is not to criticize past or current personnel practices, but only to say that this complaint reflects a confusion of categories (and hence of the relevant numbers) between the numerous elite forces and the far-from-numerous special operations forces of all kinds. The point simply is one of numbers. The higher the ratio of elite to nonelite troops, the greater the negative impact that the former are likely to have upon the quality of the latter.

Eighth, because they are unusually well endowed with warrior virtues, commanders tend to use elite units—including special operations forces—much as teenagers drive sports cars and with similar and predictable results. There are many reasons why commanders often misuse special operations forces; prominent ones include the following: ignorance on the part of commanders; an insecurity within special operations forces which encourages the acceptance of all assignments; and the need for reliable fighting units, which leads commanders to neglect the fact that some elite units also are special. In World War II, both the British and the U.S. armies, for example, focused on the elite combat capabilities rather than the special qualities of their raiding forces. Conventional minds have far less difficulty appreciating the military value of "shock troops" to perform unusually hazardous tasks than they do of special operations forces performing nonregular missions. When a war is going badly, elite-special units often find themselves assigned desperate jobs suitable to their warrior virtues, though not to their numbers, their firepower, or their ability to absorb high casualties. For example, in the final days of the Third Reich, Germany destroyed its special operations forces in the "fire brigade" role.

Ninth, consideration of the utility of special operations must take a holistic approach to the crisis, conflict, or war at issue. It is the complete structure of the war that provides the conditions which enable special operations to play a role of greater or lesser strategic significance. To illustrate, in Vietnam the dual nature of the threat—Viet Cong and People's Army of Vietnam (PAVN)—limited the potential utility of U.S. special operations. The enemy's center of gravity may have been the political infrastructure of the Viet Cong, but an exclusive focus upon that problem would have left South Vietnamese and U.S. forces vulnerable to regular operations by the PAVN. The U.S. strategic dilemma in Vietnam approximated that of a football team facing an opponent able both to run and to pass. Overconcentration to defeat either threat would leave friendly forces vulnerable to the other. The indecision which characterized British military strategy after 1778 during the American Revolutionary War provides an analogy. London could not decide whether to concentrate its naval power in home waters (to isolate the rebels from French assistance) or in American waters. In practice it did neither consistently or well, with predictable results. This ninth point is introduced for the purpose of advancing the thesis that one should plan special operations to support a single and comprehensive theory of victory. As Carl von Clausewitz observed: "But in war more than in any other subject we must begin by looking at the nature of the whole; for here more than elsewhere the part and the whole must always be thought of together."[6] An important aspect of the whole is the enemy: his nature, his objectives, his capabilities, and his strategy.

Tenth and finally, tactical success has a way of dominating serious debate over strategic utility. Indeed it may not be inappropriate to observe that success is self-validating. One can conduct special operations—in common with other kinds of operations—as ends in themselves, divorced from any master strategic plan. Virtually any special operation, though particularly any tactically successful operation, can be provided with some explanatory cover. General assertions about intended value for morale, for the cost-effective attrition of the enemy, or for field-testing of techniques, equipment, ideas, and men are all difficult to label definitively as empty excuses for instances when tactics drive strategy. Political decision makers and military planners therefore must be aware of the need for special operations to be approached as a component of a broad strategic design.

STRATEGIC UTILITY

Findings on the military utility of special operations can be grouped into the broad categories shown in Table 8.1 Findings in the first two categories— economy of force and expansion of choice—are the most important, and I term them "master claims." The concern here is to identify the strategic utility of special operations for the course and outcome of different classes of conflict; that strategic utility is indifferent as to the character of the active agent (e.g., military damage or political encouragement). The findings are augmented by general as well as specific illustration and by guidance as to their authority.

Economy of Force

Special operations can achieve significant results with limited forces. This is the first of two master claims for the strategic utility of special operations which lend themselves to employment as the framework embracing many of the more

Table 8.1
Strategic Utility of Special Operations

Master Claims	
1. Economy of force	2. Expansion of choice

Other Claims	
3. Innovation	7. Humiliation of the enemy
4. Morale	8. Control of escalation
5. Showcasing of competence	9. Shaping of the future
6. Reassurance	

specific claims. Kenneth Macksey makes a parallel point to this first claim when he concludes that "if there is a single major lesson to be drawn from the sum total of amphibious raiding operations during the Second World War it is their comparatively low cost in lives set against results achieved."[7]

1. Special operations can act as a force multiplier and augment the strength of regular forces. The SAS, SBS, and Royal Marine Commandos performed this function in Borneo from 1964 to 1966, during the "confrontation" with Indonesia and again in the Falklands in 1982. Israeli special operations in the war of independence in 1948 repeatedly stretched the effectiveness of relatively small units.

This modest sounding claim is the heart of the matter, particularly in mid- and high-intensity conflicts. Special operations forces can perform missions deftly and precisely so that the effectiveness of regular forces is greatly enhanced. The missions may be of any nature: intelligence gathering; deception and diversion; sabotage or kidnapping; and so forth. Functioning as key "enablers" for successful regular operations, special operations open the door.

2. Special operations can accelerate the pace of military success. The Abwehr's Brandenburgers and the Luftwaffe's paratroopers in Holland and Belgium during May 1940 served this end. In addition, Soviet special operations forces facilitated the advance of the Red Army and the surrender of Japanese units throughout Manchuria in August 1945.

This applies when special operations are supporting regular warfare of a mid- or high-intensity level. There will almost always be strategically useful missions for special operations forces to act as accelerators of success in regular warfare, but commanders tend to neglect the special warfare instrument when they are prosecuting war successfully. In addition, the pace of mobile warfare can outrun the time needed to plan and execute special operations.

3. Special operations can slow the pace of military failure. Otto Skorzeny's coup in Budapest in 1944 which helped keep Hungarian forces loyal to the Axis is a leading illustration of this underexamined and underemployed option.

Again, this point applies to special operations in support of regular warfare in large-scale conflict. Whether or not special operations can help slow the pace of an unfolding failure and even help turn military events around must depend upon the scope, scale, and pace of that failure.

4. Special operations can themselves secure operational and even "strategic" objectives, particularly in single-mission events. The February 1943 raid on the German heavy-water supply from Norway, the successful Entebbe hostage rescue by Israeli special forces in July 1976, and the unsuccessful Iranian hostage rescue mission of April 1980 are cases in point.

This claim applies to all levels of conflicts.

5. Special operations can prepare the battlefield for success in regular operations of war. Partisan operations in Russia in 1943–44; by the SAS, Special Operations Executive (SOE), and the Office of Strategic Services (OSS) in France in June 1944; and by the OSS in Italy in the spring of 1945 all fit this claim.[8]

This claim applies most to conditions of ongoing or imminent mid- or high-intensity warfare, but it may also prove true for low-intensity conflict when special operations forces soften up an area for subsequent regular military operations.

6. Special operations can wage war economically. The SAS in the Western Desert in 1942, the OSS in the Kachin Hills of Burma in 1944, the SOE in France, the SAS, SBS, and Royal Marine Commandos in Borneo in 1964–66 all illustrate this point.

In conflicts of all kinds, special operations forces can conduct operations at a fraction of the cost of regular forces. Special operations are not, of course, cost free. But, provided the distinction between special and elite units is not forgotten, special operations require minimal national assets. This claim is based on two comparisons: first, that of strategic return with the scale of the investment and second, that of the scale of investment in special operations forces with the scale of effort necessary if regular forces attempted the missions.

7. Special operations can have a disproportionate impact on a battle, campaign, or war when the balance of regular forces is fairly even. The SAS (as well as the Long Range Desert Group and Popski's Private Army) in the Western Desert in 1942 and the Soviet partisan/Spetsnaz operations in support of the counteroffensive at Kursk in July 1943 are examples of this claim.

In mid- or high-intensity conflicts, special operations can work either as an economical equalizer or—better still—as critical leverage for victory.

8. Special operations can solve a political or military problem quickly as well as cheaply. Skorzeny's rescue of Mussolini in 1943, the SAS in Oman in 1959, and the activities of the SAS and SBS in Borneo in 1964–66 fit this description.

For some operational-level tasks in mid- or high-intensity conflict, only special operations forces can perform the mission quickly. Special operations forces are uniquely suitable for execution of *coups de main*. Rarely is swift success attainable in low-intensity conflict, but special operations provide the shortest path to victory, conditions being permissive (e.g., with no North Vietnamese regular army in the background).

9. Special operations can deny swift military, and hence political, success to an enemy. Wingate's Chindits in Burma in 1943 and even the Green Berets in Vietnam in the early 1960s might fit this description. Special operations forces can help deny victory by sustaining a conflict, albeit on a small and stealthy basis, or by slowing the pace of the enemy's success (as in point three above).

In this way special operations forces can generate strategic utility in conflicts of all kinds.

10. Special operations can seize individuals and equipment that are difficult or impossible to reach by regular operations. Apart from Otto Skorzeny's kidnapping exploits, the British commando raid on the Lofoten Islands (February 1941) and the airborne raid on Bruneval to grab German radar equipment (February 1942) showed how special operations could seize enemy personnel, equipment, and documents.[9] The Israelis emulated these examples in the war of attrition with Egypt in 1968–69.

Again, this unique special operations capability is relevant to conflicts of all kinds.

11. Special operations can impose disproportionate losses on the enemy. The SAS and OSS in France, Italy, and the Balkans in 1944 had this effect; while the Chindits and Merrill's Marauders in Burma in 1943–44 also wrought great pain on the enemy.

In all kinds of conflicts special operations can impose a discouraging and unfavorable ratio of losses upon an enemy. However, this kind of utility is more appropriate to an attritional style of war—most likely of a mid- or high-intensity character. Relative body-counts are not usually of key significance in low-intensity conflicts.

12. Special operations can seize the initiative and put the enemy on the defensive. Amphibious raids by British commandos in 1940–44, the operations of the SAS, OSS, and SOE in southern and western Europe in 1942–45, partisan and Spetsnaz activities on the eastern front, and U.S. cross-border raids in Southeast Asia after 1964 all served this strategic purpose. In 1917, German financial support and administrative arrangement for Lenin's return to Russia were a political operation with profound military significance. In World War II, British raiding activities and the

mandate for SOE also fitted this mission. Skorzeny's English-speaking infiltrators in the Ardennes offensive of December 1944 had the purposes both of helping accelerate the German advance and of creating panic in the enemy's rear. The military consequences of psychological warfare—as in Vietnam or Desert Storm or the attempt to subvert Austria-Hungary's polyglot armed forces in 1918—further illustrate this claim.[10]

This claim for strategic utility is not specific to type of conflict or character of mission; rather, it highlights the importance of the unorthodox in special operations.

13. Elite forces, including special operations forces, can substitute for absent or incompetent regular forces. French airborne units (*les paras*) in Indochina and Algeria compensated for the subaverage martial qualities of many conscript and colonial soldiers.[11] The Israeli Defense Forces (IDF), for another example, have always needed to "fight smarter" to win against larger Arab numbers.

In all kinds of conflicts commanders can assign special operations forces to missions which offset the limitations of regular forces. For reasons amenable to explanation by culturally empathetic military sociologists, some countries at some times have responded to military demands beyond the average competence of their average forces by creating elite units which include, and invite confusion with, special operations forces. Lack of understanding of the true character of special forces can encourage the creation of elite units which, while they have great fire-brigade value, if too large can damage further the average quality of the armed forces as a whole. For reason of their small numbers, special operations forces cannot do this. (They can spur resentment, but that is another matter.)

14. Special operations can deceive and perhaps immobilize the foe. German special operations forces throughout Holland during the invasion of 1940 helped fix Allied attention on the north, which encouraged the Allies to implement the disastrous Plan D (the advance to defend the line of the River Dyle) and distracted Allied intelligence from the Ardennes and the Meuse at Sedan. In Operation Titanic on 5–6 June 1944, eight SAS men helped deceive the Germans about the details of the Overlord invasion (as a small part of the immense Fortitude deception operation). Some SEAL operations on the coast of Kuwait in 1991 paralleled the 1944 Fortitude plan.

Special operations forces can threaten senior commanders. Skorzeny's falsely reported threat to kill Eisenhower all but paralyzed Supreme Headquarters Allied Expeditionary Forces (SHAEF) in December 1944; the tactically abortive Son Tay prisoner of war (POW) raid in November 1970 made North Vietnamese leaders anxious about rear-area security; while Israeli antiterrorist strikes into Beirut—particularly the Aviv Neurim operation of April 1973— told Israel's enemies that they could exist only in peril. In another sense, special operations forces can distract and divert enemy forces in their rear area, thereby causing a diversion of military strength from the battlefield—Maquis-OSS operations in Brittany in June 1944 provide classic illustration of this point.

Deception is not specific to any special warfare mission or level of conflict. Nonetheless, the most spectacular employment of special operations forces for the purpose of deception has been in conflicts of high- and mid-level intensity. Given that surprise is absolutely critical to all special operations, the relevance of deception is self-evident.

15. Special operations can entice the enemy into an overextension of forces. Classic instances include Brig. Gen. James A. Doolittle's raid (a special operation if ever there was one) on Tokyo on 18 April 1942 and Brig. Gen. Orde Wingate's first Chindit expedition into Burma (February–April 1943). The Doolittle raid "finally quashed the opposition" in Tokyo to Yamamoto's plan of campaign, which was to draw the U.S. Navy into a climactic fleet battle, that is, the Midway gamble.[12] Just as Doolittle's raid had demonstrated the vulnerability of the Japanese home islands to carrier-based attack, so Wingate's Special Force in 1943 proved to the Japanese that their position in Burma was vulnerable to overland attack and that the jungle-covered hills of the Indo-Burmese border were passable.[13] As a consequence, the Japanese ruined themselves in Burma by their 1944 expedition to invade India.

By design, though probably more often by accident, special operations can prod an enemy into self-destructive behavior. The shock of a special operation against an area considered secure can trigger an unwise and unbalanced response. Needless to add, it is exceedingly difficult to craft special operations with the precision necessary to entice an enemy into overextending himself. This form of strategic utility applies to all kinds of conflicts and to special operations of an independent or of a supporting nature.

16. Special operations can apply military pressure quietly and perhaps even with some plausible deniability. Special operations can enable a state to apply military pressure when other kinds of military activity are politically impracticable. In the 1960s, both the United States in Southeast Asia and Britain in the "confrontation" with Indonesia faced severe political opposition to waging mid-intensity combat, yet doing nothing was also deemed unacceptable.

In peacetime and even in wartime, special operations provide a unique capability to apply pressure when no other class of military action is politically feasible. In peacetime and against unfriendly neutrals in time of war, special operations are potentially the only kind of operations that one can conduct.

17. Special operations can find and reach elusive or hard-to-hit targets; they can function as the ultimate "smart weapon." From Gestapo headquarters and critical railroad tunnels in World War II to Scud missiles in the Gulf War, special operations can have a degree of precision in targeting that is unmatched. Special operations forces are an agile, real-time, intelligent, and discriminating instrument of grand and military strategy. Whether it was Skorzeny's SS

commandos rescuing Mussolini from the Gran Sasso in 1943 or the SAS finding Argentinian helicopters in the Falklands, special operations forces offer distinctive utility for precise targeting.[14]

This kind of strategic utility can have massive force multiplication value for regular forces and is not specific to type of conflict. Also, special operations as a "smart weapon" can be effective in supporting or in stand-alone tasks.

Expansion of Choice

Special operations can expand the options available to political and military leaders. Policy without means is just wishful thinking. In peacetime special operations are uniquely capable of providing policymakers with options for direct action (e.g., hostage rescue or counterterrorist strikes) in support of political goals. In wartime special operations increase the choices available to military commanders. For example, the 1940 German air-landing assault on the roof of the Belgian fort of Eban Emael by Para Assault Detachment Koch facilitated the prompt crossing of the Meuse canal and enabled the pace of the invasion of Belgium and France to proceed at the planned rate. In wartime, unlike peacetime, there are often regular force alternatives to a special operation, but those alternatives require much greater resources.

In theory, there are always alternatives to the use of force—diplomacy, economic sanctions, and the like. In practice, however, there are some situations that one cannot resolve successfully without resort to physical coercion. The availability of a special operations capability means that a country can use force flexibly, minimally, and precisely. The realization by the enemy that one has a special operations capability can have beneficial effects on calculations made abroad. In time of war, both in its independent and supporting roles, special operations enhance the flexibility with which one can use force. Special operations offer a low-cost solution to precisely targeted problems, and they can greatly enhance the feasibility of success in regular military operations. From World War II to the Gulf War of 1991, the examples are legion.

Innovation

Special operations can demonstrate new tactical doctrine, equipment, and military methods. Special operations can be a laboratory for innovation. The entire history of the IDF provides an extreme example of this claim. A special operations ethos has pervaded the IDF from its founding. Special operations forces have been leaders in setting requirements for lightweight equipment and personal weapons that are rugged and possess a high rate of fire. The British Combined Operations Directorate in 1940–43 was especially effective at military innovation, while the cooperation between Orde Wingate's Chindit

Special Force in Burma and the USAAF's No. 1 Air Commando was a model for emulation by regular forces.

Because of the demanding nature of their missions, special operations forces must push the limits of excellence in military training and equipment. The small scale of special operations and the high risk that attends its missions mean that there is a need for "equalizing" techniques and equipment. Regular forces can frequently adopt equipment and methods which work well for special operations forces. This is particularly true for conditions of high- and mid-intensity conflict.

Morale

Special operations can raise morale and encourage a sustained political will.

1. Special operations can personalize conflict and create heroes. The clash of armies and army groups tends to be too vast for it to engage the imagination. The small scale and often heroic deeds of special operations forces bring war to a level to which most people can relate. In both world wars governments and their supportive media sought to raise domestic morale by personalizing the struggle through the promotion of heroes. Special operations have been a rich source of such heroes. In World War I, Britain feted T. E. Lawrence (of Arabia) and Roger Keyes (leader of the St. George's Day 1918 raid on Zeebrugge), as well as air "aces." In World War II, Britain celebrated Orde Wingate of Chindit fame and Guy Gibson (leader of the "dams" raid), while the United States did the same for James Doolittle, William O. Darby (of Darby's Rangers), and Frank Merrill (of Merrill's Marauders, also known as the 5307th Composite Unit [Provisional]).

This claim applies mainly to protracted high-intensity conflict. Moreover, the claim applies especially to high-intensity conflict where the general course of the conflict to date has not been encouraging.

2. Special operations can make the point that a powerful and feared enemy can be outfought on his own terms and thereby be denied moral ascendancy. Wingate's first Chindit expedition in 1943 is a classic example of this strategic function. In the words of one historian, "the overall effect of the Chindits was to encourage the whole army."[15] Doolittle's carrier-launched B-25 raid on Tokyo showed that the Japanese were not alone in the ability to strike suddenly and competently over a great distance.

Again, this claim has an all but unique applicability to a high-intensity and, just possibly, a mid-intensity conflict of considerable duration. However, there can be cases in low-intensity conflict where it is important to demonstrate to friends and foes that our forces can match or defeat the enemy.

3. Special operations can demonstrate national toughness. National security can be a matter of respect as well as of actual military capabilities. In Palestine

in the 1930s and 1940s, the Jewish Special Night Squads, the Haganah, and (after 1941) the Palmach conducted special operations which were also political statements of a national will to survive. British commando operations in 1940–41 made the same point.

The enemy's respect for your military prowess is the basis of deterrence.

Showcasing of Competence

Special operations can enhance the political standing of the country by demonstrating military prowess.

1. Special operations can showcase military competence for deterrent effect, particularly by a deep, bold strike. Between wars or during a protracted hiatus within a war, one can employ special operations to make a statement about military prowess. Ariel Sharon and his Unit 101 performed this function for its deterrent effect in 1953, after a period of IDF ineptitude in raiding. The hostage-rescue raid on Entebbe airport by Israel's Unit 269 in 1976 had strategic utility as a deterrent to other would-be kidnappers.

From its 1930s experience in Palestine, the IDF has believed that the demonstration of the enemy's vulnerability in his rear area is good for national morale. Wingate designed his first Chindit expedition to be a "strategic" blow, both militarily and politically. The abortive Son Tay POW rescue attempt by the United States in 1970 carried messages important for morale (i.e., we really care about our POWs and we can reach deep into North Vietnam).

Understanding of the potential of deterrence in low-intensity conflict is not widespread. Nevertheless, the military prowess and political will which special operations can demonstrate could deter some opponents of the United States from acting. At a higher level of concern, U.S. military performance can help shape official and popular views abroad of the U.S. capacity for collective action. In both peace and war there is strategic value in persuading one's opponents that they are not safe anywhere.

2. Military competence is a prerequisite for deterrent effect. The successful assault on the Iranian embassy in London on 6 May 1980 by the SAS augmented an already formidable reputation in the antiterrorism field. The recognition abroad of a country's special operations competence is a political bank account of considerable value.

If special operations forces have a reputation for effectiveness, their use—or even just the announcement of their commitment—can have a deterring effect. The British prime minister's announcement in January 1976 that he was sending the SAS into South Armagh (Ireland) is an example of a potent political gesture with special operations forces. In 1964 and after, U.S. OPLAN 34A for cross-border special operations in Southeast Asia could not bear the political traffic that was asked of it.[16] For good reason, the Irish Republican Army (IRA) feared the SAS; in the mid-1960s Hanoi was not impressed with what its foes allowed themselves to attempt with special operations.

A reputation for the successful conduct of special operations will enhance a country's political standing. It should not be forgotten that states behave toward each other in security matters on the basis of generalized judgments about capacities, competence, and interests. Special operations are a way of asserting an interest in a manner that speaks clearly, yet risks breaking the least possible amount of china (among the military options, that is to say). As a superpower with global interests and a vital role to play as organizer for collective security, the United States needs all the political respect that special operations can supply.

By definition this claim applies only to peacetime or to conditions of low-intensity conflict. Special operations can make a political point only when their message is not overwhelmed by other events.

Reassurance

Special operations can reassure an angry or fearful public or ally that something is being done. Special operations can serve as politically expressive blows; they can function as a safety valve for an angry and frustrated public. Even if special operations are not planned or conducted competently, they can still help people cope with frustration. Desert One of 1980 was a failure and something of a political humiliation, but many people were proud that the United States had made the attempt. If a government is under pressure to act, special operations enable it to be seen doing something between the making of speeches and application of manifestly minor sanctions, and the conduct of full-fledged war.

Very occasionally the tactical failure of special operations may even be preferable, that is, yield more strategic utility, for a government than would tactical success. The disastrous Anglo-Canadian raid on Dieppe on 19 August 1942, for example, helped validate British policy and strategy toward a second front. Had Dieppe been a tactical triumph, London would have been embarrassed. Operation Rice Bowl of 1980, the U.S. rescue attempt which ended at Desert One, could have been something of a no-lose venture for President Carter. If it succeeded, he would take the credit. If it failed, he would take the credit for trying and would be proved right in the eyes of many people for having been so reluctant to launch the attempt.

Special operations as politically expressive blows have utility in all types of conflicts. The necessary political condition for this claim is simply one of public and perhaps official frustration. In such circumstances special operations will provide one answer to the question, What can we do?

Humiliation of the Enemy

Special operations can embarrass an enemy and make him lose face without triggering a much wider war. Special operations can damage an enemy's reputation by making him be seen to fail; they can thereby achieve a psychological (or moral) ascendancy.

Special operations can inflict exemplary punishment as well as actual loss. In spirit, at least, raids upon the libraries and art treasures of enemy leaders in the intercity and civil wars of Renaissance Italy illustrate this point.[17] During the war of attrition with Egypt in 1968–70, Israeli commandos attacked one of the "crown jewels" of the Egyptian economy, the Naj Hamadi transformer station and bridge which were 320 kilometers inside Egypt. These are examples of a state being revealed as unable to protect its assets.

Deep-penetration raids by Israeli commandos during the war of attrition were particularly humiliating to Egypt, because they affronted the pride and dignity of Nasser's government and because they were conducted by small light-infantry units. The individual warrior dimension to the typical light-infantry exploits of special operations forces make them especially well suited to humiliate a foe who takes pride in the martial qualities of his soldiers. It is one thing to be beaten by Israeli technology—or Israeli-improved American technology—but it is quite another to be shown to fail against handfuls of Israeli soldiers on the ground. The Doolittle raid on Tokyo in 1942 and Wingate's Chindits in 1943 were both humiliating to the Japanese. The former demonstrated that even the home islands were not safe, while the latter showed the Japanese that they could be outmarched and outfought. The Japanese had come to believe their own propaganda that they were supermen. Wingate and later Merrill showed them that they were wrong. In the words of a participant-historian: "The Wingate expeditions in 1943 and 1944 went a long way towards destroying the myth that the Japanese were some kind of supermen, able to dominate the jungle without apparent effort. Oceans of ink have been spilt about Wingate, and the Chindits, some praising him, some decrying. But that one fact about him is incontrovertible: he put an end to the myth of the Japanese superman."[18]

This claim for the strategic utility of special operations applies to all levels of conflict and to both independent and supporting missions. Whatever the character of the conflict, a moral ascendancy over the enemy means that they are already half defeated, because they no longer believe they can win. Special operations can be designed to demoralize the enemy.

Control Escalation

Special operations can limit the scope and intensity of a conflict.

1. Special operations can control escalation. Whatever the strategic utility generated, special operations by definition are small in scale. It is much easier for a foe to choose to ignore small-scale operations than large-scale regular operations. Also, special operations make it more likely that the enemy will respond with a similarly low level of violence. The British during a "confrontation" with Indonesia in Borneo in 1964–66 and the IDF throughout its history have exemplified the discreet use of force for the dampening of escalation dangers, while still meeting their objectives.

A political message and deterrence were the purposes behind the cross-border raiding by Israel in the 1950s, 1960s, and 1970s, by Britain in Borneo in 1964–66, and by the United States under OPLAN 34A after 1964 in Southeast Asia. In none of these cases did the raiding trigger an escalatory response. Naturally, whether or not escalation ensues is a function of the total context of the conflict at issue.

In high-intensity war the counterescalatory value of special operations is probably irrelevant. But in low- and particularly mid-intensity conflicts, special operations can provide major alternatives to the escalation of the combat.

2. Special operations can succeed while inflicting and suffering only a few casualties. Cultures differ in their attitudes toward casualties. Nonetheless, the small scale, tight focus, and precision of special operations all but guarantee that casualties on both sides will be low. Since high casualties, particularly among "the innocent" (i.e., unwanted "collateral damage"), are an especially potent fuel for escalation, the precision of special operations is an important factor for the control of conflict. The British government in 1964 required its armed forces to defeat the Indonesians with a low-casualty strategy,[19] while Israel throughout its history typically—though not at the outset of the October War of 1973—has pursued an offensive irregular style of war well suited to its outnumbered condition.

The less popular a conflict, the greater the political sensitivity to casualties. It follows that the necessarily small tactical scale of special operations is uniquely appropriate in protracted low-intensity conflicts, when public support is frequently ambiguous. Also, the general character of special operations—of finesse, stealth, and precision, rather than brute force—can provide a military option for policymakers when no other alternatives are likely to be both effective and low in the casualties they claim.

Shaping the Future

Special operations as a contributor to unconventional warfare can help shape the future course of political events. The first four specific claims pertain to the value of special operations in or as a part of unconventional warfare in the context of high- or even mid-intensity conflict.

1. Special operations can prepare the political ground in wartime for postoccupation power struggles. In Yugoslavia in World War II, Britain's SOE played a vital role in shaping the political future of the country. SOE helped Tito to survive and defeat his internal and German and Italian foes, thereby strengthening his prestige as the liberator of Yugoslavia. As the liberator of his own country, Tito was uniquely positioned to resist Soviet imperialism.

2. Special operations can shape people's views of their occupier and of the war as a whole. By providing "resisters with backbone, with steely support to uphold the good cause against the bad,"[20] SOE, OSS, and Spetsnaz operatives both encouraged subject peoples to resist and obliged the occupier to wage war against the inhabitants of what could have been quiet rear areas. (Note, however, that conditions have to be favorable—special operations cannot function as specified here in all political and military contexts.)

3. Special operations enable a temporarily disadvantaged state or regime to regain or retain some political control over its people under enemy occupation. Soviet partisan activity behind the German lines had political control of the inhabitants as a major objective. The heavy hand of the Soviet state could be felt in the occupied U.S.S.R. via the agents of Moscow sent into the German rear areas.

4. Special operations demonstrate political will and commitment. Special operations demonstrate a continuing political interest in an area. To insert special operations forces into a country is a more tangible and impressive gesture of political interest than bombardment from the air or the sea. SOE and OSS activities throughout Europe and Asia in World War II had this objective. But the strategic value of special operations will not be significant in the absence of a local belief in our eventual victory.

5. Special operations can alter the cast of players and their relative slate of assets in the politics of a particular country or region. Political warfare, with the assistance of special operations, can undermine an enemy regime. Imperial Germany altered the cast of leading actors in Russian politics in 1917 in order to destroy Kerensky's pro-Allied government. Italy waged political-psychological warfare in 1917–18 to undermine the fragile cohesion of the Austro-Hungarian Empire. In World War II, the OSS in Vichy-controlled North Africa sought to promote French political leaders as alternatives to General Charles de Gaulle.

One can design special operations of a military or political-psychological nature for the purpose of securing strategic effect on the political level of conflict; this can be achieved in conflicts of all kinds.

THE OTHER SIDE OF THE COIN: THE POTENTIAL STRATEGIC DISUTILITY OF SPECIAL OPERATIONS

This analysis views the strategic utility of special operations as a continuum possessing both positive and negative values. Many of the broad claims for strategic utility identified above carry implicit meaning for potential disutility. This section presents some of the negative values of special operations.

First, special operations have the potential to alert the enemy to the prospect and perhaps the direction of an attack by regular forces. For example, "The Delta Force team's assault caused the alarm to be raised all over the island [of Grenada]. Key points were reinforced as local army and militia men prepared for the U.S. invasion."[21] While special operations forces can perform a vital function in deception and intelligence-gathering missions, their presence in the enemy rear can increase the wariness of one's opponent. In the Falklands campaign in 1982, British regular force commanders were concerned over what conclusions the enemy might draw from the activities by special operations forces that they detected. Even when military planners are careful to avoid tipping operational intentions through the use of special operations forces, there always remains some risk of the enemy correctly deciphering the purpose behind a pattern of deception. Nonetheless, the record of special operations yields only a few cases where special operations forces alerted the enemy to an attack by regular forces.

Second, if it is true that special operations can enhance political respect, it is likewise true that failure can diminish national standing. The point has been made already that positive strategic value can derive even from special operations that are tactical failures. But for that to be the case, heroism may have to compensate for operational failure so that public perceptions of the raiders or their political sponsors are favorable.

When one launches a special operation against a background of perceived military failure—for example, the Iranian hostage-rescue mission of April 1980—the potential risk or benefit to national standing may be equal. The Desert One debacle reinforced foreign and American perception that the U.S. military establishment was "the gang that could not shoot straight." When political leaders risk national prestige with a special operations coup, they need to weigh carefully the quality of their country's military instrument. One should recall the "special operations paradox" cited earlier.[22] A country that resorts to a special operation in order to refurbish a tarnished military reputation must consider whether its special warfare establishment is likely to perform to greater strategic effect than its regular forces. There are exceptions, but as a general rule, a country unable to wage war as a whole effectively is not likely to conduct special operations competently. When a nation employs special operations forces, or elite forces more generally, in lieu of regular forces that are either missing, incompetent, or otherwise not available, the final outcome in the war is unlikely to be positive. The problem will not lie with the special operations forces, but rather with strategy or the armed forces as a whole.

Third, there have been cases when the strategic value of special operations has been offset by public revulsion to the brutality of the means employed. Due to the high-risk character of special operations, they are not well known for gentlemanly conduct, and military discipline can be difficult to apply. The experience of irregular operations behind the enemy lines by small groups of soldiers can produce a code of behavior that does not serve the national political cause well at all.

For example, French special forces in Indochina and Algeria contained "thugs" who frequently functioned as private armies. Brutality, warlordism, and private armies are by no means hazards unique to special forces. But the character of conflict that special forces wage and the circumstances in which they wage it render the peril of strategically dysfunctional thuggery unusually severe. Hard situations call for hard men and hard methods. Again, however, this is only a caveat—a warning of danger. There is reason to believe that the thuggish behavior of French elite forces in Algeria was as unnecessary for success, indeed was counterproductive, as it was historically unusual among special operations. As a general rule, decent treatment of civilian bystanders (possible allies) and of enemy prisoners is very much in the self-interest of special operations forces.

Fourth, it is worth emphasizing that when one expands special operations forces beyond handfuls of heroes to the level of brigades or more, those forces are all but certain to drain critical high-quality personnel from the regular forces. It is perilous to generalize on this subject, because of the variableness of local and historical circumstances. However, there can be no doubt that after being established in World War II, Britain's SAS and SBS have since been kept so restricted and so well integrated within the regular military establishment that this caveat on "skimming" does not apply. But in 1940–43, British Army Commandos did become much too large relative to their potential net strategic value. Indeed, growth in their numbers obscured their true military function. (The creation of the SAS was specifically in reaction to the growing unwieldiness of the commandos.) The history of the U.S. Army's Ranger battalions and of the Marine Corps raider battalions similarly has shown the ill effects of ambivalence over military functions. To repeat, special operations forces, by definition, are small in scale and are dedicated to the performance of "special" high-risk, high-payoff tasks with a minimal quantitative commitment of human and material resources. If those forces are allowed to grow because of the fallacious belief that if a few special operations forces are good, a great many must be a lot better, then the much expanded forces understandably will be given missions suitable to battalion- and brigade-size entities. There may be a need for elite shock troops in quite large numbers, but those troops are not special forces.

Fifth, it is a universal human trait to resent people and organizations whose designation as being somehow "special" carries unflattering implications about the nonspecial character of others. If special just means specialized, that is one thing. It is quite another to advertise special forces as unusually elite in their martial virtue as well as in their recruitment. In the words of an SAS memoir, "[e]litism is counter-productive, it alienates you from other people and we depend on a working relationship with many other groups."[23] Perception of a "prima donna" quality to special forces rapidly escalates to an active and mutual antagonism with negative consequences for operations. The result will be the use of special forces on inappropriate missions, while regular-irregular antipathy may preclude the exploitation of their tactical success.

Sixth, few political leaders can resist the promise of the apparently free lunch—the great result for little effort. It can be perilous to advise political leaders that special operations forces "can produce results that far outweigh their numbers. . . . You can demand anything of them, any God damn thing you can name, and you can name it with impunity, without any hesitation. But it takes good leaders, good training, people who know their business."[24] These expansive claims, in this case advanced by an experienced commander of special operations forces, are not true as stated. At least, one must qualify the claims by reference to the conditions friendly for the prospects for success.[25] Some political leaders have romanticized war of a personalized and "special" character and have taken literally the kinds of generalized claims for the utility of special operations that people make. Given the frequently politically embattled position of special operations forces vis-à-vis regular forces, there is a general reluctance by leaders of special operations forces to emphasize their limitations.

One might recall the point advanced in Chapter 7 that special operations forces require protection from the enthusiasm of their political sponsors, as well as from their critics. There are circumstances when the tactical success of special operations is improbable or when tactically successful special operations would have little strategic value.

Seventh, by their nature special operations possess the ability to embarrass their political masters. In times of nominal peace, and even in some distinctly "limited" wars, the conduct of special operations *in the enemy's territory* carries political implications that can be positive, negative, or both. When one side uses neutral or otherwise nonbelligerent countries as sanctuaries, the temptation exists for the other side to level the playing field by operating in those sanctuaries clandestinely, covertly, or perhaps even overtly but in a controlled way. Examples of this phenomenon abound, but U.S. cross-border activities in Southeast Asia in the 1960s and early 1970s and activities by the British in Kalimantan in Borneo in 1964–66, in the Irish Republic in the 1970s, and on the mainland of Argentina in 1982 all highlight the relevant incentives, risks, and sensitivities.

Eighth, mention was made earlier in this chapter of the strategic utility of special operations as a tool for the humiliation of the enemy. The negative side of that function is that it might cause the targeted foe to escalate the political situation. A problem with the demonstrative punitive theory of deterrence is that measured punishment may stimulate a determination to wreak vengeance rather than teach the lesson that aggression does not pay. This is not an argument against the political demonstrative value of special operations, but it suggests that before one targets a regime for punishment, one should take care to ensure a total context of deterrence and defense for the discouragement of escalation. Every target regime will have some escalatory options. It is the responsibility of the policy planner to ensure that special operations fit within the strategic view of the conflict as a whole.

Finally, special operations may have the effect of strengthening the resolve of an enemy, rather than softening him up. Whenever war is taken to the enemy, the possibility exists that the strategic result will be the reverse of what one intended. If one raids an area friendly to the enemy, the likely political outcome is an increased dependence of the population on the government (the people's protector). Raiding can help legitimize, for reasons of security, a more intrusive pattern of political control. There is reason to believe that the U.S. cross-border activities in Southeast Asia in the 1960s, particularly into North Vietnam, had the net effect of strengthening Hanoi's political grip. With respect to special operations into enemy-occupied territory, one must not forget the risks which local resisters face. Special operations may oblige occupied peoples to commit themselves in a war wherein prudence suggests that neutrality is the safest course vis-à-vis their distant allies. However, the conduct of special operations may result in people committing themselves in favor of an oppressive occupier for the sake of their families. Moreover, the reprisals which an occupying power may conduct can generate hatred not only against that occupier, but also against the country which set in motion the events which resulted in the reprisals. Very few of the relevant histories of World War II, for a case in point, attempt a strategic and human/moral accounting of the price paid by subject peoples for their support of special operations activities.[26]

These nine caveats are simply that, warnings. None of these nine detract from the strength of the claims advanced earlier for the strategic utility of special operations. Indeed, those claims when drafted took these caveats fully in mind. Moreover, just as there are caveats pertaining to the utility of special operations forces, so there are caveats relevant to the unique strategic value of air power or sea power, for example, as earlier chapters of this book have made explicit. Furthermore, the claims for utility outlined above depend upon favorable conditions. Neither these caveats nor those conditions contradict the argument advanced for the multifaceted strategic utility of special operations.

A BALANCED ASSESSMENT

As Chapter 7 suggested, it is useful to organize the assessment of the strategic utility of special operations forces on the basis of four questions. It should help to make sense of the claims, arguments, points, and caveats about the strategic utility of special operations forces if one asks: (1) What is it that only special operations forces can do? (2) What is it that special operations forces can do well? (3) What is it that special operations forces tend to do poorly? (4) What is it that special operations forces cannot do at all? Answers to these questions are given in Table 8.2.

It is possible to argue that special operations forces are of greatest strategic utility in peacetime or in low-intensity conflicts, which are the contexts wherein they uniquely provide military or paramilitary options to policymakers with acute security problems. Nonetheless, one must reject that argument. The reason lies in discerning the difference between absolute and relative strategic value. Relative to all other military capabilities, special operations forces certainly will dominate in peacetime and low-intensity conflict conditions. But, the absolute strategic value of special operations forces in a mid-intensity conflict, let alone a high-intensity one, is likely to outweigh their value in wars of low intensity. Nonetheless, low intensity does not mean low importance. Furthermore, the contexts of peacetime or of low-intensity conflict are the most common. Strategic utility in mid- or high-intensity conflicts generally is hypothetical. The strategic value of special operations forces depends not just on how well or poorly they perform, but also on how important for the war as a whole are their assigned missions.

Of the broad findings in this chapter on strategic utility, the two most important categories are economy of force and expansion of choice. Much of what special operations can accomplish uniquely—though not necessarily wholly independently—or which they tend to do well bears more or less directly upon these two central ideas. It is the closeness of fit between the character of special operations forces and of special operations—properly understood—and the idea of economy of force which propels these judgments. However, just as it would be foolish to confuse the force multiplication potential of special operations with actual achievement, it would also be foolish to look for some allegedly decisive value in the strategic utility of such

Table 8.2
Utility of Special Operations Forces

1. *What, uniquely, can special operations do?*
   - Establish and maintain personal contact with people in enemy-occupied territory and encourage and support them in their struggle to be free.
   - Wage unconventional warfare—as guerrillas or as counterguerrillas.
   - Execute clandestine, and hence deniable, coups.
   - Humiliate an enemy, on the ground, person to person, deep in his supposedly secure hinterland.
   - Secure and update in real time precise intelligence on enemy targets not accessible to airborne or space sensors.
   - Solve politically sensitive security problems swiftly, precisely, and cheaply.

2. *What can special operations forces do well?*
   - Embarrass an enemy.
   - Wage conflict relatively (to regular forces) cheaply—with reference to resources committed and casualties (on both sides).
   - Act as a very economical force multiplier for the rest of the armed forces.
   - Deceive, distract, and disrupt the enemy, again at low cost.
   - Protract resistance even in circumstances of comprehensive, if temporary, defeat.
   - Provide tangible local evidence of continuing political commitment to a conflict.
   - Seize the initiative, if only briefly, and put the enemy on the defensive.
   - Capture and retrieve (or interrogate) small numbers of people or physically small items of equipment from enemy territory.
   - Entice the enemy into operational, strategic, or political error (e.g., overextension).
   - Control escalation.
   - Innovate in military method and equipment.
   - Raise friendly morale by daring deeds.
   - Send a political message for deterrence by demonstrating the will and ability to strike painfully.
   - Reassure the public that something is being done.

3. *What do special operations forces tend to do poorly?*
   - Attrite the enemy in large numbers.
   - Seize and hold distant objectives.

4. *What are special operations forces unable to do?*
   - Defeat large enemy forces on their own.
   - Win mid- or high-intensity conflicts by themselves or even play decisive roles in such conflicts. (Special operations forces can generate great strategic utility in mid- and high-intensity wars, but those conflicts are team efforts.)

operations. In most cases of national need and certainly in conditions of high- or mid-intensity warfare, special operations forces will more than pay their way if they contribute significantly to final victory. The historical record indicates that that is a more than reasonable expectation.

NOTES

1. The findings and overall argument in this chapter rest upon the evidence developed in the form of historical case studies in Colin S. Gray, ed., *Special Operations: What Succeeds and Why? Lessons of Experience, Phase I*, Final Report (Fairfax, VA: National Institute for Public Policy, June 1992).

2. A superb, methodologically innovative study related in approach to this analysis is Allan R. Millett and Williamson Murray, eds., *Military Effectiveness*, 3 vols. (Boston: Allen and Unwin, 1988).

3. This observation applies with particular clarity to Desert Storm 1991.

4. Kenneth Macksey, *Commando Strike: The Story of Amphibious Raiding in World War II* (London: Leo Cooper, 1985), p. 212.

5. Field-Marshal Viscount Slim, *Defeat into Victory* (London: Papermac, 1986; first pub. 1956), p. 547.

6. Carl von Clausewitz, *On War*, ed. and trans. Michael Howard and Peter Paret (Princeton, NJ: Princeton University Press, 1976; first pub. 1832), p. 75.

7. Macksey, *Commando Strike*, pp. 208–9.

8. See Gray, ed., *Special Operations*, chaps. 4, 6, and 7; M. R. D. Foot, *SOE in France: An Account of the British Special Operations Executive in France, 1940–1944* (London: HMSO, 1966); and George C. Chalou, ed., *The Secrets War: The Office of Strategic Services in World War II* (Washington, DC: National Archives and Records Administration, 1992).

9. See R. V. Jones, *Most Secret War* (London: Coronet Books, 1979; first pub. 1978), chap. 27.

10. See Paul A. Smith, Jr., *On Political War* (Washington, DC: National Defense University Press, 1989), chap. 5.

11. See Gray, ed., *Special Operations*, chap. 8; Roger A. Beaumont, *Military Elites in the Modern World* (Indianapolis, IN: Bobbs-Merrill, 1974), pp. 103–11; and Eliot A. Cohen, *Commandos and Politicians: Elite Military Units in Modern Democracies* (Cambridge, MA: Harvard University, Center for International Affairs, 1978), pp. 62–63, 65–70, 81–83.

12. H. P. Willmott, *The Barrier and the Javelin: Japanese and Allied Pacific Strategies, February to June 1942* (Annapolis, MD: Naval Institute Press, 1983), p. 118.

13. See John W. Gordon, "Wingate," in John Keegan, ed., *Churchill's Generals* (New York: Grove Weidenfield, 1991), p. 293.

14. Ray E. Stratton and August G. Jannarone, "Toward a Strategic Targeting Doctrine for Special Operations Forces," *Air University Review* 36, no. 5 (July/August 1985): 24–29, is useful.

15. Gordon, "Wingate," p. 295.

16. See Gray, ed., *Special Operations*, chap. 9.

17. See ibid., chap. 3.

18. James Lunt, *The Retreat from Burma, 1941–1942* (Newton Abbott, England: David and Charles Publishers, 1989; first pub. 1986), p. 285.

19. See Gray, ed., *Special Operations*, chap. 10.

20. Foot, *SOE*, p. 359.

21. James Adams, *Secret Armies* (London: Pan Books, 1989; first pub. 1988), p. 238. In the context of Operation Desert Storm, the U.S. Department of Defense has offered the opinion that "use of Special Operations capabilities requires difficult tradeoffs between the potential political risk that often accompanies the conduct of special operations and military advantage they can generate. Pre-hostility and cross-border operations can provide both tactical and operational level advantages to general purpose force commanders; however, inadvertent disclosure or compromise of these activities can signal strategic objectives, incurring both military and political repercussions." *Conduct of the Persian Gulf Conflict: An Interim Report to the Congress* (Washington, DC: U.S. Department of Defense, July 1991), pp. 5–6. The understandable, if frequently exaggerated, fears of military commanders in this regard tend to have a blunting effect upon the special warfare instrument. More often than not, military commanders would appear ignorant of or indifferent toward the opportunity costs that they incur by an all but reflexive "leashing" of special operations forces prior to the formal opening of hostilities.

22. See Chapter 7.

23. Andy McNab, *Immediate Action* (London: Bantam Press, 1995), p. 381.

24. Col. Arthur D. "Bull" Simons, the leader of the 1970 Son Tay POW rescue mission, quoted in Benjamin F. Schemmer, *The Raid* (New York: Avon Books, 1976), pp. 287–88.

25. See Gray, ed., *Special Operations*, chap. 17.

26. It is interesting and perhaps reassuring to read in Foot's history of the Special Operations Executive that "[e]veryone, from the king and the prime minister down to the humblest sub-sub-agent, was perpetually obsessed with the problem of reprisals, as they might be wreaked by an axis secret police force against the innocent abroad" (p. 61). The argument that the human cost of popular resistance to Nazi occupation was incomparably higher than was its strategic value to the Allied cause is advanced in John Keegan, *The Second World War* (London: Hutchinson, 1989), chap. 26. Keegan is scornfully dismissive of "a powerful lobby of historians, some of whom were its former officers," who, he alleges, have "puffed" the strategic significance of SOE (p. 495). Foot, it should be noted, served in the SAS, not in SOE.

Chapter 9

Special Operations Forces and Defense Planning

In a brilliant analysis in May 1954 that merits continuing appreciation, Samuel P. Huntington wrote as follows:

> The fundamental element of a military service is its purpose or role in implementing national policy. The statement of this role may be called the *strategic concept* of the service. Basically, this concept is a description of how, when, and where the military service expects to protect the nation against some threat to its security. If a military service does not possess such a concept, it becomes purposeless, it wallows about amid a variety of conflicting and confusing goals, and ultimately it suffers both moral and physical degeneration.[1]

Of course, special operations forces do not comprise a service, and in these times, wherein "joint," even "combined," endeavors are high in favor, one must look to the overall effectiveness of military forces. Nonetheless, Huntington's argument remains relevant. Special operations forces contribute effectiveness to the great enterprises of state, either in joint efforts or on autonomous missions, through application of their own distinctive character and virtues. To adapt Huntington's formulation, there is need for a strategic concept of special operations forces. That concept has to identify tersely and accurately what is distinctive and what is distinctively valuable about those forces. The concept must stake out a unique mission or mission area and preferably provide some general clues to the basic nature of special operations forces, yet it should not be framed so as to be competitive with other distinctive elements of military power.

Although this formulation is far from comprising the totality of what they do, special operations forces have as their strategic concept the conduct of small-scale, high-risk/high-payoff, unorthodox operations that are outside the bounds of regular warfare. Depending critically upon surprise—to compensate for their modest numbers and firepower—special operations forces undertake missions that regular forces either cannot perform or cannot perform at acceptable cost. In addition to surprise, the success of special operations typically depends upon appropriately unconventional training and equipment. In peacetime those operations are likely to be conducted for purposes, and in conditions, of great political sensitivity.

Associates of the strategic concept just stated are the two master effects or consequences of special operations capabilities developed in Chapter 8. Those effects are economy of force and expansion of choice. Special operations forces are by no means unique among military instruments in being able to act economically as force multipliers and as option expanders, but their nature (modest costs, small scale, precision, and flexibility) renders them distinctively valuable in these key regards. Of the five well-established primary missions for special operations forces—foreign internal defense, special reconnaissance, direct action, counterterrorism, and unconventional warfare—only foreign internal defense lacks a strong flavor of direct action. The discussion in this chapter focuses upon special operations forces and what the country may require of them, rather than upon special operations per se.

THE NEW SECURITY ENVIRONMENT

Notwithstanding the many uncertainties of the emerging, post–Cold War security environment, the structure and functioning of that environment are easier to predict than are the specific implications for U.S. policy. The problem is not only to divine the shape and workings of the emerging security environment, but also to determine what roles the United States will want to play. Advocates of special warfare often describe the capabilities in question and proceed to characterize the shape of the security world to be, but fail to connect the two intelligibly. For the puzzle to be assembled so as to constitute a coherent picture, none of the principal pieces must be neglected.

The new security environment, the changing U.S. domestic context, and the evolving capabilities of U.S. military power (including special operations forces) will each lack a general meaning for U.S. foreign policy. For example, to observe the former Yugoslavia in a condition of complex civil and international war is not to identify any particular U.S. foreign policy. Similarly, to note what U.S. military power *could* do in a specific case is not synonymous with high-policy choice. Capability can influence decisions on behavior, just as foreign misbehavior influences foreign policy choices. But, still, a critical filter is absent. That filter traditionally is called the national interest or is treated plurally as national interests.

It is common to find assertions that national interests are at risk; it is less common to find consensus over how much they are at risk and, as a consequence, what ought to be done about that alleged fact. Bold statements on the subject of preferred action should rest upon the availability of instruments of grand strategy. The pieces of the puzzle addressed here can be expressed as follows:

- What is happening in the world?
- How much does the United States care about a particular development or event?
- Shall the United States act—and to accomplish what?
- What instrument or instruments of policy shall be used?
- If the military instrument is used, what role, if any, should special operations forces play?

The new security environment can be discussed as if it were something "out there," beyond the national frontiers, but in fact the United States is an integral part of that environment (like man in "nature"). Certainly the United States looms large in the security environment of many other states. States and their security environments interact, but some states have much more of a shaping effect upon their environment than do others. The question of just how malleable the external world is, or should be, to U.S. wishes has long been a highway of public debate.

It is important to begin this analysis with frank recognition of a key, but largely unappreciated, quality to this era. Namely, the 1990s are not a post-war period, as some would like to think, but rather an interwar (and hence prewar) period. In 1919, Great Britain adopted the assumption that it would not be involved in a major war for ten years; this "ten-year rule" enjoyed official blessing until 1932.[2] Today, it is no exaggeration to say that there is a broad consensus in the United States upon such a ten-year rule, while many people probably would be willing to sign on for twenty- or even thirty-year variants, and a few nurture the conviction that major war truly is obsolescent, if not definitively obsolete. It may be of interest to note that several times in U.S. history an extravagantly optimistic view of a peaceful future for the nation has been popular. The 1870s and 1920s provide leading examples of the recurring popularity of this belief. Nothing in the past proves anything about the future, since the course of history is unique and deeply contingent. Nonetheless, an awareness of history at least encourages humility and caution in the face of the temptation boldly to predict a radically different future.

Popular democracies perennially have difficulty keeping their swords sharp in a long period of peace. There are several examples from U.S. history of the armed forces descending precipitately from the first rank in quantity and quality to near impotence in a handful of years. The willingness of a democracy to reduce its ready military prowess in the absence of a clear and present danger should not be underestimated. If more and more people slip into the column of endorsing ten-year, then twenty-year, then thirty-year rules or more, the U.S. armed forces increasingly will reflect the fact. Those armed forces are an expression and an instrument of American society.

If the utility of U.S. special operations forces in the new security environment must flow from responses to the demands of policy, what are the more important features of that still-emerging environment?

1. *Continuity in goals and methods of statecraft.*[3] Without denying the fact of massive cumulative change in the structure of the international system, there is no evidence to suggest that the character of international politics and security relations is in transition to some order resting upon alternative organizing principles. Time after time in international history, old "orders" have gone and new "orders" have come. The teams and relationships may be different in the future from those of the Cold War era, but there is every reason to believe that the "game" of security politics will continue along familiar lines, for familiar goals, and by familiar methods. The use or threat of force and the value of alliance, as contrasted with genuinely collective (all but universal) security guarantees, are not obviously in general decline.

The idea that major war will go the way of the duel into social obsolescence is simply a pleasing speculation. If anything, military power may well be more useful a tool of statecraft in this post–Cold War era than was the case from 1945 until 1990, given the absence of plausible powder trails to a nuclear World War III. The fact that military conquest as the path to national greatness and pride is unfashionable in what used to be known as Western Europe (before the geopolitical concept of Eastern Europe lost its meaning) is not solid evidence of any general trend.

Implications for special operations forces: There are no general transnational trends unique to the 1990s in the realm of the legitimacy or illegitimacy of force. The utility of special operations forces must depend upon choices in foreign policy. The evaporation for a while of the possibility of high-intensity conflict leaves intact, in principle, the possibilities for U.S. participation in the kinds of lower-intensity conflicts for which special operations forces are especially well adapted.

2. *Unusual salience for economic strength and economic rivalry.*[4] This feature of the new security environment is not new, nor does it point to insights uniquely relevant to the post–Cold War world. Muddled thinking underlies the proposition that the advanced industrial states are entering, or have already

entered, a new security environment wherein economic antagonisms will take the place of yesterday's political-military rivalries. Economic rivalry and quests after an economic security defined in a distinctly non-defense-oriented way are the products of a permissive political-military context. Britain and the United States were great trading rivals for much of the first half of the twentieth century. Because their political relations, reflecting a compatibility of vital interests, were fundamentally amicable, there was never a plausible prospect of Anglo-American armed conflict.[5] Humankind is not evolving from conditions of political-military conflict toward or actually into political-economic conflict. Neither individuals nor states are governed wholly by economic considerations. The least criticism that might be ventured of the proposition that "geoeconomics" is replacing geopolitics is that it is premature.[6]

The new salience of economic strength and economic rivalry, which has attracted half-baked political-economic theories of international politics, reflects the current permissive political climate, as could be said of the 1920s. The demise of a former dominant pattern in political-military power relationships, and a subsequent liberty on the part of former and still-formal allies to advance parochial economic interests are not the same as the triumph of economic over military power. Military power has to be an expression of mobilized economic power. To claim that the 1990s are witnessing some allegedly novel significance for economic strength misunderstands both the present and the past. After all, the U.S.S.R. and the Russian empire failed in the 1980s for reasons that were at least as much economic as political. The economic failure is revealed beyond doubt. The latest Russian revolution is still unfinished business.

To those politicians and theorists who have leapt upon the bandwagon of economic security, one can only say that they have strange views of the course of modern history. The U.S. economy was the most fundamental reason the North won the Civil War and the Allies won the two world wars. The point is that there is much less that is novel to this feature of the new security environment than meets the casual eye.

Implications for special operations forces: The current absence of a major scale of active military rivalry among the great powers carries no general implication for the strategic utility of U.S. special operations forces. It is only through the U.S. foreign policy response to the new security environment that special operations forces acquire strategic relevance. Although in theory the disappearance of credible connections between small-scale violence and nuclear holocaust renders world politics much safer for conduct of the former, in practice the incentives for the United States to be active or proactive in the world are changing and diminishing. No general conclusions should be drawn regarding the future utility of strategic operations forces from the current high visibility of political-economic, as contrasted with political-military, antagonisms.

3. *Absence of superpower and great-power political-military rivalry.* This is a historically unique condition. It is not particularly unusual for there to be a period wherein contemporary commentators discern scant risk of major war, but it is unprecedented in modern times for there to be no noteworthy political-military antagonism among the great powers. Realistically viewed, the great powers of the 1990s are the United States, Russia, China, Germany, and Japan. With the minor exception of border controversy between Japan and Russia, there are no very meaningful strategic relations among these polities, let alone political-military antagonisms. The ongoing Russian revolution has unraveled the international security system familiar for half a century. Many plausible possibilities exist for the return of balance-of-power security politics, but at this time the pattern of future rivalry is not predictable. The capabilities for dangerously rogue behavior, however, along with ample political motives and historical opportunity, will be present in abundance in Europe and Asia.

Implications for special operations forces: The absence of superpower or even great-power rivals to the United States in the 1990s means that the risks of special operations are far less than heretofore. There is no powder trail to nuclear holocaust. Similarly, there is no global rival to exploit any local embarrassment a special operation might cause. The other side of the coin is that the localization of security issues restricts the significance of local success. There is less to lose, but less to win.

4. *The United States as the solitary superpower.* There is a sense in which the United States always was the only multidimensional, "full-service" superpower. With the Cold War interred and the principal adversary of yesteryear consigned to history's garbage heap, there is a nontrivial possibility—indeed an emerging probability—that the United States inadvertently may contribute to the losing of the peace, notwithstanding having just won the Cold War. In the absence of a clear and present great-power danger, it is more likely that far from succumbing to some alleged "imperial temptation,"[7] the United States will behave as if permanent peace has arrived. Americans have an admirable track record in undertaking and succeeding with great enterprises, but their performance has been less assured on tasks that call for finesse and subtlety.[8] (Historically, the uneasy relationship between the U.S. Army, indeed the U.S. armed forces as a whole, and special operations forces makes this point.)[9] The United States has become used to enjoying hegemonic security relationships, first in the Americas, then globally with anti-Soviet polities. The idea of exercising a subtle cooperative, consensual guardianship over an international system struggling to settle upon new patterns of security is not an idea that sits well with U.S. taxpayers. It is one thing to organize, lead, arm, and partially bankroll a global alliance against the evil empire of the U.S.S.R. It is quite something else to play the role of helpful guardian to economic rivals who are striving, in part, to liberate themselves from their condition as security wards of U.S. superpower.

U.S. foreign policy in the aftermath of the Cold War lacks a concrete sense of true north, although the U.S. government appreciates well enough that the compass bearing for significant danger points to some maldistribution of power in the hands of polities unfriendly to U.S. interests.

Implications for special operations forces: Since U.S. foreign and defense policy lacks a dominant functional or regional focus, so too must the missions of U.S. special operations forces. Given the versatility, readiness, flexibility, option-expanding, and force-multiplying merits of those forces, the fact of a disparate array of actual or potential duties is a matter of limited significance.

5. *Adaptation of Cold War security structures*. Organizations and modes of behavior must adjust to change or risk becoming obsolescent and ineffective. NATO, the most successful collective defense organization in history, has evolved in detail continuously from its founding in 1949. Few coalitions created for a specific purpose succeed in surviving the passing of that purpose. Occasionally a coalition is transformed into an empire, as happened with Athens in the Delian League in the 470s and 460s B.C.,[10] but more often a grand alliance either dissolves in acrimony or just withers and dies when the political glue provided by yesterday's threat evaporates. Successful coalitions carry the seeds of their own destruction.

At present, the trend in international security structures is generally benign. Cold War–era alliance and mutual security ties have not been overturned precipitately (with the exception of U.S.-Filipino relations), but rather have been adjusted in the light of new conditions of regional security. It is recognized widely on both sides of the Atlantic that the most significant of NATO roles now are to keep the United States actively engaged in security in Europe and, as a consequence, to reduce or foreclose upon the dimensions of the traditional "German problem." From the time of Otto von Bismarck's inauguration of the new German empire in 1871 until the fall of the Third Reich in 1945, the central problem of European security was an overly powerful Germany.

NATO retains its familiar orientation toward collective defense, though it is under some pressure to tilt toward a collective security system. The alliance is focusing upon regional instabilities and helps uniquely to keep the United States actively engaged on the European continent.[11] There is no guarantee, however, that the pace of U.S. regional force-structure reductions and homeward pattern of redeployment will not assume an all but free-fall character in the absence of clear and present major peril. The reasons remain potent for continued U.S. participation as a player in regional power balances. But there is little in U.S. history to suggest the willingness of the polity to play a multidimensional ordering role when dominant scenarios of national peril are absent. In principle, the disappearance of Soviet threats to U.S. survival interests allows the country to redefine permissively those interests it elects to treat as vital, which is to say worth fighting to protect or advance. In practice, though, the ending of Soviet threats had a ripple effect which downgraded most erstwhile vital interests to the categories of major or even just "other" interests (see the next section). During the Cold War, much that was deemed vital, worth fighting for, was so precisely because it bore directly upon the Soviet-U.S. struggle. If there is no single, dominant, life-or-death struggle as the national-security centerpiece, it is difficult to argue persuasively that any event abroad should trigger U.S. military action.

Implications for special operations forces: In a period when the intensity of many U.S. interests is eminently debatable, it is hard to explain plausibly to people familiar only with unambivalent menaces that special operations forces provide a uniquely useful array of low-visibility, or high-visibility but politically welcome, small-scale options to support policy. The full array of missions for special operations forces—that is, collateral mission areas[12] as well as foreign internal defense, special reconnaissance, counterterrorism, unconventional warfare, and classic direct action—covers a wide spectrum of policy-responsive activity in an era when perils are diffuse and often indirect and distant. No better example exists than that provided by the shifting NATO missions in Bosnia. Special operations forces are supporting the NATO-enforced "peace" in Bosnia across the board of their established structure of tasks.

6. *Increase in regional and local instability in Europe and the Middle East.* Yugoslavia was a train wreck waiting to happen since the founding of that multinational state in 1919 as a much expanded Serbia. The end of the Cold War meant that neither the U.S.S.R./Russia (the traditional protector of the Serbs) nor NATO played a strong hand in shaping events in Yugoslavia, while "Europe" is still in the process of becoming a strong security system. The implosion of the Soviet imperium, of the Soviet Union, and then even of the Russian empire occurred with remarkably little violence (relative to the potential, that is—or relative to conditions in the former Yugoslavia). Because of isolation and unique conditions, it is not obvious that sub-Saharan Africa or South America will be prey to more instability than would have occurred with the Cold War continuing. Of course, assistance by the U.S.S.R. and its surrogates and by the anti-Soviet Chinese made trouble in Africa, but that continent has trouble enough of a purely indigenous kind. Instability can be imported, but in Africa it is endemic for reasons of the politics of modernization and systemic poverty.

The ending of the Cold War in so rapid and thoroughgoing a manner inevitably has transformed Europe from geopolitically the most stable continent to the least stable. Even the geopolitical terms used for forty-five years no longer apply. Central Europe, or *Mitteleuropa*, a concept that had no political reality from 1945 to 1990, could become a force to be reckoned with again.[13] In the Middle East, as in Europe, the good news that Soviet policy no longer contributes to regional instability is offset by the bad news that that policy no longer restrains regional clients.

It would be agreeable to record that the renewed power of nationalism and of ethnic, religious-sectarian, and cultural identity—particularly in Central Europe, the Balkans, and the Middle East—is more than counterbalanced by the growth in free-market economies and popular democratic institutions. The jury is still out, and is likely long to remain out, on that macroscopic holistic issue. At present such progress as there has been toward democracy in formerly Soviet Europe, Africa, and Central and South America looks distinctly patchy, fragile, and reversible. From the Andes to the Balkans to the Gulf, it would be heroically premature to proclaim the end of history "as such."[14]

Implications for special operations forces: The facts of disorder and instability are undeniable. Both in regions long troubled and in areas where communities have been newly liberated to express their separate ambitions, these are, as the Chinese proverb would have it, interesting times. The question is not whether there are deeply troubled regions in the world, but rather whether such troubles matter very much to the United States. The fact of a disorderly region carries no inherent meaning for U.S. policy. As fuel for U.S. policy consideration, however, and as possible trigger for U.S. decisions to employ special operations forces, regional and local instability is rising rather than declining.

7. *Growing proliferation of high-technology weaponry, including weapons of mass destruction*. "Assertive disarmament" works, as the U.S.-led grand coalition demonstrated in Desert Storm and subsequently.[15] It is scarcely less obvious that classical measures of arms control do not work. The reason is sadly prominent in both logic and historical experience. Most of the arms control devices and proposals that appeal to responsible Americans have zero appeal in the capitals of most interest to U.S. arms control policy. Would-be rogue polities, such as Iraq and Iran, do not wish to eschew the pleasures of ownership of late-model and mass-destructive weaponry. Furthermore, from their particular points of view, they are correct. The problem is not weapons; it is the political ambitions that generate the requirements for weapons. In the aftermath of the Cold War there is a global surplus of high-technology weapons and weapon-making industrial capacity. Regardless of which, if any, theory of arms control has merit, the facts are that the world is well stocked with weapon suppliers eager to sell, with regional and local powers (and substate communities) eager to purchase, with weapons available for acquisition, and with unscrupulous middlemen.[16] There is no distinctive problem with the proliferation of missile systems or of the knowledge of nuclear, biological, and chemical (NBC) weapons. Rather, the problem is the political instability and disorder already discussed.[17] It is as certain as anything can be that the proliferation of ballistic missile and NBC technologies will proceed, at best slowed at the margin by arms control measures. Those particularly troubling weapon technologies can no more be kept out of the hands of would-be disturbers of regional order in the future than bombing aircraft, submarines,

and heavy artillery could be banned or restricted to "responsible" (or "civilized")[18] polities in the 1918–39 period. The proliferation of missile and NBC technologies could well alter U.S. risk-benefit calculations vis-à-vis intervention in local or regional political quarrels.

Implications for special operations forces: To search for, gather intelligence upon, and damage or destroy particular weapons often is cited mistakenly as a novel mission for special operations forces. In fact, there are many historical precedents. When feasible, sabotage of a foe's "trump" weapon always has been attractive. Two cases from 1942–43 serve to make the point. On 27–28 February 1943, an SOE team sabotaged the German "heavy water" facility at the Norsk Hydro plant in Versork, Norway. Exactly a year earlier (27–28 February 1942) a team from the British Second Battalion, Parachute Regiment, jumped on to St. Bruneval on the Channel coast of France and seized and escaped with vital components of a German "Wurzburg" radar. The ability of special operations forces to capture vital physical evidence, sometimes including key people, is a unique virtue.

Policy demand is certain to increase for assistance from special operations forces by way of special reconnaissance and direct action vis-à-vis the proliferation of high-technology weaponry, including weapons of mass destruction.[19] The intensity, urgency, and frequency of this policy demand must rest ultimately upon broad considerations of policy. One can imagine a United States more introspective than at present adopting a laissez-faire attitude toward weapon proliferation. The implications for U.S. special operations forces of weapon proliferation must be sought through the prism of national-security policy, not narrowly with reference to such proliferation per se, as if that proliferation had some immanent policy meaning.

8. *A U.S. focus on domestic matters.* The 1990s are witnessing a concentration of U.S. political energy far more upon domestic than foreign matters. In today's perspective, the most salient questions are how fast and how far will this process of domestication proceed. Thoroughly introspective, even isolationist, views are not yet in command in the United States, but nativist sentiments are distinctly popular. Major foreign peril is not in evidence today, nor is it likely to be for many years to come. The homeward trend is in good measure both inevitable and desirable in the wake of success in the Cold War and changing economic relationships. The pace and breadth of U.S. national security adjustment to the ending of the Cold War has been responsibly deliberate to date. A key problem is to try to understand this period. If these years are best approached as an interwar era, as I believe, should the United States plan on the basis of a ten-, twenty-, or thirty-year rule?

The challenge is for the country to "come home" by way of force-level reductions and redeployments in a purposive way and not simply as a desirable end in and of itself. But purposive adjustment to the still-emerging new security environment presumes some knowledge of, or willingness to guess prudently about, the structure and character of the new world and the role of the United States in it. Much work remains to be done on those fronts. It is not assumed pessimistically here that the future of world politics must be as bloody and disorderly as the past. But this analysis rests upon the observation that a mammoth transition from bad old ways to good new ways, if feasible at all—which I doubt—requires a quality of vision and performance in statecraft that is not in evidence today.

Implications for special operations forces: The relative strategic utility of special operations forces should be enhanced by U.S. military consolidation at home, in the context of cumulatively large reductions in regular forces. Being necessarily light in numbers and equipment, special operations forces are inherently easier to move rapidly over long distances than are regular forces. However, mere mobility or availability does not necessarily mean utility. The fact that regular forces will be less readily available for employment in large numbers on short notice around the periphery of Eurasia does not mean necessarily that special operations forces can substitute for them. After all, no matter what the security context, special warfare has distinctive features and capabilities that cannot be ignored. Nonetheless, it is plausible to argue that as the U.S. armed forces assume a new, leaner shape, the availability of high-quality special operations capabilities will attract unusual policy attention.

There are severe limits on the ability of special operations forces to substitute for general-purpose forces, but a leaner and more mobile U.S. military establishment, not to mention one better educated about the meaning of special warfare (if this is not a heroic assumption), is likely to make more extensive and imaginative use of special operations forces than has been the rule in the past.[20]

9. *A new politics of (possible) ecological change*. Scientists disagree about the dynamics and consequences of ecological change. However, a broad analysis such as this would be deficient were it to ignore what may become an accelerating trend in political stresses flowing from adverse climatic change. There is no way of knowing as yet who is correct in the contemporary debate over the alleged greenhouse effect or purported global warming. Suffice it to say that defense planners are on notice that climate-driven policy demands at least are on the distant horizon, with minor harbingers already extant.

Implications for special operations forces: On a minor scale—in the great scheme of things—special operations forces have the mission of being on, or of actually constituting, the cutting edge of U.S. policy response to natural disasters. Humanitarian relief in distant as well as nearby climes is a mission well fitted to the flexibility, mobility, and skill mix of special operations forces. If the global climate deteriorates in some of the ways predicted, then there will be more and more policy utility to the ability of special operations forces to provide prompt assistance. If broad-gauged ecological change does occur, as it has in the past, then the political consequences for international order and security could be very troublesome. For example, it is more likely than not that the *Völkerwanderung* of steppe peoples which, by the ultimate effect of its successive waves, brought down the (Western) Roman Empire in the fifth century A.D. was triggered by catastrophic changes in grazing conditions in central Asia.[21] Also, it might be recalled that Egypt once was the granary of the Roman Empire.

Trends can be identified, as in this section. Similarly, it is possible to characterize both the new security environment into which the United States is moving and the kind of events that the U.S. government most likely would classify as triggers for action. The task then is to apply understanding of the capabilities of special operations forces to the jobs to be done and the outcomes desired. Those are not modest undertakings, but neither do they require the impossible, that is, the prediction of the future in detail.

NATIONAL INTERESTS

The strategic value of special operations forces to the United States is a function not only of the quality and appropriate quantity of the special warfare establishment, but also of the foreign policy choices exercised. Those choices rest upon American political and strategic culture in action, rather than exclusively upon trends in world affairs. Rarely are those trends blessed with self-evident meaning, and even more rarely is it plain beyond a reasonable doubt what Americans ought to try to do about them. The value of special operations forces is largely a dependent variable. The U.S. government first has to decide to allow special operations forces to perform in the field on missions that are important. Second, there is the question of the quality of performance on those missions. Special operations forces may perform superbly on missions of little importance, or they may perform poorly because the political-military establishment assigns them to "mission(s) impossible." National interest, or national interests, is the concept that is key to unlocking the otherwise uncertain relationship between a polity and its security environment.

Even though it has an unhelpfully formalistic pedagogical odor about it, the concept of national interest is inescapable. The tasking of special operations forces derives directly from judgment about national interests. The judgment may be careful or casual, arrived at via extensive bureaucratic due process in policy making or by snap instinctive decision, but the end result is the same. Special operations forces will or will not be employed because of high-level decisions on where the national interest lies and how intense it is.

A good deal of the unhelpful heat could be removed from public policy debate were more discipline to be exercised over discussion of national interest. At root, national-interest analysis operates as a critical discriminator, serving to advise the body politic about the importance of a particular event. Unfortunately, such analysis alone cannot be permitted to run policy, because decisions to act must accommodate prior judgments about probable effectiveness. From time to time policymakers will discern accurately a seriously adverse foreign development, but be unable to do anything effective about it. As the key to constructive thought about national interests, with a view to improving understanding of the origins of policy and strategy demand for the services of special operations forces, readers are reminded of the fourfold categorization that was introduced briefly in Chapter 6 (see Table 6.1). It may be recalled that (U.S.) national interests may be thought of as coming at four levels of intensity:

1. *Survival interests* are interests that must be protected (by any and all means) if the country is to endure physically and politically.

2. *Vital interests* are interests so important that they are worth fighting to defend.

3. *Major interests* are interests that it is difficult, though not impossible, to justify fighting to defend or advance.

4. *Other interests* are interests that it is virtually impossible to argue plausibly are worth fighting to protect.

This simple hierarchy is much clearer in principle than it is in practice. In the real world of difficult policy decisions it is often not certain just how intense the U.S. interest is, and neither is it certain that a particular grand-strategic instrument (e.g., military force) can be effective, no matter how worth fighting for an interest may be. An almost perfect example of a difficult case for U.S. policy was provided in August 1990 with Iraq's seizure of Kuwait. The prolonged, divisive, and diplomatically unhelpful domestic U.S. debate over policy and strategy expressed the fact that the opinion-shaping elite could not agree on whether the case at issue was a *vital* or a *major* U.S. interest.

An important complication to national-interest analysis is that, with the exception of the rarefied realm of survival interests, all relevant considerations are relative rather than absolute. To protect or advance an interest entails the assumption of risks as well as the prospect of gain or disadvantage. In addition to a judgment about the intensity of a U.S. interest as, say, *major* or *other*, analysis of the probable costs of success in its protection can be critical. For a variety of motives, a government may be tempted to solve a policy problem by direct action by special operations forces. After all, in the right conditions, special warfare offers the glittering prize of an effectiveness that is heroically and favorably disproportionate to the scale of effort committed.

Since the country's assets of all kinds are finite, even fixed, at any one time, a decision actively to defend some interest may imply a decision not to defend others. The reverse can be true, of course. The Johnson administration decided to defend South Vietnam because it believed that the rest of Southeast Asia was at stake, also. The framing of the policy question is critical: where shall we fight, not shall we fight.

Thinking about the new security environment of this decade, and particularly about the features discussed in the previous section, it is essential to distinguish framework from shifting content and principles from detail. The end of the Cold War means neither that there has to be a crisis in U.S. foreign policy nor that world politics has altered radically. After all, there is a long history of the rise and fall of great empires, of which the Soviet-Russian has been merely the most recent. At a high level of generality national interests endure, even though the detail of their contemporary concern or expression will vary. The evolving trends of the 1990s and prognostications for the next century should be accommodated within a settled structure of national-interest analysis. The United States should know in principle where its vital or major interests lie (and why) and not have to wait for the passage of future events to reveal them.

There is no generally recognized methodology for determining the identity and intensity of national interests. In practice, the domestic political process of policy making provides authoritative, albeit frequently contested answers (e.g., should we provide military aid to the Nicaraguan Contras? Military assistance to Bosnia?). That practice, notwithstanding undisciplined public rhetoric, tends to be driven by the application of three decision rules bearing upon (1) the distribution of power among or within states; (2) U.S. reputation and standing in the world; and (3) the direct welfare of Americans. The first is by far the most important of the decision rules guiding the course of policy. These are not standard official formulations, but they explain better than does any alternative brief list of considerations why and how U.S. governments behave in broad terms in foreign affairs and national security policy. The judicious application of one or more of these considerations, or algorithms for action/inaction, provides the most useful guide to the policy sources of U.S. demand for the strategic services of special operations forces. Trigger events (see the next section) in the new security environment for U.S. policy, grand-strategic, and military-strategic decisions are more likely than not to warrant ascription as such because they touch directly upon one or more of these three considerations.

Distribution of Power

Regardless of the ideological rationales provided, all of the major U.S. exercises of force in this century have been undertaken in order to correct an actual or impending maldistribution of power in Europe or Asia or both. Expressed as a principle that points to U.S. survival/vital interests, this consideration would have been entirely reliable as a predictor of U.S. participation in the three world wars (two hot, one cold) of the twentieth century, as well as in Korea, Vietnam, and Kuwait-Iraq.

States have three choices when facing an actual or plausibly impending imbalance of power in favor of a presumptive foe: they can seek to restore the balance, they can try to jump on the bandwagon, or they can endeavor to stand aside. Geography and the scale of national capabilities have allowed the United States an apparent degree of policy latitude unusual among states. In practice, however, U.S. administrations repeatedly have chosen to balance, even over-balance, potentially unfriendly maldistributions of power in Eurasia. Whether or not the geopolitical precept has been recognized explicitly in Washington, the United States, following the prolonged British example, has sought to balance power in, rather than with, Europe and Asia.[22] Not all imbalances of power must have implications inimical to U.S. interests. But trends in the distribution of power in Europe and Asia constitute the single most likely source of trigger events for the active engagement of U.S. national security strategy. The lesson from this is not to watch China, or Russia, or Ukraine, or Iran, but rather to watch the changing distribution of power within, between, and among regions.

Reputation in the World

This decision rule usually can be traced to the other considerations treated here but still the question of reputation merits individual treatment. Just as for people it is said that reputation is a valuable attribute, so this consideration is deeply significant for polities also. Reputation is a matter not only of foreign assessment, but also of self-respect. Motives for policy usually are mixed. States will take action for the sake of their good name both as an issue with expected pragmatic consequences and as an issue of honor and emotional commitment. The enemies of Americans, from the British in the 1770s through the Iraqis in 1990–91, repeatedly failed to understand the depth of a democracy's attachment to its own need to defend its honor.

It is neither possible nor necessary to separate consequentialist from absolute arguments here. A superpower United States is rarely obliged to enforce its wishes physically. An important reason why military coercion is a rare event is that disadvantaged states are unwilling to wage hopeless contests. The better the U.S. reputation for carrying out its promises and threats, the less often it will need to perform in the field. The closest analogy would be to a company's credit rating. Admittedly, reputation is a matter of perception supported by rough calculation, but it is not a free-floating value manipulable at will.

A hostage rescue mission by special operations forces may be ordered because it is right in an absolute sense to attempt to save people (and particularly Americans) in peril, because it is important for U.S. standing in the world that the United States should not appear helpless in the face of terrorists, and because it is important to discourage hostage taking in the future. It would be a serious mistake to dismiss this second decision rule as unworthy of statesmanship. When, by default, a country acquires and assumes a lead role as guardian of international order and civilized values, and it is the only possible organizer of multinational coalitions for demanding collective security tasks, its reputation becomes an unusually precious commodity. Few people or governments doubt what the United States or a U.S.-led coalition could do. The question typically is what Americans will choose to do.

When the matter is raised of special operations forces as a strategic asset, this consideration of national reputation and how it may need to be supported should loom prominently. The historical episodes that shape foreign and domestic perception of national reputation generally will be modest in scope yet symbolically suggestive in function. For example, success or failure in a hostage rescue mission or in the conduct of a low-intensity conflict can help shape assessments of national will and competence far beyond the confines of those actions themselves.

Welfare of Americans

This third decision rule means that events in the new security environment likely to trigger U.S. decisions to use force will include situations where individual Americans are in danger. Statecraft usually is a cold-blooded business, but popular democracies can act in anger. By and large there will be relevant policy issues beyond the obligations of the U.S. state to its citizens, but it would be unwise to ignore the ability of the human level of concern to drive policy. The nature of special operations and special operations forces renders them uniquely suitable as candidate agents of policy and grand strategy for dealing with a range of human-level problems in world politics. The small scale and tightly focusable character of special operations forces mean that they are likely to be the instrument of first choice for proportionate action, tactical considerations permitting.

A previous section of this chapter identified nine trends that are shaping a new security environment. Now it is necessary to proceed beyond trend identification and specify the U.S. role in the world of the 1990s,[23] the global insecurity conditions likely to generate U.S. policy and strategy demand for the services of special operations forces, and, finally, the classes of plausible trigger events that could lead to U.S. employment of its special warfare capabilities.

Some observers of U.S. foreign policy lament what they discern as a gaping hole at its center. With the Soviet Union defunct and its state and would-be state successors internally preoccupied, the United States lost the keystone in the arch of forty-five years of its national security policy, the concept and practice of an anti-Soviet containment. It would be erroneous, however, to believe that the United States requires a replacement-in-kind for the anti-Soviet containment doctrine. The error would lie in misunderstanding the most fundamental level of policy determination. Containment was only a derivative instrumental concept and doctrine for the guidance of policy. Why was the Soviet Union to be contained? Because Soviet power threatened to dominate Europe and Asia. The end of the Cold War, therefore, does not leave the United States floundering without an organizing principle for the shaping of national security policy. The organizing principle still holds: to prevent, oppose, or correct Eurasian imbalances of power likely to work to the U.S. disadvantage.

It is a general rule of statecraft that polities seek such influence over their external environments as they can achieve at tolerable cost. Roles in the world are the complex product of opportunity, capability, and preference. Most countries at most times are more constrained than they are at liberty to play significant roles helping shape their foreign security environments. By virtue of its size and power potential, its recent history and the expectations at home and abroad that flow from that history, and its historically unusual opportunity to play alone as a true superpower unchecked by another superpower, the United States is almost embarrassed by an overly full menu for policy choice. So many are the domestic moral, legal, and cultural constraints upon U.S. exercise of its power that Americans are wont to forget just how much influence for good or harm or both they can exercise. A giant is used to being a giant. Also, the American giant is so used to being checked by Soviet power or by fears of igniting powder trails of inadvertent escalation to nuclear war that creative and bold statecraft is much at a premium. In the aftermath of the Cold War, and notwithstanding domestic problems, some of them systemic, the foreign policy question for the United States is not so much What can we do? but rather What should we do?

The core of the answers, which can accommodate a wide range of alternative and complementary rhetorical flourishes, is as follows:

- The defining concept of the U.S. role in the world in this decade (at least) is that of chief guardian of a global "liberal" order.

- The principal menace to that global order will be the rise of new, or old but revived, centers of power (states or coalitions of states) which threaten to create regional imbalances of power.

- As the only possible guardian of last, and often even of first, resort and as the organizer of "posses for peace," the United States will need to play a multiregional antihegemonic role with vigilance.

- The good name or reputation of the United States as a just and reliable protector will be critical for its "creditworthiness" in the conduct of global security business.

- Because of the U.S. global security role as guardian of a widely appealing practice and vision of order, individual Americans and their assets will have merit as hostages and targets in the eyes of some of the envious, the angry, the frustrated, and the ambitious. Americans and American assets are worth imperiling precisely because the United States is a country whose policy is worth influencing.

CONDITIONS THAT GENERATE DEMAND FOR SPECIAL OPERATIONS FORCES

In an obvious sense, conditions around the world are always ripe for alleviation or resolution by the services of U.S. special operations forces acting either autonomously or as an integral part of wider military operations. But a condition of disorder is not necessarily justification for forceful U.S. policy response. Although the United States has been bequeathed by historical accident the leading guardianship role for international order and civilized values, it is not the world's policeman. For conditions abroad to generate demand for the services of U.S. special operations forces, national-interest analysis has to intrude rigorously. The external conditions of disorder which might lead to U.S. special warfare activity have to be conditions that positively engage the decision rules discussed earlier. Does a potentially menacing imbalance of power (local, regional, or global) loom as a distinct possibility? Is U.S. reputation involved in the matter at issue? Are Americans or American assets directly at risk? Therefore, to discover the foreign conditions that would promote special operations forces into live policy contention, one has to marry general appreciation of the emerging security environment to focused enquiry that applies these three questions.

For so long as global security politics do not orbit about a central superpower rivalry, local and regional quarrels are exactly that, local and regional. The United States can intervene in local or regional disturbances in fairly confident expectation that the outcomes will not have meaning beyond the areas in question (though the consequences for U.S. reputation could be significant).

It is precisely that isolation of local and regional events in a world now spared powder trails to a nuclear World War III that reduces the intensity of relevant U.S. national interests. General judgments such as that always are subject to variable applicability in specific cases. The mixture of Persian Gulf oil, weapons of mass destruction, and the security of Israel rendered Iraq in 1990–91 a special case by any reasonable definition.

This discussion suggests trigger events which could lead U.S. policymakers to choose to employ special operations capabilities. What follows are not predictions of dire events to come or of policymakers choosing to employ special operations forces. Rather, this is a synthesis of historical evidence, current features and apparent trends, and prudent guesswork about the future. The purpose is to identify the conditions in which special operations forces could well seem to policymakers to provide useful answers.

BALANCE -OF-POWER PROBLEMS

An Interwar Period

It is only elementary prudence for the United States to assume that these years are seeded with the origins of the next balance-of-power struggle. With Europe between security systems, with Russia in the midst of an incomplete revolution, and with the Balkans in the throes of mayhem unprecedented in time of general European "peace" since 1912–13, there is no other prudent assumption that U.S. policymakers can make.

With reference to U.S. special operations forces, this first condition argues for a full-service military establishment vis-à-vis a potentially first-class (i.e., a heavily nuclear-armed super state or coalition) foe that menaces the balance of power in Eurasia. The identity of such a hypothetical foe is uncertain, but the leading candidates, rank ordered by probability of emergence, have to be (1) a Russia seeking restoration of empire and dignity and (2) a Germany supporting potential victims of Russia. Whatever the geopolitics of a future balance-of-power struggle, the possibility of such a conflict has to impact U.S. force planning today. The greater that impact is allowed to be, the more likely it is that the United States could take early preventive measures to slow or arrest a slide toward this highly undesirable condition.

Regional Roguery

Even in the current absence of superpower rivalry, regional disorder promoted by rogue polities can have wide implications. Few cases of regional roguery will manifestly license U.S. military action as did Saddam Hussein's obtuse bid for glory in 1990–91, but that case, extraordinary though it was, should have served as a wake-up call to those who had seen the future and found it peaceful. It is admittedly unusual for a regional antagonism to have the inherent wider meaning granted in the Gulf instance by oil, but there are many possible regional, even local, crises that predictably would engage U.S. national interests intensely.

Regional disorder in the Caribbean and Central America, for example, is close to home for the United States, has consequences expressed by ethnic-political special interests inside the United States, and is in a region characterized by long traditional self-appointed U.S. guardianship. Consider as well the leading other—non-Gulf—Middle Eastern regional quarrel, over who gets how much of Palestine. Standard national-interest analysis does not function in this case. Were Israel *in extremis*, the United States would fight to protect it. More to the point, the United States is irretrievably engaged in the Middle East in the linked and tension-ridden roles of honest-broker-peacemaker and last-ditch guarantor of Israel.

Apparently strictly regional disorder in Southeast or East Asia, or indeed in Europe (e.g., the Baltics or the Balkans), again must engage U.S. national interests intensely. The reason would be not so much the immediate stakes in the conflicts at issue, but rather the potential effect of regional or local crises upon possible great-power or superpower antagonisms and upon the terms of conflict more broadly. When rogue behavior goes unrestrained, let alone unpunished, that visible fact encourages roguish traits elsewhere. (Given Russia's recent loss of imperial territory and the other irredenta that litter the map of central, eastern, and southern Europe, the importance of this topic would be difficult to exaggerate.) Also, the use of weapons of mass destruction in a regional conflict would erode supposedly global norms against such employment.[24] The use of special operations forces in the Gulf War of 1991 shows how invaluable such forces can be in regional conflicts. Special warfare was waged against Scuds, against strategic command and control, in aid of the air campaign, and—*inter alia*—against Iraqi morale.

Local Disorder

The regional problems that can have global ramifications always have local roots, as all of foreign policy is made at home somewhere. Whatever its origins, local disorder pertaining to the internal security of individual countries typically will be of interest to the United States at most in the last category ("other") of relative intensity. Local disorder, however, can manifest itself in the seizure of American hostages or property, can attract predatory neighbors, and might engage world attention as a herald of one trend or another. The issue is not whether there will be conditions of local disorder from Bosnia to Peru (via Moldova, Ukraine, Chechnya, Georgia, Somalia, and Cambodia, to cite but a few among the recently hotter spots), but whether those local conditions are likely to precipitate a policy response by the United States which includes action by special operations forces. No coherent, detailed answer can possibly be provided, but the three substantive decision rules already advanced yield useful guidance. For example, if the case in question is disorder in Georgia encouraged from outside by Russian agencies, one has to apply the template of U.S. national-interest analysis and ask if (1) the regional or international distribution of power is at stake, directly or plausibly indirectly; (2) U.S. reputation as guardian or protector of order is at risk; and if (3) Americans are in immediate peril.

With the important exception of the employment of special operations forces as surrogate diplomats in a wide range of military training and civil assistance roles, it is safe to argue that single-country, local disorder is likely to generate demand for special operations response only when broader issues are believed to be at stake. Operation Just Cause of December 1989, for example, was conducted in a country almost uniquely intimately related to the United States, connected by geography and engineering to profound U.S. strategic interests, and over an immediate issue that pervades American society and influences all of U.S. policy toward the Andean and Central American states. Panama in 1989 was not a precedent or a model; it was *sui generis*. It follows that the frequency and urgency of U.S. policy interest in special operations forces as an agent of grand strategy vis-à-vis local disorders abroad must be driven by the presence or absence of larger regional or global challenges. Viewed truly in local isolation, conditions of disorder around the world will not lead the U.S. government to dispatch special operations forces into action.

Transnational, Nontraditional Security Threats

This fourth category refers to such sensitive problems as drugs and narcoterrorism, international and transnational organized crime, terrorism of all kinds, and even economic "warfare." The importance of these security threats is relative to what else is menacing the country. Compared with categories one and two above, this fourth class of problems fades rapidly in significance. Nonetheless, this category of conditions does present a set of challenges to which some of the qualities of special operations forces are uniquely well suited among military agents. The leading role in each of the nontraditional areas has to be taken by police forces, U.S. and foreign. However, it transpires that the police activity required seriously to trouble the more competent drug-peddling, terrorist-criminal, and even economic espionage (and trade law–evading) organizations has to contain a distinctly paramilitary element. Indeed, the differences between politically sensitive special operations forces in the SAS or Delta Force mode and paramilitary elite police units can be more a matter of political culture and national preference than of mission. Whether or not a country elects to provide them in special warfare guise, some of the capabilities of special operations forces will be needed in the future as a complement to traditional police forces and police methods.

The skills of special operations forces will not be required very often to solve problems created by drug lords or terrorists, but when that policy requirement comes down, there are likely to be no acceptable grand-strategic substitutes for "special" action. The 1970s and 1980s demonstrated both the necessity for true professionalism in special operations capabilities and the costs of amateurishness. In the exacting realm of special operations, only the best is good enough, and only the best will command the confidence of politicians.

"911"

Individuals, families, communities, and countries all face unpredictable emergencies. Whether or not any interests more intense than "other" can be identified as being at stake, the reputation of a superpower is readily engaged in the policy issue of an international relief or rescue effort. It is only with modern transport and communications, overlying considerable organizational abilities, that emergency assistance on a truly global, all-season, (almost) all-weather basis is possible. Because the United States is the power with global reach—including unmatched maritime, air, and space assets—it is as inevitable that "911" calls should come to Washington, D.C., today as it was that they came to London (much delayed, notwithstanding the arrival of the electric telegraph) in the last century.

Emergencies come in different sizes, but they have the common characteristic of erupting with little or no warning. Many kinds of military organizations could be useful in human and political emergencies, but special operations capabilities enjoy some obvious advantages. For example, special operations forces are

- maintained in high readiness to move and act
- mobile
- small in scale
- prepared to live off the country (or carry only modest quantities of necessary supplies with them)
- provided with excellent communications equipment
- skilled in providing administrative assistance (in military government or civil affairs), as well as humanitarian aid

- as well trained in self-defense as any small deployment of troops can be, and able to provide local security in their deployment area
- trained to be sensitive to alien customs, beliefs, and circumstances
- uniquely alert to the political dimensions to foreign deployment
- characterized by mature, self-sufficient people

The point is not to claim that special operations forces are wholly uniquely useful in emergency conditions, which would not be true. But it is to claim that for most international emergencies not of a traditionally military kind, special operations forces provide the best available fit of means to need. It is safe to claim that politically and naturally created emergencies will occur in the future. In this interwar or postwar era, there will be fewer inhibitions both upon those in need calling the United States and upon the United States being willing to respond (because there will be little fear of adverse regional or global consequences). The argument that the United States has less to win in this era by foreign commitment is a half-truth, but it is also close to irrelevant in the specialized context of emergency assistance. The United States will respond to foreign emergencies as a matter of general moral obligation or duty to international society; to sustain its own self-respect as a good neighbor; for general reputation and good will; and to help keep military capabilities usefully occupied with real-world "training" in a period of peace.

TRIGGERS FOR THE EMPLOYMENT OF SPECIAL OPERATIONS FORCES

The rich detail of history, not to mention the awesome implications of chaos theory,[25] all but invariably confounds the would-be rational, long-range defense planner. The best that can be done is to identify accurately enough the question to be answered. In this case the question is What events plausibly could trigger decisions by the United States to employ special operations forces? The decision-making process is outlined in Figure 9.1.[26]

Even when they are regarded as an independent strategic asset rather than as an adjunct to regular military forces, special operations forces are only one of the many instruments of U.S. grand strategy. To respond to the various conditions of insecurity that ultimately could trigger the employment, U.S. policy and grand strategy would be all but certain to have resort to several tools (e.g., diplomacy, economic sanctions or assistance, and possibly some regular military deployment and maneuvering for political effect).[27] Illustrative triggers for special operations forces also could be triggers for the use of other instruments of grand strategy. Special operations forces should be viewed as integral to a wide range of U.S. military threats and actions in conflicts of all

Figure 9.1
Strategic Demand for U.S. Special Operations Forces Effectiveness

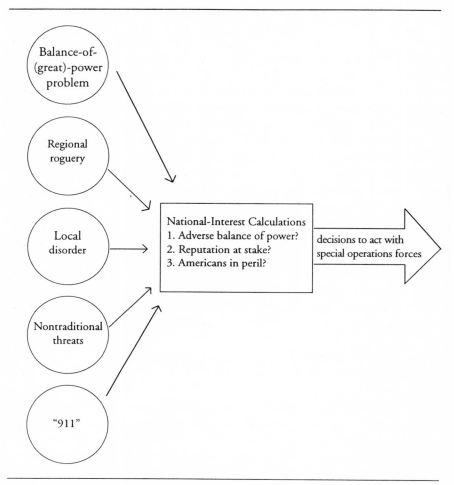

levels of intensity. Also, special capabilities can feature in U.S. responses in peace and war and could function independently or as close adjuncts to regular forces.

It follows that special operations forces, special operations, and the activity of special military personnel (which frequently is not classic direct action) have operational relevance across the board of political-military behavior. Far from comprising exotic capabilities and actions to be employed rarely as a "silver bullet" triggered by some desperate necessity, special operations forces are now a regular and traditional instrument of grand strategy and a regular component in theater war plans. There will always be the possible policy demand for a "silver bullet" special operation. Indeed, the ability of handfuls of highly trained people to penetrate hostile territory and perform a politically sensitive mission of the greatest danger and strategic significance does and should inspire the strategic concept that legitimizes and explains special warfare. First-class special operations forces have many politically important skills and strategically desirable attributes, but it is well to recall what most clearly distinguishes such forces from other military agencies. Each military career specialty can be identified and praised for its importance in different ways, but each has a concept at its core. To repeat the definition offered at the beginning of this chapter, special operations forces have as their strategic concept the conduct of small-scale, high-risk/high-payoff, unorthodox operations that are outside the bounds of regular warfare. It is essential that this distinctive strategic concept should not be ignored, but it is no less essential that the raid-of-the-decade notion should not obscure the less obviously heroic tasks that special operations forces should be expected to perform.

It would be agreeable for neat analysis if the strategic utility of special operations forces scaled inversely with the physical size of conflicts. Such an idea is not only incorrect and historically falsifiable, but it reflects a fundamental misunderstanding of when, how, and to what effect special operations work strategically. It is true that special operations forces are more and more likely to play leading roles relative to other military instruments as the threats and emergencies—as in Table 9.1—descend from the "balance of (great)

Table 9.1
Relevance of Special Operations Forces and Missions Across Threat and Emergency Zones

	FID	SR	DA	CT	UW	PSYOP	CA	CMA
Balance-of-(great) -power problems	X	X	X	X	X	X	X	X
Regional roguery	X	X	X	X	X	X	X	X
Local disorder	X	X	X	X	X	X	X	X
Nontraditional threats	X	X	X	X		X		X
"911"							X	X

FID—foreign internal defense; SR—special reconnaissance; DA—direct action; CT—counterterrorism; UW—unconventional warfare; PSYOP—psychological operations; CA—civil affairs; CMA—collateral missions areas.

power" down to the "911" level. But special operations forces should have missions at each of these threat levels, while the absolute significance of their missions in balance-of-power or regional threat zones would be likely far to outweigh the fact that they might be operating largely in a combined-arms context. Functioning integrally in joint and combined-arms operations in balance-of-power or regional conflicts would not preclude special operations forces from being employed in independent (classically "strategic") missions of a special-reconnaissance or deep-raiding (e.g., sabotage, hostage taking, POW rescue, enemy equipment seizure) character. Table 9.1 matches the standard listing of special operations forces missions with the different threat and emergency categories.

The purpose of Table 9.1 is to present vividly the point that the mission architecture for special operations forces, no matter how subdivided, is relevant across the whole range of potential threats and emergencies which could trigger U.S. decisions to act. The problem of illustration of argument is dominated by an excess of candidates, not by a dearth.

Balance-of-(Great)-Power Problems

The full range of missions for special operations forces would be needed to support deterrence of and conduct in a new global struggle against a super-power antagonist. Geopolitically, this antagonist must arise in Eurasia and menace, initially, the balance of power on that bicontinental landmass. Every-thing that U.S. special operations forces planned to perform in the context of Soviet-American rivalry and the Cold War writ large applies in this grand case. For the purposes of force-level planning, investment in equipment, and training, this discussion tells the special operations community to assume a superpower enemy. Foreign policy analysis also advises not to assume five, ten, or twenty years notice that a new balance-of-(great)-power struggle is coming.

Illustrative trigger events or trends could include the following:

- Another coup in Moscow leading to the establishment of a regime determined to restore much of the great Russian empire lost in 1991 or of the Soviet imperium lost in 1989.

- Antagonism between Russia and some formerly Soviet republics—espe-cially Ukraine and the Baltics—leading the latter to seek support for their independence. The growing insecurity of the states in the east, no matter who was most responsible, could well lead to rearmament in west-central Europe, including a nuclear dimension (essential to neutralize the Rus-sian nuclear arsenal).

- The emergence of a militarily modern, superpower China—a condition unprecedented since the time of the Ming Dynasty (1368–1644). In keeping with its Confucian political culture, such a China may have only modest regional ambitions. Nonetheless, the appearance of so powerful a China geopolitically "behind" the new Russia and overshadowing trade-dependent Japan could not fail to have a major ripple effect upon the whole structure of security in Asia and Europe. A fragile Russia confronting renewed Chinese demands for the return of territories lost to the tsars in the nineteenth century would be assailed opportunistically at the same time by other geopolitical threats. The occupant of the White House in such a period could anticipate early morning calls from Moscow.

Regional Roguery

Logically, illustrative cases in this category will comprise relatively early stages of potential category one problems. By analogy, if a balance-of-(great)-power problem is a hurricane, regional roguery is a tropical storm with hurricane potential. During the Cold War, truly regional security problems frequently were disaggregated into state-by-state components for the express purpose of minimizing the peril of a tropical storm becoming a hurricane. U.S. policy and strategy toward Vietnam, South and North, rather than Indochina as a whole (including Laos and Cambodia), is a classic case in point. The October 1973 war between Israel and its Arab neighbors is an example of a genuinely regional conflict.

Illustrative trigger events or trends could include the following:

- An Iranian bid for influence or even imperium over the formerly Soviet Islamic republics of central Asia
- An Iranian bid for revenge, prestige, and greater territorial holdings at the expense of a still-weak Iraq
- Another Balkan war, with its center of territorial gravity in Macedonia and Kosovo
- Another Indo-Pakistani conflict
- Another Korean war
- Any of half-a-dozen conflagrations within the periphery of the former U.S.S.R.

Local Disorder

If the analogies of categories one and two above as referring, respectively, to security hurricanes and tropical storms have any appeal, local disorder may be likened to a tropical depression (unlikely to develop into a major hurricane, but still pregnant with possibilities). The structure of this argument clarifies the connections among global, regional, and local security disturbances. Neorealist theorists of international relations assert that world politics must be viewed as a system-dominant architecture.[28] That means that the ramifications of local or regional disorder will be determined by overall patterns in the distribution of power and particularly by the quality of political polarity (bipolar or multipolar). By way of contrast, this chapter argues that although the overall character of the international system can be critically important (e.g., there was no bipolar superpower rivalry inhibiting U.S. regional policy toward Iraq in 1990–91), disturbances at the local and regional levels can reshape overall (balance-of-power) security architecture.

Illustrative trigger events or trends could include the following:

- Chaos in Russia (and several other former Soviet republics)
- Chaos in China
- Civil war in Lebanon, the former Yugoslavia, Slovakia (with its Hungarian minority), Romania, Egypt, Iraq, Iran, Panama, Nicaragua, and so on
- Political disturbances or civil war in countries important to the United States on criteria critical to the national interest

The range of activities that might be conducted discreetly (and discretely) by U.S. special operations forces include providing or training others to provide personal security for political leaders and security for vital installations (power plants, bridges, radio stations, and transportation assets such as airplanes, airports, ships, ports, and locks). Special operations forces have a well-established multifaceted function in the realm of foreign internal defense. Just how urgent such defense may prove will depend significantly on developments at the global and regional levels of potential conflict. How "local" is local disorder? What are the regional implications of a particular local disorder and how much does the United States care?

Transnational, Nontraditional Security Threats

Nontraditional is a description that can mislead. The threats encompassed in this category—drug trafficking and narcoterrorism, other forms of terrorism and transnational criminal conspiracies, and economic warfare—are by no means new. These threats to Americans, even to the fabric of American society and to American prosperity, are, however, not usually considered suitable candidates for military attention. The fact is that the shadow world of drugs, organized and well-armed criminals, terrorism, and economic warfare is a world where police, intelligence, and military prowess all meet. There is no objectively correct answer to the question of whether these threats should be handled by military or by civilian agencies. As a general rule it is the American way to combat drugs, terrorism, organized crime, and economic "warfare" more as police problems than as challenges to the armed forces. Nonetheless, the armed forces and particularly their special operations forces have skills and capabilities complementary to police prowess.

Illustrative trigger events or trends could include the following:

- Transnational drug trafficking that has the consequences of both turning inner cities in the United States into war zones and of ruining the lives of many American young people
- A drug industry so profitable that it shapes the political, economic, and social destiny of countries of interest to the United States
- The functioning of transnational terrorist organizations that are partially sponsored by pariah states and that have the power to destabilize countries or whole regions
- Acts of terroristic violence that kill, maim, or otherwise menace American citizens
- Transnational criminal syndicates, including drug traffickers that, albeit only for financial profit, can influence the course and quality of local or regional political and social development
- A climate of economic competition among states and trading coalitions so intense that industrial/scientific espionage and tariff (trade-law) evasion become significant for American prosperity

"911"

By their nature, emergencies are not routine events. But emergency calls for assistance of the kind that U.S. special operations forces can provide readily have become generically routine. As noted above, special capabilities have a character all but tailormade for a wide range of emergency responses. To cite just one class of relevant activity, special operations forces have a major military role in (military) search and rescue. That capability can be as valuable for civilian as for military emergencies.

Illustrative trigger events or trends could include the following:

- Natural disasters anywhere on earth (e.g., tidal-surge damage in the Bay of Bengal or hurricane relief in Florida). If the pessimists are even partially correct on the subject of a deteriorating global climate, the special operations forces mission of providing emergency humanitarian aid will grow.

- Manmade disasters, such as those in Iraq, Somalia, Rwanda, and the former Yugoslavia

This discussion does not amount to advocacy of a particular view of the utility of special operations forces, though no secret is made of the belief here that special capabilities to perform strategically useful missions extend across the full spectrum of threats to U.S. national interests. The presentation above has been restricted to (1) description of the most likely U.S. role in the world; (2) identification of the conditions of national and international security liable to generate U.S. policy responses that could include the activities of special operations forces; and (3) discussion of possible trigger events or trends for the employment of U.S. special operations forces.

SPECIAL OPERATIONS FORCES AS A STRATEGIC ASSET

Special operations forces are a national strategic asset, but the exact meaning and implications of that premise require careful articulation and illustration. To provide that detailed analysis, this section proceeds by two routes: first, the strategic-asset postulate is explored with reference to principles for the guidance of defense planning; and second, the mission structure for this new era of special operations forces—that is, their strategic value vis-à-vis the threat spectrum presented in Table 9.1—is reconsidered. It is important to know how special operations forces can express the principles of defense planning and how their missions can alleviate or resolve threats.

Special Operations Forces and Principles for the Guidance of Defense Planning

The thirteen principles presented earlier in Table 6.3 are the distilled product of strategic-theoretical, historical, military-practical, and even plain common-sensical streams of evidence. These principles can be questioned at the margin, but that would hold true for any such set of characteristics for armed forces.

A caveat attends the list of principles. The principles have been derived to help guide force planning in toto, not only special operations forces (in Chapter 6 they were cited to help elucidate the strategic value of air power). This caveat is not a limitation upon the value of the principles; rather, it is a strength. A longstanding problem for special operations forces in many countries is that they have been treated as a capability apart. Too often, those forces have not been regarded or employed as integral to the regular military establishment, able to function both independently and in roles adjunct to and supportive of large-scale military operations. No military capability can score a perfect ten for fit with all plausible national needs or strategic desiderata at the levels of grand and military strategy. Although special operations forces are a strategic asset with utility right across the threat spectrum, they are not a panacea. Such forces are not the solution to every challenge to national security. What follows are brief explanations of the ways in which special operations forces express or advance the principles that should guide defense planning. These principles are policy-neutral vis-à-vis what Clausewitz referred to as the (political) "logic" of war;[29] in and of themselves they have nothing to say on such subjects as intervention in the former Yugoslavia or the prudent level of residual U.S. forces to be retained in Europe and Korea. In addition, these principles themselves do not specify how much air power and so on, relative to land, maritime, and space power, the United States should maintain. Again with gratitude to Clausewitz, these principles speak mainly to the "grammar" of war, to considerations that transcend political agendas and trends in tactical-technological relationships.

The flexibility possible in the employment of special operations forces is key to their significance as a strategic asset. Because they are small in number, light in weaponry and logistical train, able to act effectively in a wide range of environments, and capable of decisive action in imperfectly anticipated situations in response to only general orders, special warfare capabilities can achieve a speed of employment and secure a measure of surprise unattainable by conventional forces.

U.S. special operations forces should have the following characteristics:

1. *Capable of winning* in the wars to which they are committed; this translates minimally as the ability to deny important strategic advantage to an enemy. Special operations forces are the only U.S. forces (excluding bombardment assets)[30] that can be employed globally within hours, using the reach of air-sea power as well as information from space systems. Special operations forces can attain nuanced strategic objectives rapidly. Antiterrorism, hostage rescue, seizure or sabotage of weapons of mass destruction, disruption of enemy command structures without significant collateral damage, and seizure of key terrain are among the activities that those forces can perform and which have the potential to shape the course and outcome of an entire conflict.

2. *Sufficient in number* to be employed to decisive military effect. Because of the inherent qualities of special operations forces, often they can have decisive effect with very low numbers. This means that there are many cases where the political contexts, domestic and international, find intervention by special operations forces far preferable to larger alternatives. Indeed, there are instances wherein these forces provide the only politically practicable option.

3. Of a kind, scale, and character of behavior such as to *enjoy and merit acceptability at home.* Special operations forces and special warfare have a long and honorable history in the United States.[31] Special warfare capabilities, though relatively low in dollar cost in the defense budget, have a dispropor-

tionate positive public appeal as the embodiment of individual warrior virtues. The distinctly human-level, people-intensive character of special operations renders these forces uniquely valuable as exemplary guardians of society's values and virtues.

4. Suitably *diverse* as to allow for adaptability to unexpected conditions. Special operations forces depend on high-quality and rigorously trained people rather than on large numbers of specialized machines and extensive, tailored organizations; it follows that special operations forces are significantly more adaptable to unexpected conditions than are other kinds of military forces.

5. Technologically advanced, that is, *modern,* for the generation of effectiveness in action overall. Because of their quality and small numbers, there are cases wherein special warfare personnel derive combat utility from the newest technology well before comparable equipment can be introduced into regular forces in sufficient numbers and with sufficient training time gainfully to exploit the same equipment in combat.

6. Able to be *applied quickly,* when necessary. Special operations forces are shaped, trained, and maintained to be the most ready and easily transportable element of flexible military power. They are conceived with objectives that include targets whose vulnerability may be only fleeting (e.g., as intelligence sources briefly indicate their location).

7. *Logistically supportable* for an optimum, or unexpectedly imposed, operational tempo. Special operations forces are designed to achieve much of their combat power through achieving an operational tempo decisively quicker than that manageable by conventional forces. This prospect is enhanced by superior deployability. It is in the nature of first-class special operations forces that they will evade and offset a materially much stronger foe by surprise, speed in execution, and prompt disruptive effect.

8. *Adaptable*, or tailored *to* threat environment *geography*. Because special operations forces are designed around the qualities of toughly trained and mature personnel, rather than a large equipment park, they are highly adaptable to adverse conditions.

9. Able to *cope with surprise* and dampen surprise effect. By flexibility and mobility, special operations forces are well suited to achieve a rapid response to surprise. Special operations cost a small investment of force. Losses tend to be small and controllable and in most cases may be recouped by subsequent action at larger force levels without threat to overall strategic objectives. Although special operations forces, along with the remainder of the military establishment, may be caught by surprise, they are well designed to deny an enemy some of the beneficial operational or strategic effect of such tactical surprise as he may achieve. Special operations forces can help limit an enemy's gains, slow him down, harass his rear areas, and create fear, or the reality, of operational overextension on his part. Special warfare should be integral to

military plans and operations, whether friendly forces are advancing, withdrawing, or holding.

10. Able to *focus a maximum potential of military power* on any given conflict. While special operations forces are organized to produce the most intense military effect possible, even more important is the sharpness of the focus of special operations on strategically significant objectives. Special warfare achieves strategic effect by leverage, not by brute force.

11. Capable of holding at risk an enemy's *center of strategic gravity* and of protecting their own. In some cases when an enemy's center of gravity is compactly definable and accessible, special operations forces are unique in their ability economically to place that center of gravity at risk. Similarly, special operations forces are suited to react quickly to the need to protect important friendly assets. There are several different ways in which excellent special operations can assault an enemy's center of gravity. For example, special warfare can threaten the lives or liberty of enemy leaders; challenge the reputation of an enemy regime by conducting raids that are politically humiliating; and affront the enemy's self-esteem and alter his terms of analysis (in favor of pessimism). The potential of special operations forces to "go for the jugular" of an enemy's center of gravity is far more extensive than most countries have ever licensed in practice. This topic would reward careful study.[32]

12. Sufficiently *flexible* to cope well with the kinds of missions that tend to rank low on service priorities (e.g., low-intensity conflict tasks). This is the essence of special operations forces: the ability to ensure that no opponent can challenge the United States in a way that evades the capabilities of the U.S. armed forces. Terrorism and other forms of unconventional warfare are broad classes of events that tend to leave conventional armed forces without relevant targets at which to strike. Special operations forces are indispensable to cover the low end of the threat spectrum.

13. *Worthy of respect* in valuation of would-be foes. Conventional forces embody the attributes of technical competence, large numbers, and logistical prowess important to a major, integrated war effort, while special operations forces embody and express the qualitative excellence of the individual soldier that ensures across-the-board respect from any opponent. Furthermore, special operations forces with a well-advertised deep-raiding capability and doctrine can help undermine a putative foe's sense of personal and institutional security. It is important, indeed in some cultures it is essential, that American fighting men should be respected, as contrasted with the general respect that pertains to the overall weight of U.S. military power.

This discussion is intended only to outline the special dimension to the military capabilities implied by the thirteen principles for the guidance of defense planning. The claims just advanced for special warfare capabilities are not presented to be competitive with other kinds of military forces.

What stands out from this analysis is the unique niche that special operations forces fill in rounding out the necessary array of military and political-military capabilities. In much the same way and for the same reasons, for example, that it is essential to consider the air power or space power dimensions to virtually every national security problem, so the special operations dimension should be considered also. In some cases, special operations forces (or air power or space assets) will be of little or no easily identifiable relevance, but the educated habit of applying a special operations perspective will produce recognition of otherwise unnoticed applications for special warfare.

Missions for Special Operations Forces and Future Threats

The method adopted here is a straightforward examination of the missions for special operations forces in the context of the threat and emergency categories specified in Figure 9.1 and Table 9.1. The point can hardly be made too strongly that this discussion of the utility of special operations forces in the new security environment is dominated by threat analysis. There are three broad questions. First, which security problems will the United States face or choose to face? Second, which missions and individual tasks will special operations forces be allowed to attempt? Third, how well will those forces perform? The answer to the third question cannot be treated as foreordained. One of the plainest lessons of recent history is that unless a special warfare establishment is properly nurtured and wisely used, the inherently risky character of its more heroic missions assuredly will arise to mete out due punishment (recall the attempted Iranian hostage mission of 1980).

1. *Balance-of-(great)-power problems.* Although small events can have large and unpredictable consequences, this topmost category of threat essentially is a potential struggle of the biggest battalions. One can speculate illustratively about important special warfare missions in a World War III, but it is hard to find missions likely to shape, let alone define, such a struggle as a whole. This is not intended to demean the potential strategic value of a contribution by special operations forces. Indeed, often there is an inverse relationship between the absolute and the relative strategic value to the country of the performance of special operations forces. The tasks that those forces undertake as *the* strategic instrument of high policy, in other words when they are the concluding executive agency of the United States, are likely to be tasks of relatively modest importance. By way of contrast, special warfare contributions—both independent and closely adjunct—to the deterrence or waging of a large regional or a global conflict most probably will be modest relative to the contributions of regular forces, but distinctly immodest absolutely. When there is more at stake there is more to win, even when the role is only that of a modest team player.

The logic of this argument is historically well supported. For example, many historians have noticed the unprecedented—then or since—scope and scale of special warfare in World War II, but have proceeded to judge that extensive effort as relatively unproductive of identifiable strategic effect. In part the problem was the one identified by U.S. Army historian David W. Hogan, Jr.: "for the most part, the conventional Allied campaign in the Mediterranean proceeded as if special operations never existed. The relative insignificance of such activities reflected both American inexperience and a chronic shortage of material and manpower resources. But the basic cause was the absence of any doctrine of special operations."[33] Hogan also notes that "[e]xcept for some isolated instances, conventional U.S. generals discarded special operations in Europe and focussed almost totally on conventional warfare once their forces had consolidated beachheads in North Africa, Italy, and France."[34] The problem for special operations forces in major conflict, as Hogan implies, is that the scale of the enterprise appears to outrun the strategic significance of small units, no matter how tactically excellent they may be.

To say that the role of special operations forces in major conflicts is that of modest team player is not in any sense a put-down. In fact, it would be a considerable achievement were U.S. commanders to employ special warfare capabilities systematically and effectively in their proper supporting ("door-opener") missions, while political and higher military authorities licensed the occasional, truly bold, independent "strategic" special operation. When there is more to win or lose, when the stakes are as high as they can be, both the opportunities for and the constraints upon special warfare will be much larger than usual. It is a familiar paradox for special operations forces: when they could generate the most strategic utility (ahead of active hostilities, say), they are likely to be the most severely harnessed by a nervous government and by conventional military commanders.

When large-scale nuclear war looms as a distinct possibility, and a clash of nonnuclear arms must engage at least tens of divisions, hundreds of ships, and thousands of aircraft, the scope for the significance of special operations will appear to many to be smaller than in fact it is. The relative prominence of special activities will be less in a great balance-of-power conflict than in situations of local disorder. Nonetheless, those dimensions of the larger conflict that diminish the relative contribution of special operations forces also multiply the scope for special operations and magnify their absolute potential strategic value. As Table 9.1 indicates, there are no missions for special operations forces prospectively irrelevant to a great balance-of-power struggle. Superpower or great-power rivals will find that even the counterterrorist skills of some small fraction of their special warfare establishments are in demand in a context of actual or prospective global war. For example, twice in this century Germany provided material sponsorship for Irish and other terrorists against

Britain, while Warsaw Pact countries similarly saw to the training, care, and feeding of a large and diverse segment of the international terrorist subculture. It is a general rule in politics that the enemy of my enemy is my ally-of-convenience.

2. *Regional roguery*. As the focus and geopolitical scope of conflict narrow, so it becomes more likely that tactically excellent special warriors will be able to make a critical and identifiable strategic difference to the course of hostilities. In great conflicts, both sides typically have been so well endowed with a diversity of assets on a large scale that the outcome could only be secured by an attritional style of warfare. Special operations forces can make useful contributions to victory in attritional combat, but those contributions are likely both to be swamped by the sheer scale of the fighting and to be placed at a discount because of the substitutions or adjustments the foe can make. It is worth noting that with trivial exceptions, the general course of World War I was all but designed to be proof against influence by special warfare. The point is not that special operations forces, had they existed, could not have functioned, but rather that it is less than obvious that there were suitable targets for their attention.

Almost at the opposite extreme from World War I was the Gulf War of 1991.[35] True, Desert Storm was very much a theater-level operation of big battalions, but it was also a war of decisive maneuver. Coalition special operations played recognizably important—if not literally vital or decisive—roles to facilitate the grand and military strategy of the war. Special operations forces facilitated and supported the air campaign that was the leading edge of the coalition war effort; served as significant evidence of coalition determination to protect Israel (by hunting for Scud missiles on the ground in Iraq); contributed critically to deception and psychological warfare operations; functioned more than just usefully in an unusual forward liaison role with Arab forces; helped organize and sustain Kuwaiti resistance to the invader; and so on.

The Gulf War of 1991 was of course unique. The more-than-minor contribution of special operations forces to coalition success, however, need not be unique. By themselves, special operations cannot wage and win a large-scale regional conflict, but neither are they merely a "nice to have" addition to regular-style military campaigning. In regional conflicts special operations forces can function both as important key-turning, door-opening facilitators and enablers for conventional success and as quasi-independent agents of direct operational, strategic, and even political effect.

The specific conditions of each conflict, as well as the quality of the special warriors in question and of the conventional forces that they might assist, always will be critical to the merit in special operations. It is necessary to consider both what special operations forces can do well and what specifically needs doing in a particular historical case. Not only do such forces have to be fit to be employed in the most demanding of military missions, but also political and military leaders have to know how to use them and must have confidence in their prowess. In many instances special operations forces will compete with other kinds of forces to perform tasks that all agree must be performed, while some of the more important stand-alone special operations would work strategically more as accelerators of victory (or brakes upon the pace of defeat) than as indispensable keys to victory. History is replete with cases of commanders electing to take a brute-force, methodical path to victory, rather than assuming apparently high, and gratuitous, risks with less reliable cunning plans.

3. *Local disorder.* Local disorder refers to war, disturbance, or instability within a single country, albeit frequently with one or more of the belligerent parties demanding secession. This category of threats to U.S. interests would exclude the wars in Korea, Vietnam (i.e., Indochina or Southeast Asia), and the Gulf (1991). By way of contrast, the Dominican Republic in 1965, Grenada in 1983, Panama in 1989, and today the former Yugoslavia would all count in the column of local disorder. The contemporary tragic drama in the Balkans is a textbook example of local disorder teetering on the brink of regional conflict.

Table 9.1 claims that the entire mission structure for special operations forces is relevant for the "local disorder" category just as it is for the categories of balance-of-power struggle and regional conflict. Typically what distinguishes the special operations story in local disorder, however, is the centrality of their potential strategic contribution. Although one can identify a myriad of apparently lost opportunities for special operations in major wars, the merit in a leadership role for special operations forces in many cases of local disorder has been undeniable even to military establishments not known for their affection for special warfare and its warriors.

The issue here is the structural difference between, say, a Vietnam after mid-1964 and Iraq-Kuwait in 1990–91, and Grenada in 1983 and Panama in 1989. The Grenadian and Panamanian cases plainly provided conditions that were user-friendly for a large, even dominant, role for special warfare. There are conflicts wherein the seizure of a handful of sites and facilities, and perhaps even of one person, will shape the course of an entire war. Similarly, there will be cases of low-intensity conflict, probably including some modest measure of cross-border support for the insurgents, for which virtually the missions of special operations forces alone will be relevant to meet the strategic demand from policy.

In-country disorder involving actual or incipient civil war maximizes the salience of the ethical dimension to military behavior. The problems of just war will be more than matched by the dilemmas of just conduct in war. Even in the near regional conflict in the Gulf in 1991, U.S. political and military leaders were uncomfortable with the casualty rate inflicted upon undeniably enemy soldiers, let alone upon enemy civilians.

On the rare occasions when the United States will be motivated to intervene in a local conflict, it is a safe prediction that for political viability the intervention will have to be swiftly executed and exceedingly discriminating in its application of lethal force. More often than not, special operations forces will be the military instrument of choice to reach, grasp, and neutralize the enemy's center of strategic gravity. There will be the odd exception to that rule. However, it is intriguing to speculate from the proposition that the United States should intervene in local conflicts only when special warfare capabilities can be employed decisively. If special operations forces are judged unlikely to be effective in a particular case, the reasons could prove enlightening for policy direction overall.

4. *Transnational, nontraditional security threats.* Police and intelligence agencies typically lead in responses to the national security problems that flow from drug trafficking, other manifestations of organized crime, terrorism, and unscrupulous and illegal forms of competitive economic behavior. Nonetheless, when the proper roles of the FBI, CIA, the Drug Enforcement Agency, the Treasury Department, and others are duly noted, the fact remains that special operations forces are a major and on occasion indispensable resource for policy.[36] With respect to the shadowy region wherein internationally organized crime meets those motivated to commit crimes for political reasons, special operations capabilities should be integral to the total response strategy. When transnational, nontraditional menaces are difficult to find, reach, grasp, and neutralize, police and intelligence agencies need all the help they can obtain.

The inherently military character of special operations forces can raise political difficulties abroad that purely civilian agents of policy would sidestep. However, it is in the character of special warriors (and special operations) to leave few footprints. Employment of special warfare yields the benefits as well as the (political) limitations of a military force. Generalizations are not useful on this subject. Case by case, special operations forces can be judged to offer either net advantage or net disadvantage. Most often, they will be contributing together with other members of a team that includes U.S. and sometimes foreign intelligence and police agencies.

Common sense and historical experience suggest that most special missions (see Table 9.1) in principle are relevant to U.S. responses to transnational, nontraditional threats. Those authorities suggest also that the special warriors' direct-action mission to neutralize such threats is likely to be involved in "third and long" situations, wherein there is political consensus upon the need for desperate measures.[37] The point is not to argue, for example, that special operations offer the answer to terrorism, transnational crime, and attempts at evading economic sanctions, but rather that well-equipped and well-trained special warriors have capabilities that police agencies generally lack. Special warfare commitment to team efforts to counter these kinds of threats may not be large in relative terms, but that commitment often will be literally essential. The contribution of special operations forces can include intelligence gathering and the reliable, prompt transmission of information, interdiction of the transnational foe's lines of communication, and sabotage or seizure of key equipment, products, and people.

5. *"911."* In all respects, special operations forces have characteristics close to ideal for responding quickly to emergency calls for help in the face of natural or manmade disasters. Embodying the principle of economy of force, relatively small bodies of special operations forces have become the instrument of first choice when the government needs to provide emergency relief. These forces are far from uniquely capable of providing emergency assistance—many branches of the armed forces have served in this capacity—but they have proven to be by far the most suitable rapid-response agency in most events. Special operations forces are postured to move quickly, they concentrate a variety of relevant skills in a modest number of soldiers, they are trained to cooperate with people of different cultures, and they can provide more local physical security in dangerous contexts than can any body of soldiers similar in size.

SPECIAL OPERATIONS FORCES AND NATIONAL SECURITY POLICY: AN AMBITIOUS ANALYSIS

This chapter has explained the structure of U.S. national security today and the fit of special operations forces within that structure. This discussion neither advocates special operations of particular kinds nor seeks to prescribe a national security policy that would be greatly in need of the strategic assistance of those activities. The implications of this analysis lie in the whole architecture of the argument. Although these are not conclusions in a conventional sense, they highlight the key points and the chain of logic.

First, it is essential to be clear about the strategic concept of special operations forces. If that clarity is lacking on the part of the armed forces, political leaders, and even the special warfare community itself, then the strategic utility of special operations forces must be much diminished.

Second, the strategic value of special operations forces in the new security environment of the 1990s cannot be assessed via a context-free study of those forces themselves. To describe the instrument, in no matter how glowing terms, does not speak to the notion of whether or not the country requires the services of that wonderful instrument. Only a holistic analysis of all of the major pieces of the national security puzzle can lead to confident understanding of whether, how, where, and when special warfare should fit.

Third, just as free-floating praise of special warfare capabilities would be irrelevant, so careful analysis of the new security environment or of U.S. foreign policy also would miss the mark. The challenge is to locate the proper structure for relating special warfare capabilities to external security. The relevant mechanism is national-interest analysis. Other things being tolerably equal, the U.S. government is moved to act in the world when (1) it discerns a threatening imbalance of power, (2) it believes that U.S. reputation is on the line, or (3) when Americans are in peril. These are not by any means perfect decision rules, but assuredly they are good enough to capture most of what national-interest analysis needs to capture.

Fourth, somewhat ambitiously, this chapter has explored the sources of demand for the services of special operations forces. To that end the discussion identified plausible U.S. roles in the new security environment (following the analysis of trends in the 1990s and of how the United States identified and categorized the intensity of its national interests); classified roughly by intensity and scale the insecurity conditions or threat zones likely to generate strategic demand for the employment of special warfare capabilities; and cited some illustrative trigger events or trends that could ring the bell for the use of those capabilities.

Fifth, when the mission architecture for the special operations forces is plotted in a matrix against the full range of threat and emergency categories (Table 9.1), the scope and persistence of the strategic relevance of those forces are blindingly apparent. Before proceeding to assess just how useful they can be in particular contexts, the chapter interpreted special qualities in light of the thirteen principles applicable for the guidance of defense planning.

Sixth, special operations forces were appraised for the relative weight of their likely strategic contribution to the alleviation or solution of national security problems, category by category, across the full spectrum of threat and emergency.

None of the separate pieces of the analysis in this chapter makes much sense individually; it is the whole edifice that bears the interpretation. The discussion explains the connections which should obtain among evolving world security conditions, U.S. national interests, U.S. choices in national security policy, and special warfare capabilities as one among many instruments of policy. The structure of explanation here explicitly connects special warfare through policy making to conditions in the outside world. The analysis is not obviously sensitive to detailed changes either in policy and strategy or in world conditions. Indeed, substantial cumulative change is assumed for both domestic and external affairs.

NOTES

1. Samuel P. Huntington, "National Policy and the Transoceanic Navy," U.S. Naval Institute *Proceedings* 80, no. 5 (May 1954): 483 (emphasis added).

2. The war cabinet minutes of 15 August 1919 stipulated as follows: "It should be assumed for framing revised estimates, that the British Empire will not be engaged in any great war during the next ten years, and that no Expeditionary force is required for this purpose." Quoted in N. H. Gibbs, *History of the Second World War, Grand Strategy*, Vol. I, *Rearmament Policy* (London: HMSO, 1976), p. 3. Also see John Robert Ferris, *Men, Money, and Diplomacy: The Evolution of British Strategic Policy, 1919–26* (Ithaca, NY: Cornell University Press, 1989), especially chap. 2.

3. For different views see Ken Booth, "Security in Anarchy: Utopian Realism in Theory and Practice," *International Affairs* 67, no. 3 (July 1991): 527–45; Robert Jervis, "The Future of World Politics: Will It Resemble the Past?" *International Security* 16, no. 3 (winter 1991/92): 39–73; and Colin S. Gray, *Villains, Victims and Sheriffs: Strategic Studies and Security for an Inter-War Period, An Inaugural Lecture* (Hull, England: University of Hull Press, 1994).

4. See James Schlesinger, "New Instabilities, New Priorities," *Foreign Policy*, no. 85 (winter 1991/92): 3–24; and, for a skeptical view, Colin S. Gray, "Global Security and Economic Well-being: A Strategic Perspective," *Political Studies* 42, no. 1 (March 1994): 25–39.

5. A different judgment underpins Christopher Hall, *Britain, America and Arms Control, 1921–37* (New York: St. Martin's Press, 1987). Emily O. Goldman, *Sunken Treaties: Naval Arms Control Between the Wars* (University Park: Pennsylvania State University Press, 1994), especially p. 12, n. 7; and Erik Goldstein and John Maurer, eds., *The Washington Conference, 1921–22: Naval Rivalry, East Asian Stability, and the Road to Pearl Harbor* (London: Frank Cass, 1994), are useful also. Still on the maritime theme, John B. Hattendorf and Robert S. Jordan, eds., *Maritime Strategy and the Balance of Power: Britain and America in the Twentieth Century* (New York: St. Martin's Press, 1989), is uniquely valuable.

6. Edward N. Luttwak, "From Geopolitics to Geoeconomics: Logic of Conflict, Grammar of Commerce," *National Interest*, no. 20 (summer 1990): 17–23, remains fashionable.

7. Robert W. Tucker and David C. Hendrickson, *The Imperial Temptation: The New World Order and America's Purpose* (New York: Council on Foreign Relations Press, 1992).

8. For reasons explored in Samuel P. Huntington, "Playing to Win," *National Interest*, no. 3 (spring 1986): 8–16.

9. See Alfred H. Paddock, Jr., *U.S. Army Special Warfare, Its Origins: Psychological and Unconventional Warfare, 1941–1952* (Washington, DC: National Defense University Press, 1982).

10. See P. J. Rhodes, "The Delian League to 449 B.C.," in D. M. Lewis et al., eds., *The Cambridge Ancient History*, Vol. V, *The Fifth Century B.C.*, 2nd ed. (Cambridge: Cambridge University Press, 1992), pp. 34–61.

11. Much of what there is to reveal is revealed in "The Alliance's New Strategic Concept," *NATO Review* 40, no. 5 (October 1992): 25–32. Whether or not the United States can, or should, be kept interested in European security via NATO in its familiar form is a theme central to "The Future of NATO," *Journal of Strategic Studies* 17, no. 4 (December 1994).

12. "Collateral Mission Areas. SOF's [special operations forces] additional collateral activities missions are security assistance, counterdrug activities, peacekeeping, personnel recovery, special activities, coalition warfare, and antiterrorist and other security activities including measures to protect individuals and property from terrorist attack. In these areas, SOF share responsibility with other forces as directed by the geographic combatant commanders." William J. Perry (secretary of defense), *Annual Report to the President and the Congress* (Washington, DC: U.S. Government Printing Office, February 1995), p. 227.

13. James Kurth, "Things to Come: The Shape of the New World Order," *National Interest*, no. 24 (summer 1991): 3–12, is insightful.

14. See Francis Fukuyama, *The End of History and the Last Man* (New York: Free Press, 1992).

15. "Assertive disarmament" is the concept which covers the preventive or preemptive forcible neutralization or destruction of a putative foe's armament. The Israeli air raid upon Iraq's nuclear reactor at Osiraq in June 1981 is a classic illustration of this concept at work in practical form. Unfortunately or otherwise, the probability of the United States adopting a policy of truly assertive disarmament toward nuclear-proliferant polities is not high. A similar sad judgment is registered in Eliot A. Cohen, "Comment," *National Interest*, no. 34 (winter 1993/94): 37–38. Brad Roberts, "From Nonproliferation to Antiproliferation," *International Security* 18, no. 1 (summer 1993): 139–73, stands out amongst a large literature. Les Aspin, "Counterproliferation and Threat Reduction," in *Annual Report to the President and the Congress* (Washington, DC: U.S. Government Printing Office, January 1994), pp. 34–50, may appeal to some.

16. See Janne E. Nolan, *Trappings of Power: Ballistic Missiles in the Third World* (Washington, DC: Brookings Institution, 1991); Richard A. Bitzinger, "The Globalization of the Arms Industry: The Next Proliferation Challenge," *International Security* 19, no. 2 (fall 1994): 170–98; and David Mussington, *Understanding Contemporary International Arms Transfers*, Adelphi Papers, no. 291 (London: International Institute for Strategic Studies, September 1994).

17. Two superior analyses by Kathleen C. Bailey are *Doomsday Weapons in the Hands of Many: The Arms Control Challenge of the '90s* (Urbana: University of Illinois Press, 1991); and *Strengthening Nuclear Nonproliferation* (Boulder, CO: Westview Press, 1993). For an excellent debate on the value, or otherwise, of nuclear proliferation for stability, see Scott D. Sagan and Kenneth N. Waltz, *The Spread of Nuclear Weapons: A Debate* (New York: W. W. Norton, 1995).

18. On the explicit standard of "civilization" in customary international law, see Gerrit W. Gong, "China's Entry into International Society," in Hedley Bull and Adam Watson, eds., *The Expansion of International Society* (Oxford: Clarendon Press, 1984), p. 179.

19. See Aspin, *Annual Report*, pp. 34–50.

20. The sad tale is told well in Paddock, *U.S. Army Special Warfare, Its Origins*.

21. See H. H. Lamb, *Climate, History, and the Modern World* (London: Methuen, 1982). For the Roman example, see E. A. Thompson, *A History of Attila and the Huns* (Oxford: Clarendon Press, 1948); and Hans Delbrück, *History of the Art of War*, Vol.

II, *The Barbarian Invasions* (Lincoln: University of Nebraska Press, 1990; first pub. 1980), Book II.

22. Nicholas J. Spykman, *America's Strategy in World Politics: The United States and the Balance of Power* (Hamden, CT: Archon Books, 1970; first pub. 1942).

23. See the section in Chapter 6 on "Obligations of Primacy."

24. The concept of a nuclear taboo is important in Lewis A. Dunn, *Containing Nuclear Proliferation*, Adelphi Papers, no. 263 (London: International Institute for Strategic Studies, winter 1991). For a frontal assault on the merit in the concept see Colin S. Gray, "The Second Nuclear Age: Insecurity, Proliferation, and the Control of Arms," in Williamson Murray, ed., *Brassey's Mershon American Defense Annual, 1995–1996* (Washington, DC: Brassey's, 1995), pp. 135–54. The notion of a nuclear taboo is a pious hope, and a dangerous pious hope at that. Belief in the authority of a nuclear taboo amounts to self-deception.

25. See James Gleick, *Chaos: Making a New Science* (New York: Penguin Books, 1988; first pub. 1987); David Ruelle, *Chance and Chaos* (New York: Penguin Books, 1993; first pub. 1991); Alan Beyerchen, "Clausewitz, Nonlinearity, and the Unpredictability of War," *International Security* 17, no. 3 (winter 1992/93): 59–90; and Stephen H. Kellert, *In the Wake of Chaos: Unpredictable Order in Dynamical Systems* (Chicago: University of Chicago Press, 1993).

26. Please note that Figure 9.1 shares the conceptual framework expressed earlier in Figure 6.3. Where possible throughout this book I am proceeding from a common methodology and set of ideas.

27. See the place of trigger events as represented in Figure 6.2.

28. Kenneth N. Waltz, *Theory of International Politics* (Reading, MA: Addison-Wesley, 1979). But see Robert O. Keohane, ed., *Neorealism and its Critics* (New York: Columbia University Press, 1986).

29. Carl von Clausewitz, *On War*, ed. and trans. Michael Howard and Peter Paret (Princeton, NJ: Princeton University Press, 1976; first pub. 1832), p. 605.

30. As a general rule, the immediate military options reduce to bombardment by ballistic or air-breathing vehicle or the insertion of teams of special warriors. The latter can be logistically effectively self-sustaining for a while, they are light (and therefore mobile), and they should be ready. There are times when bombardment is not the preferred response.

31. See the essay by Michael Vlahos, "Special Operations and American Culture," in Colin S. Gray, ed., *Special Operations: What Succeeds and Why? Lessons of Experience, Phase I*, Final Report (Fairfax, VA: National Institute for Public Policy, June 1992), chap. 14.

32. Following discussion with some of the official historians of World War II, especially with historians of intelligence matters, I am baffled as to why much more effort was not committed by the Allies to attempts on Adolf Hitler's life. Until recently I had assumed that I just did not know much of what was planned, let alone attempted. Now I am convinced that little was planned and very little was attempted. Rarely in any of history's great struggles was the life and performance of one person more significant than was the case of Adolf Hitler in World War II.

33. David W. Hogan, Jr., *U.S. Army Special Operations in World War II* (Washington, DC: Department of the Army, Center of Military History, 1992), pp. 32–33.

34. Ibid., p. 138.

35. The relevance of special operations forces to coalition problems in Desert Storm is emphasized suitably in General Sir Peter de la Billière, *Storm Command: A Personal Account of the Gulf War* (London: HarperCollins, 1992), especially pp. 191–92, 199, 221–25, 227, 267–68. De la Billière, the British commander in the Gulf, had spent virtually his entire military career in the SAS. The contrast with senior opinion in the U.S. Army could hardly have been more stark. Rick Atkinson writes about "the deep suspicion held by many military commanders towards elite forces" (p. 142). *Crusade: The Untold Story of the Gulf War* (London: HarperCollins, 1994; first pub. 1993). Atkinson offers the familiar quotation from British World War II Field-Marshal William J. ("Bill") Slim on the reliance of armies upon their "standard units," not upon "a few bodies of super-soldiers." In the Gulf War of 1991, however, both personality clashes and regular-irregular tensions continued the longstanding unease in the U.S. Army's handling of its special warriors. Notwithstanding the tradition of irregular (domestic) frontier warfare, U.S. military culture in this century has never been very comfortable with its special forces.

36. This point is developed in Colin S. Gray, "Combatting Terrorism," *Parameters* 22, no. 3 (autumn 1993): 17–23.

37. If the government of a democratic polity sanctions direct action by special warriors, it is a fair bet that the mission will hover between very difficult and impossible. In other words, special operations forces typically will be licensed to conduct direct action only in very tough cases. The test of the tough case is the one that really matters, as I have argued by way of criticizing arms control, for example (in *House of Cards: Why Arms Control Must Fail* [Ithaca, NY: Cornell University Press, 1992]).

Part IV
Conclusions

Chapter 10

Strategy and the Revolution
in Military Affairs

Few blindingly original and startling insights illuminate these pages; the challenge is more to keep lit the flame of a properly strategic mindset than it is to ignite new fires. An important argument is not necessarily original, any more than an original argument has to be important. Because old truths can be forgotten, mislaid, misapplied, ignored, or explicitly defied, their periodic repetition or even rediscovery is useful. Every chapter of this book, usually in major key, sometimes in minor, illustrates the validity of the three binding themes identified in the Introduction: the ubiquity of strategy and strategic effect; the pervasively joint character of war and defense preparation; and the distinctiveness of each form of military power in its advantages and limitations. Chapter by chapter this discussion has put flesh on the bare bones of these worthy mantras (to mix metaphors).

~

If strategy is king, he is a constitutional monarch. By way of illustration of this theme, consider Paul Kennedy's judgment on British performance in World War I: "Yet the more the subject is examined, the clearer it becomes that the problem was not about strategy so much as the *practical application* of that strategy; that is, tactics and operations."[1] Kennedy offers a persuasive contrasting summary judgment on German performance with the thought that "[a]t the strategic level . . . the Teutonic genius for war peters out quickly."[2] All too often, alas, the same judgment could be applied to the United States. For but the most recent example, in the Gulf War of 1991 the United States had a sound vision of the desirable, made surefooted policy choices, and orchestrated a historically memorable triumph of military operational art. Unfortunately, the military success was disconnected from the desired political effect, and policy making in Washington, D.C., became almost casual at the vital strategic moment. The result was a victorious campaign which yielded too little strategic and political benefit. Because of memories of Vietnam, the undue influence of General Colin Powell, who for all his political astuteness did not have a sophisticated view of how and why force may need to be exerted (he could not transcend his Vietnam experience), and careless decision making, strategic effect was not well calculated in 1991.

As a constitutional monarch, to develop the analogy, strategy functions well only when it serves legitimate ends that its subjects (national or alliance resources, exploited through logistics, tactics, and operations) are able and willing to pursue with a reasonable prospect of success. Strategy may direct as it will, but if the broad vision and the specific goals of high policy are impracticably demanding of strategic effect, then strategy must fail. Strategy has to be "done" by people and machines at the sharp end of war, at the tip of the spear. Strategy, per se, can be neither wise nor foolish. Judgments as to wisdom or folly can be affixed to strategy only in the context of policy goals and tactical and operational competence. Endeavors to discuss the merit in strategy, treated in isolation, would be akin to evaluating the performance of a bridge that was free-standing, quite disconnected from anything at either end.

Strategy is hard to do well, hard to teach, and—for many people—even hard to understand. Although there are many reasons why this should be so (some of which were suggested in Chapter 1), probably the most fundamental and persisting is the awkward fact that strategy lies between the profession (or trade) of politics and the profession of arms. Strategy is the bridge between politics and soldiering, but it is neither of those activities. Excellence in the military arts is no guarantee of superiority in strategy, which is why even an unblemished career in tactical and then operational levels of command provides no assurance of fitness for the highest of commands, where politics and force meet. Military professionals ever are prone to condemn "amateur strategy" and "amateur strategists," and frequently they have a point.[3] The most irresponsible of schemes can be proposed by civilians who are utterly ignorant of Clausewitz's "grammar" of war.[4] To be fair, however, it is not self-evident that the skills of the military professional are conclusively adequate to meet the challenges of strategy. Strategy is about the cashing of military threat or action for desired political consequences—in Clausewitz's words, to repeat the words quoted in Chapter 1 above, "the use of engagements for the object of the war."[5] It is not always a simple matter to determine whether a particular string of engagements, no matter how victoriously concluded, will produce the object of the war—witness the political half-success of Desert Storm in 1991.

$\sim$

The variety of topics pursued in these *Explorations in Strategy* illustrates my view that strategy is a realm for all seasons, all environments, and all functions that bear upon the relevance of force to statecraft. With only the most minor of passing exceptions, the subjects treated here have been recent, contemporary, or forward-looking. There is no inherently good reason why that should be so, save only for the necessarily modern character of the subject of *nuclear* deterrence—though not of deterrence per se, of course—air power, and even special operations. For all the antiquity of warfare with a truly special character, special operations forces organized, trained, and employed as such are a post-1939 phenomenon. The clusters of chapters in this book on air power (Part II) and special operations (Part III) represent ambitious efforts to explore the strategic meaning and value of different kinds of military power. My purposes might have been served almost as well by clusters of chapters on siege warfare and cavalry raids (*chevauchées*) in the Latin East in the High Middle Ages[6] or sea power in the eastern Mediterranean in the seventh and eighth centuries.[7] The intellectual discipline is the same. The analytical approach employed in the chapters on air power and special operations should lend themselves, with only modest adaptation, to the study of other military capabilities or functions even in other historical periods (where relevant).

But how plausible can readers find my claims for the value of historically diverse study in the face of the contemporary argument that the United States is leading the charge to implement a new revolution in military affairs? If the future belongs to the "information warrior"—at least pending arrival of the next revolution—whose force multiplier is the microchip and whose micro-processing capability leverages military power in all its diverse forms,[8] what salience for the future can be claimed for the topics discussed above?

The short answer is that the coming of "third-wave" or information-age[9] warfare (or "I-war"), even if the new phenomenon delivers much of what its prophets advertise—the desirable and the undesirable—simply adds fresh material for explorations in strategy. It matters not to the strategist whether the subject is stone-age warfare, industrial-age warfare, or now information-age warfare. The eyeballs of a cavalry scout and thermal sensors on a satellite perform essentially the same function. Warfare has changed dramatically in the course of this century, and it changed not much less dramatically in the nineteenth century, while certainly early modern Europe witnessed changes in military technology and associated techniques that historians have called a military revolution.[10]

Those who are historically challenged are wont to approach each revolution or candidate revolution as though it were the end of history, the last move, the maturing of the absolute and final. Of course there are no final moves in military affairs any more than there are in other branches of human behavior and misbehavior. If information warfare is "third-wave" warfare, we can be confident that a fourth wave is lurking around the corner in the twenty-first century to enrich either the Tofflers (again) or their successor interpreter-popularizer-prophets. The truly wide-eyed enthusiast for "I-war" would do well to check his enthusiasm against the powerful paradoxical logic of strategy that was so well explained in Edward N. Luttwak's cautionary 1987 masterpiece, *Strategy: The Logic of War and Peace.*

The extended defense community in the United States, which is to say the government, its contractual dependencies, and other defense professionals, is vulnerable to a somewhat uncritical enthusiasm for the idea of the month, year, or decade. In the late 1980s, as the excitement over the Strategic Defense Initiative at last diminished, there was great excitement following discovery of the supposedly novel notion of "competitive strategies." The central problem with competitive strategies was that it comprised discovery of what should have been devastatingly obvious.[11] It was the intellectual equivalent of proceeding at great fanfare into outer space and then announcing that one had found that environment to be extremely cold. By its very nature, strategy should be competitive. Anyone who needed to discover that fact should be disqualified from playing any significant role in strategy formation or guidance. Discussion of the new military revolution is beginning to assume some ominously familiar disturbing features.

It is commonplace to argue that a society wages war, and prepares to wage war, in ways that express its nature. Inevitably, a United States which leads the world into the information age is likely to be a United States on the global cutting edge of capability to wage "I-war." This is neither good nor bad, though it could prove on balance to be fortunate or unfortunate in some different contexts; it simply is a fact. U.S. society and its armed forces are one.[12] There is a sense, therefore, in which even efforts at constructive criticism of the "I-war" movement, fashion, and fad are just pointless. The United States is what it is, for good and for ill. For the record, it is probably important to register at this juncture that in broad terms I agree with the hypothesis of an "I-war" military revolution.[13] Indeed, in studies focused especially on space warfare I have urged full recognition of the contingent revolutionary implications of the new information age.[14] The computer, like gunpowder and nuclear fission and fusion, is here to stay. As usual, the problem is not so much with the key idea itself (yes, strategy should be competitive), but rather with the pathologies which can come to dominate it.

The following paragraphs describe some of the leading problems with current discussion of the third-wave, information-age warfare hypothesis.

Gee whiz! Although enthusiasm and a measure of excitement are necessary propellants for change, they have never been of much utility for strategic enquiry. The dazzle of new technology, the appeal of shiny new weapons (or weapon possibilities), and even the mind-numbing effect of what can venture close to technobabble all tend to dull the critical strategic faculties. It can be difficult to remember that technologies, weapons, and even weapon systems do not wage war. In any particular period a society has a particular system of war which has at least as much political and social content as it has technological. As with air power and then with armored and mechanized ground forces—though generally not with nuclear weapons—revolutions in warfare typically have phases of overpromise and underperformance, maturity for competitive success, and then declining stand-alone value as ways to blunt their cutting edges are discovered and fine-tuned. Information-age warfare is still in the phase of discovery and excited prophecy. Prophets can overstate a good case as when Colonel Campen claimed that the Gulf War "was the first information war."[15] He qualified that claim immediately when he conceded, "[n]ot that information hasn't always been a key element in war, it has been—the Battle of Britain being one example of the use of radar information to position a virtually destroyed Royal Air Force." Campen then proceeded to claim that the Gulf War was different from all previous wars in that in 1991 "[i]nformation was a target. . . . It was the first war with a notion that an enemy could be brought to his knees by denial of information."[16] He was not wholly in error, though his misreading of the RAF's condition in August–September 1940 does not inspire confidence in his credentials as historian; still, he was overreaching with a good argument and risking avoidable error.

The nature of war. One can argue that nuclear weapons, the nuclear revolution, changed the nature of war, though even in that extreme case there are reasons to be cautious before advancing sweeping claims.[17] However, the idea that today "[t]he very nature of war is changing" because of the information-led military revolution[18] is thoroughly implausible. If the concept of war is understood to refer to organized violence undertaken for political purposes, how could information-age weapons alter the nature of the subject? Whether the organized violence is applied, metaphorically speaking, with a sledgehammer or a scalpel, it remains organized violence conducted for political ends. Even if the claim is scaled back to the proposition that the character of war is changing, it is not obvious that one is saying anything very important. If the Iraqi soldiers who were harried from the air in their headlong retreat from Kuwait in 1991 were given to historical reflection, they should have been struck by the merit in the notion that *plus ça change, plus c'est la même chose.* Their experience was identical in character to the plight of many Turkish soldiers in Palestine in 1918, many German soldiers in 1944, many Egyptian soldiers in 1967, and many North Vietnamese soldiers in 1972. War is hell, especially when the enemy rules the skies and you are caught in open terrain.

Ethnocentrism. Among the troubles with military revolutions is the proclivity of other polities either to partake of the same technological feast or—if necessary—to succeed in finding means to neutralize much of the strategic effect that one might hope to derive from new weaponry and ways in the conduct of war. The distinctly one-sided "I-war" waged by the United States and its allies in the

Gulf is not the kind of historical experience liable to encourage a suitable caution among strategic commentators. There is idle talk of an "electronic Pearl Harbor,"[19] but the American military establishment and American society have seen "I-war" (on CNN) and found it to be good. Quite aside from the fact that information-age weapons and methods either are or will be available to foes of the United States, it is noticeably ethnocentric, not to say strategically imprudent, for the U.S. defense community to believe that rogue polities somehow will share its newfound disdain for nuclear weapons.[20] Indeed, U.S. national security policy recognizes the awesome relevance of the unfashionable word "nuclear" in a huge diplomatic (*inter alia*) effort to discourage, even counter, nuclear proliferation. The somewhat surprising success of U.S. diplomacy in the spring of 1995 in its achievement of an indefinite extension to the Nuclear Nonproliferation Treaty regime attests to recognition of an issue which is not a little discordant with "I-age" thinking. Not to mince matters, few rogue or would-be rogue polities are going to oblige the best and the brightest American information warriors by setting themselves up to be "Iraqed" in an information war. If they are able, foes of the United States will decline to wage information war and instead will threaten or conduct operations which marginalize much of the nominal U.S. "third-wave" advantage.

The absolute, decisive, and final weapon syndrome. One of the more important reasons why a strategic mentality is advanced by historical study lies in the value of seeing strategic events in temporal context. Strategic history is the history of interacting choices made and declined and of the consequences of those choices. There may well be some defense professionals quite unreachable by efforts at education through strategic history, but happily, they are in the minority. The people and institutions to which these remarks are addressed are those who regard the new (i.e., the latest) revolution in military affairs as the last move, the final revelation. The history of warfare is replete with examples of prophets who saw war chariots, the stirruped cavalryman, the crossbow, gunpowder firearms (personal) and (field) artillery, the machine gun, the airplane, the tank, the atomic bomb, and the hydrogen bomb—to pick but a few—as the absolute, decisive, *and final* weapon (systems). The prophets of "I-war" today have an excellent case to advance, but some education in strategic history would alert them to the substantive and temporal boundaries to their claims.

∼

It is more likely than not that most readers of this book will be looking for the "trees" of most interest to them (sea power, nuclear deterrence, air power, special operations) rather than to the "wood" of strategy which connects and gives meaning to all of the "trees." Indeed, this book can be read for its contribution to the debates about, for example, sea power, deterrence, air power, or special operations forces. There is, nonetheless, a strategic integrity to this work which may appeal to a few readers. Whether or not I have succeeded, at least the endeavor systematically to apply a strategic mentality should register with some. This is not a detective novel in the English country house tradition; therefore, I will not attempt to surprise the reader with presentation of a dramatic denouement wherein it is revealed—surprise, surprise—that the butler, or strategy, did it. If the concluding thoughts to this book come as a surprise, then the preceding chapters will have failed dismally in their purpose. Tracking sequentially through *Explorations in Strategy*, I wish to highlight eight less-than-amazing points.

First, it is important to keep the meaning of strategy clear and relatively narrow.[21] There is a tradition of usage which allows sundry objects, geographical features, events, and weapons to be deemed inherently strategic. For example, the Dardanelles and the Bosporus may be held to be strategic maritime defiles, while the Khyber Pass likewise was a strategic defile on land. What was signified by such use of strategic simply was that a particular place, event, or weapon had appreciable significance for the outbreak, course, or outcome of conflict. My own strong preference, developed in Chapter 1 and displayed consistently thereafter, is for the meaning of strategy and strategic to be confined to the more restricted and clearest of the uses specified by Clausewitz. Strategy is about the threat or use of force for the political purpose of the war. In other words, armed forces *do* tactics which are given political meaning by the directing strategy. Strategic effect, which is to say leverage against a foe, can be generated by threats or by actual force of any and all kinds. The desirably joint character of most warfare is more easily forwarded when "strategic" labels are stripped from particular troops, weapons, places, and events.

Second, notwithstanding the postnuclear preference of a U.S. military establishment currently preeminent in capability for large-scale conventional warfare, we remain in a nuclear era. The 1990s are developing into a second nuclear age as policy focus shifts from yesterday's superpower standoff to endeavors to discourage or reverse horizontal nuclear proliferation. We should, of course, seek to forge a counterproliferation policy which might register the occasional success. It is scarcely less challenging, however, to keep ready enough, with short enough lead times to adequate preparedness, the nuclear-armed forces on a major scale for which strategic demand could, indeed almost certainly will, return. In their understandable enthusiasm for "third-wave" capabilities, American information warriors should not forget that old-fashioned nuclear weapons can serve as a persuasive equalizer of strategic effect for those who are electronically challenged.

Third, deterrence has become unreliable to a degree all but unimaginable from a Cold War perspective. Western powers no longer are sure just how intensely they care about certain political interests, while their comprehension of the political and strategic cultures of new candidate deterrees is modest at best. Overall, the prospects for a strategy of deterrence look decidedly less promising than was the case in the Cold War years. As more and more countries secure the capability to achieve nuclear status (declared or, more likely, undeclared but well known), these changing conditions for deterrence merit widespread appreciation. If, as I argue, deterrence is becoming ever more unreliable, there are plain implications for the value both of strategies of denial and of a policy stance of extreme caution.

Fourth, as the best of the books yet to appear on the Gulf War argues persuasively, jointness is as jointness does.[22] All that appears to be purple need not necessarily be as joint as it looks. At least six "military cultures" (ground, sea, marine, battlefield support and longer-range air, and special forces) did their several things in the Gulf War; it was bolted together, called a plan of campaign, and it all worked marvelously by redundant paths to victory against Iraq. It remains to be seen, however, just how well the U.S. armed forces, with their current powerfully joint ideology-doctrine, would perform were they to be commanded by military leaders who actually needed to make difficult choices among alternative systems of war. The true meaning of jointness continues to be hard to find, especially in a country like the United States which has a history of exceptionally poisonous interservice relations (by international comparison), and in a period when the world of the warrior is becoming ever more complicated.

Fifth, for reasons that are not entirely encompassed by the bounds of rationality, advocates for air power continue to provide evidence that they are determined never to underestimate the strategic benefit of their product. Part II of *Explorations in Strategy*, by means of a systematic enquiry into the utility of air power, effectively concluded that although air power is wonderful, it is not guaranteed to deliver success in all climes, at all times, against all foes, in all kinds of conflict. But, I must hasten to repeat, it is difficult even to conceive of a class or case of conflict wherein aerial command would not be more or less useful. By their deeds the world's air forces have made the argument for the strategic utility of air power. Contention focuses not upon that utility, which all sensible people have long granted, but rather upon the claim that air power acting independently of other kinds of forces can deliver victory. One can explain this persisting dispute with reference to the institutional insecurity of administratively autonomous air forces and to the evolving terms of engagement between action through and from the overhead flank and the continental and maritime environments below. Still, one notes the persistence of the air power claim that "if only" it were unleashed to go "downtown" Berlin, Hanoi, Baghdad and so forth, then—at long last—it could prove that Douhet was right. In the Gulf War of 1991, air power was unleashed to attack the Iraqi center of gravity "inside-outside" from the first hours of the war. Air power indeed was the key force in that war, the force to which other kinds of military power largely were only adjunct. But the air campaign independently did not deliver victory; certainly it failed in its promise to cause the downfall of Saddam Hussein's murderous regime.

Sixth, the partial revival of U.S. special operations forces in the 1980s notwithstanding, there is a pressing need for more strategic thought about the utility of those forces. The U.S. conduct of special operations over the past decade and a half has been improving, but it reflects persisting weaknesses in some of the basics of irregular warfare and, even more, a persisting misunderstanding of this style of war by "regular" military leaders. The same U.S. Army leadership which in 1990–91 did not fully trust the politicians to endorse a viable military mission against Iraq similarly did not trust their special operations command "snake-eaters" not to make more trouble than they were worth.[23] Both sets of suspicions had a common origin in the experience in Vietnam a quarter century earlier.

Seventh, to change pace but not direction, study of the multinational history of special operations leads me to emphasize the necessity for encouraging an unconventional approach to the challenges that comprise the missions for unconventional or special warfare. Too much of the history of special warfare reveals an inappropriately overriding focus upon the methods and equipment of such warfare and too little thought about unconventional choices among objectives and approaches. To give SEAL, Ranger, or other special training to people with regular, conventional minds does not miraculously turn them into special warriors capable of achieving vastly economical strategic effect. Tactical excellence is essential for special operations forces, but the measure of their strategic value will lie both in the missions of which they can conceive and in the missions they are permitted to attempt.

Eighth, new ways to commit the oldest of strategic errors continue to be found; specifically, "[t]he mode in which you are going to give battle should not become known to the enemy, lest they make moves to resist with any countermeasures."[24] Eight hundred years prior to the writing of that advice by Vegetius, Sun Tzu had advised, "[t]hus the highest realization of warfare is to attack the enemy's plans."[25] It is in the nature of strategy that it directs threats or the actual use of force to secure leverage over an enemy with an independent will who is motivated to thwart you. The sense in this utterly commonplace observation is easy to neglect in the excitement of preparing our blows against the foe. It is entirely appropriate to endeavor to prepare the battlefield, including the mind of the enemy, so that the course of a war broadly should conform to our wishes. Ideally, the enemy will be obliged to try to react belatedly to a cascade of unexpected disasters for him.[26] All of the dimensions to strategic affairs explored in this book yield painful examples of (naval, air, "unconventional") force exerted or threatened against the backdrop of an imprudently insufficient appreciation of the paradoxical nature of conflict.

Teams who decline to change their game plans invite nominally weaker opponents to find clever ways to defeat those plans. New technologies, extending through revolutions in military affairs, lose their relative potency as others engage in parallel discovery, emulate, or invest in capabilities and methods to evade and thwart the leading edge of supposedly revolutionary developments.

~

To those of us who are professional teachers, as well as students, of strategy, an intriguing question is crowding in to claim our attention and demand at least provisional answer. Whereas the 1960s, 1970s, and 1980s were characterized by pedagogical uneasiness with the relevance of prenuclear strategic history, the 1990s are registering almost the reverse phenomenon. Although there is a desperate shortage of historical perspective, now it is possible and certainly desirable to treat the Cold War era as a distinctive period with a beginning, middle (including several high points of crisis), and end. To students of strategy in the 1990s, unlike their immediate predecessors, no longer do the superpower nuclear standoff and much of its attendant theory (deterrence, limited war, arms control) look modern and self-evidently relevant. On the contrary, the Cold War decades appear historically bizarre, pregnant with abstruse and abstract strategic theory, associated with unusable and almost unimaginable engines of truly mass destruction, *yet bereft of real, tangible strategic history*. There was no nuclear World War III. No one, therefore, knows which theory of nuclear war-fighting for escalation dominance via controlled response might have been the "best buy" among those on offer. In today's classrooms, Athens' Sicilian adventure in 415–13 B.C., the First Crusade (1096–99), Sherman's march to the sea in 1864, and the execution of the amended Schlieffen Plan in 1914 are all more real and in important ways comprehensible to students than are the shifting grand designs of the Single Integrated Operational Plan (SIOP, the U.S. nuclear war plan) from 1960 to 1990.

The ending of the Cold War and of the "strategic" nuclear relationship between the superpowers (in particular) eventually will enable students of strategy to capture nuclear strategy from its erstwhile realm of unduly contemporary defense issues. At the present time, however, nuclear strategy lies somewhere in limbo. It is too recent in its still-dominant Cold War manifestation to be history, yet it is too unusual in its horrific, temporarily lapsed possibilities to be easily accommodated by the mainstream of strategic thought which flows from strategic experience. Unfortunately, there is some good reason to suspect that, with the nuclear era a permanent fact, it was not the Cold War years that were extraordinary; rather it is the 1990s which are innocent of acute great-power antagonisms. There is urgent need to make strategic sense of the nuclear history of the Cold War. If bad times do return to world politics, as historical experience indicates to be highly probable, then again we will have to know how to approach nuclear weapons strategically.

NOTES

1. Paul Kennedy, "Military Effectiveness in the First World War," in Allan R. Millet and Williamson Murray, eds., *Military Effectiveness*, Vol. I, *The First World War* (Boston: Allen and Unwin, 1988), p. 345 (emphasis in original).

2. Ibid., p. 339.

3. For a classic example see (Lt. Gen. Sir) Gerald Ellison, *The Perils of Amateur Strategy: As Exemplified by the Attack on the Dardanelles Fortress in 1915* (London: Longmans, Green, 1926). For a like view from a similar source, note the scathing references to "the amateur strategist" in Charles E. Callwell, *Experiences of a Dug-Out, 1914–1918* (London: Constable, 1921), pp. 101, 156, 186, 213, 218, 230. Sir Charles, who was the very model of a British army general staff officer, could scarcely contain himself in his literary excoriation of such amateurs at strategy as Winston Churchill.

4. Carl von Clausewitz, *On War*, ed. and trans. Michael Howard and Peter Paret (Princeton, NJ: Princeton University Press, 1976; first pub. 1832), p. 605.

5. Ibid., p. 128.

6. See Christopher Marshall, *Warfare in the Latin East, 1192–1291* (Cambridge: Cambridge University Press, 1992).

7. See Archibald R. Lewis, *Naval Power and Trade in the Mediterranean*, A.D. *500–1100* (Princeton, NJ: Princeton University Press, 1951), chaps. 1-4.

8. "Horizon," *The I-Bomb*. Text adapted from the program transmitted on 27 March 1995 (London: BBC, 1995), pp. 4, 9.

9. See Alvin Toffler and Heidi Toffler, *The Third Wave* (New York: Bantam Books, 1980); and *War and Anti-War: Survival at the Dawn of the 21st Century* (Boston: Little, Brown, 1993).

10. Michael Duffy, ed., *The Military Revolution and the State, 1500–1800*, Exeter Studies in History, no. 1 (Exeter, England: University of Exeter, Department of History and Archaeology, 1980); J. R. Hale, *War and Society in Renaissance Europe, 1450–1620* (London: Fontana Press, 1985); and Geoffrey Parker, *The Military Revolution: Military Innovation and the Rise of the West, 1500–1800* (Cambridge: Cambridge University Press, 1988).

11. For example, see Frank C. Carlucci (secretary of defense), *Annual Report to the Congress, Fiscal Year 1990* (Washington, DC: U.S. Government Printing Office, January 1989), pp. 46–48.

12. For reasons I outline in my "Strategy in the Nuclear Age: The United States, 1945–1991," in Williamson Murray, MacGregor Knox, and Alvin Bernstein, eds., *The Making of Strategy: Rulers, States, and War* (Cambridge: Cambridge University Press, 1994), pp. 579–613.

13. See James R. Fitzsimmons and Jan M. van Tol, "Revolutions in Military Affairs," *Joint Force Quarterly*, no. 4 (spring 1994): 24–31; David Jablonsky, "U.S. Military Doctrine and the Revolution in Military Affairs," *Parameters* 24, no. 3

(autumn 1994): 18–36. Andrew F. Krepinevich, "Cavalry to Computer: The Pattern of Military Revolutions," *National Interest*, no. 37 (fall 1994): 30–42; Owen E. Jensen, "Information Warfare: Principles of Third-Wave War," *Airpower Journal* 8, no. 4 (winter 1994): 35–43; and Donald F. Ryan, "Implications of Information-Based Warfare," *Joint Force Quarterly* no. 6 (autumn/winter 1994/95): 114–16.

14. Colin S. Gray, *Space Power and the Transformation of War*, Draft Final Report (Fairfax, VA: National Security Research, June 1994).

15. Quoted in "Horizon," *The I-Bomb*, p. 5.

16. Ibid., p. 6.

17. See Robert Jervis, *The Meaning of the Nuclear Revolution: Statecraft and the Prospect of Armageddon* (Ithaca, NY: Cornell University Press, 1989); and Kenneth N. Waltz, "Nuclear Myths and Political Realities," *American Political Science Review* 84, no. 3 (September 1990): 731–45.

18. William E. Odom, *America's Military Revolution: Strategy and Structure after the Cold War* (Washington, DC: American University Press), p. 47.

19. See "Horizon," *The I-Bomb*, p. 4.

20. A point registered well in A. J. Bacevich, "Preserving the Well-Bred Horse," *National Interest*, no. 37 (fall 1994): 46.

21. Judy M. Graffis, "Strategic: Use with Care," *Airpower Journal* 8 special edition (1994): 4–10, gets it right.

22. Michael R. Gordon and Bernard E. Trainor, *The Generals' War: The Inside Story of the Conflict in the Gulf* (Boston: Little, Brown, 1995).

23. Ibid., especially pp. 241–44.

24. Vegetius, *Epitome of Military Science*, trans. N. P. Milner (Liverpool, England: Liverpool University Press, 1993), p. 111.

25. Sun Tzu, *The Art of War*, trans. Ralph D. Sawyer (Boulder, CO: Westview Press, 1994), p. 177.

26. As modern jargon might express the matter, we would be operating within the enemy's decision cycle and thereby outpacing his ability to counter, let alone anticipate, our moves.

Selected Bibliography

Adams, James. *Secret Armies*. London: Pan Books, 1989; first pub. 1988.

Alger, John I. *The Quest for Victory: The History of the Principles of War*. Westport, CT: Greenwood Press, 1982.

"The Alliance's New Strategic Concept." *NATO Review* 40, no. 5 (October 1992): 25–32.

Anson, Peter, and Dennis Cummings. "The First Space War: The Contribution of Satellites to the Gulf War." *RUSI Journal* 136, no. 4 (winter 1991): 45–53.

Aron, Raymond. *Clausewitz: Philosopher of War*. London: Routledge and Kegan Paul, 1983; first pub. 1976.

Aspin, Les (secretary of defense). *Annual Report to the President and the Congress*. Washington, DC: U.S. Government Printing Office, January 1994.

Atkinson, Rick. *Crusade: The Untold Story of the Gulf War*. London: HarperCollins, 1994; first pub. 1993.

Bacevich, A. J. "Preserving the Well-Bred Horse." *National Interest*, no. 37 (fall 1994): 43–49.

Bailey, Kathleen C. *Doomsday Weapons in the Hands of Many: The Arms Control Challenge of the '90s*. Urbana: University of Illinois Press, 1991.

———. *Strengthening Nuclear Nonproliferation*. Boulder, CO: Westview Press, 1993.

Barnett, Correlli. *Engage the Enemy More Closely: The Royal Navy in the Second World War*. New York: W. W. Norton, 1991.

Barnett, Frank R., B. Hugh Tovar, and Richard H. Shultz, eds., *Special Operations in U.S. Strategy*. Washington, DC: National Defense University Press, 1984.

Bartlett, Henry C. "Introductory Essay—Planning Future Forces." In Force Planning Faculty, Naval War College, eds., *Fundamentals of Force Planning*. Vol. II, *Defense Planning Cases*, 1–8. Newport, RI: Naval War College Press, 1991.

Bassford, Christopher. *Clausewitz in English: The Reception of Clausewitz in Britain and America, 1815–1945*. New York: Oxford University Press, 1994.

Beatty, Jack. "In Harm's Way." *Atlantic*, May 1987, 37–46, 48–49, 52–53.

Beaumont, Roger A. *Military Elites in the Modern World.* Indianapolis, IN: Bobbs-Merrill, 1974.

Bergh, Godfried van Benthem van den. *The Nuclear Revolution and the End of the Cold War: Forced Restraint.* London: Macmillan, 1992.

Beyerchen, Alan. "Clausewitz, Nonlinearity, and the Unpredictability of War." *International Security* 17, no. 3 (winter 1992/93): 59–90.

Billière, General Sir Peter de la. *Storm Command: A Personal Account of the Gulf War.* London: HarperCollins, 1992.

Bitzinger, Richard A. "The Globalization of the Arms Industry: The Next Proliferation Challenge." *International Security* 19, no. 2 (fall 1994): 170–98.

Blair, Bruce G. *The Logic of Accidental Nuclear War.* Washington, DC: Brookings Institution, 1993.

Blaxland, Gregory. *Destination Dunkirk: The Story of Gort's Army.* London: Military Book Society, 1973.

Booth, Ken. "Security in Anarchy: Utopian Realism in Theory and Practice." *International Affairs* 67, no. 3 (July 1991): 527–45.

———. "War, Security and Strategy: Towards a Doctrine for Stable Peace." In *New Thinking about Strategy and International Security*, 335–76. London: HarperCollins Academic, 1991.

———. "Strategy." In A. J. R. Groom and Margot Light, eds., *Contemporary International Relations: A Guide to Theory*, 109–27. London: Pinter Publishers, 1994.

Booth, Ken, ed. *New Thinking about Strategy and International Security.* London: HarperCollins Academic, 1991.

Boyd, Charles G. "Air Power Thinking: 'Request Unrestricted Climb.' " *Airpower Journal* 5, no. 3 (fall 1991): 4–15.

Bozeman, Adda B. *Politics and Culture in International History.* Princeton, NJ: Princeton University Press, 1960.

———. *Strategic Intelligence and Statecraft: Selected Essays.* Washington, DC: Brassey's (US), 1992.

Breemer, Jan S. "Naval Strategy Is Dead." U.S. Naval Institute *Proceedings* 120, no. 2 (February 1994): 49–53.

Brodie, Bernard. *Strategy in the Missile Age.* Princeton, NJ: Princeton University Press, 1959.

———. *War and Politics.* New York: Macmillan, 1973.

Brogan, D. W. *The American Character.* New York: Alfred A. Knopf, 1944.

Brooks, Linton F. "Conflict Termination Through Maritime Leverage." In Stephen J. Cimbala and Keith A. Dunn, eds., *Conflict Termination and Military Strategy: Coercion, Persuasion, and War*, 161–72. Boulder, CO: Westview Press, 1987.

Brown, Chris. "Critical Theory and Postmodernism in International Relations." In A. J. R. Groom and Margot Light, eds., *Contemporary International Relations: A Guide to Theory*, 56–68. London: Pinter Publishers, 1994.

Brown, Neville. *The Future of Air Power.* New York: Holmes and Meier, 1986.

Builder, Carl H. *The Masks of War: American Military Styles in Strategy and Analysis.* Baltimore, MD: Johns Hopkins University Press, 1989.

———. *The Icarus Syndrome: The Role of Air Power Theory in the Evolution and Fate of the U.S. Air Force.* New Brunswick, NJ: Transaction Publishers, 1994.

Builder, Carl H., and James A. Dewar. "A Time for Planning? If Not Now, When?" *Parameters* 24, no. 2 (summer 1994): 4–15.

Bundy, McGeorge. "Existential Deterrence and Its Consequences." In Douglas MacLean, ed., *The Security Gamble: Deterrence Dilemmas in the Nuclear Age*, 3–13. Totowa: NJ: Rowman and Allanheld, 1984.

———. *Danger and Survival: Choices about the Bomb in the First Fifty Years.* New York: Random House, 1988.

Buzan, Barry. *People, States and Fear: An Agenda for International Security Studies in the Post–Cold War Era.* 2nd ed. Boulder, CO: Lynne Rienner, 1991.

Callwell, Charles E. *Experiences of a Dug-Out, 1914–1918.* London: Constable, 1921.

———. *Small Wars: A Tactical Textbook for Imperial Soldiers.* London: Greenhill Books, 1990; first pub. 1896.

Carlucci, Frank C. (secretary of defense). *Annual Report to the Congress, Fiscal Year 1990.* Washington, DC: U.S. Government Printing Office, January 1989.

Chaliand, Gérard. "Warfare and Strategic Cultures in History." In Gérard Chaliand, ed., *The Art of War in World History: From Antiquity to the Nuclear Age*, 1–46. Berkeley: University of California Press, 1994.

Chalou, George C., ed. *The Secrets War: The Office of Strategic Services in World War II.* Washington, DC: National Archives and Records Administration, 1992.

Chant-Sempill, Stuart. *St. Nazaire Commando.* Novato, CA: Presidio Press, 1987; first pub. 1985.

Churchill, Winston S. *The World Crisis, 1911–1918.* 2 vols. London: Odhams Press, 1938.

Cimbala, Stephen J. *Extended Deterrence: The United States and NATO Europe.* Lexington, MA: Lexington Books, 1987.

Clark, Ian. *The Hierarchy of States: Reform and Resistance in the International Order.* Cambridge: Cambridge University Press, 1989.

Clausewitz, Carl von. *On War.* Edited and translated by Michael Howard and Peter Paret. Princeton, NJ: Princeton University Press, 1976; first pub. 1832.

Clodfelter, Mark. *The Limits of Air Power: The American Bombing of North Vietnam.* New York: Free Press, 1989.

Cohen, Eliot A. *Commandos and Politicians: Elite Military Units in Modern Democracies.* Cambridge, MA: Harvard University, Center for International Affairs, 1978.

———. "Comment" [on nuclear proliferation]. *National Interest*, no. 34 (winter 1993/94): 37–38.

———. "The Mystique of U.S. Air Power." *Foreign Affairs* 73, no. 1 (January/February 1994): 109–24.

Cohen, Eliot A., and John Gooch. *Military Misfortunes: The Anatomy of Failure in War.* New York: Free Press, 1990.

Collier, Basil. *A History of Air Power.* New York: Macmillan, 1974.

Colson, Bruno. *La culture stratégique Américaine: L'influence de Jomini.* Paris: FEDN/Economica, 1993.

Corbett, Julian S. *The Campaign of Trafalgar.* London: Longmans, Green, 1910.
———. *England in the Seven Years' War: A Study in Combined Strategy.* 2 vols. London: Longmans, Green, 1918; first pub. 1907.
———. *Some Principles of Maritime Strategy.* Annapolis, MD: Naval Institute Press, 1988; first pub. 1911.
Cowles, Virginia. *The Phantom Major: The Story of David Stirling and the S.A.S. Regiment.* London: Collins, 1958.
Craven, Wesley Frank, and James Lea Cate, eds. *The Army Air Forces in World War II.* 7 vols. Chicago: University of Chicago Press, 1948–58.
Creveld, Martin van. *Technology and War: From 2000 B.C. to the Present.* New York: Free Press, 1989.
———. *Nuclear Proliferation and the Future of Conflict.* New York: Free Press, 1993.
Davis, Paul K., ed. *New Challenges for Defense Planning: Rethinking How Much Is Enough.* Santa Monica, CA: RAND, 1994.
Delbrück, Hans. *History of the Art of War.* Vol II, *The Barbarian Invasions.* Lincoln: University of Nebraska Press, 1990; first pub. 1980.
Dewar, James A., et al. *Assumption-Based Planning: A Planning Tool for Very Uncertain Times.* MR-114-A. Santa Monica: CA: RAND, 1993.
Dougherty, William A. "Storm from Space." U.S. Naval Institute *Proceedings* 118, no. 8 (August 1992): 48–52.
Doughty, Robert Allan. *The Seeds of Disaster: The Development of French Army Doctrine, 1919–1939.* Hamden, CT: Archon Books, 1985.
———. *The Breaking Point: Sedan and the Fall of France, 1940.* Hamden, CT: Archon Books, 1990.
Douhet, Giulio. *The Command of the Air.* New York: Arno Press, 1972; first pub. 1942.
Dror, Yehezkel. *Crazy States: A Counterconventional Strategic Problem.* Lexington, MA: Heath Lexington Books, 1971.
Duffy, Michael, ed. *The Military Revolution and the State, 1500–1800.* Exeter Studies in History, no. 1. Exeter, England: University of Exeter, Department of History and Archaeology, 1980.
Dull, Johathan R. *The French Navy and American Independence: A Study of Arms and Diplomacy, 1774–1787.* Princeton, NJ: Princeton University Press, 1975.
Dunn, Lewis A. *Containing Nuclear Proliferation.* Adelphi Papers, no. 263. London: International Institute for Strategic Studies, winter 1991.
Dunnigan, James F., and Austin Bay. *From Shield to Storm: High-Tech Weapons, Military Strategy, and Coalition Warfare in the Persian Gulf.* New York: William Morrow, 1992.
Dupuy, Trevor N., ed. *International Military and Defense Encyclopedia.* 6 vols. Washington, DC: Brassey's (US), 1993.
Emme, Eugene M., ed. *The Impact of Air Power: National Security and World Politics.* Princeton, NJ: D. Van Nostrand, 1959.
Fall, Bernard B. *Street Without Joy.* New York: Schocken Books, 1972; first pub. 1964.
———. *Hell in a Very Small Place: The Siege of Dien Bien Phu.* New York: Da Capo, 1985; first pub. 1967.

Ferris, John Robert. *Men, Money, and Diplomacy: The Evolution of British Strategic Policy, 1919–1926.* Ithaca, NY: Cornell University Press, 1989.

Fischer, David Hackett. *Historians' Fallacies: Toward a Logic of Historical Thought.* New York: Harper and Row, 1970.

Fitzsimmons, James R., and Jan M. van Tol. "Revolutions in Military Affairs." *Joint Force Quarterly*, no. 4 (spring 1994): 24–31.

Foley, Charles. *Commando Extraordinary.* London: Longmans, Green, 1954.

Foot, M. R. D. *SOE in France: An Account of the British Special Operations Executive in France, 1940–1944.* London: HMSO, 1966.

———. "Special Operations/I." In Michael Elliott-Bateman, ed., *The Fourth Dimension of Warfare.* Vol. I, *Intelligence, Subversion, Resistance*, 19–34. Manchester, England: Manchester University Press, 1970.

———. *SOE: An Outline History of the Special Operations Executive, 1940–46.* London: Mandarin, 1990; first pub. 1984.

Force Planning Faculty, Naval War College, ed. *Fundamentals of Force Planning.* 3 vols. Newport, RI: Naval War College Press, 1990–92.

France, John. *Victory in the East: A Military History of the First Crusade.* Cambridge: Cambridge University Press, 1994.

Freedman, Lawrence. "Terrorism and Strategy." In Lawrence Freedman et al., *Terrorism and International Order*, 56–76. Chatham House Special Paper. London: Routledge for the Royal Institute of International Affairs, 1986.

———. "Whither Nuclear Strategy?" In Ken Booth, ed., *New Thinking about Strategy and International Security*, 75–89. London: HarperCollins Academic, 1991.

———. "Strategic Studies and the Problem of Power." In Lawrence Freedman, Paul Hayes, and Robert O'Neill, eds., *War, Strategy, and International Politics: Essays in Honour of Sir Michael Howard*, 279–94. Oxford: Clarendon Press, 1992.

Freedman, Lawrence, and Efraim Karsh. *The Gulf Conflict, 1990–1991: Diplomacy and War in the New World Order.* Princeton, NJ: Princeton University Press, 1993.

French, David. *The British Way in Warfare, 1688–2000.* London: Unwin Hyman, 1990.

Fry, Michael G. "Historians and Deterrence." In Paul C. Stern et al., eds., *Perspectives on Deterrence*, 84–97. New York: Oxford University Press, 1989.

Fuller, J. F. C. *Armament and History: A Study of the Influence of Armament on History from the Dawn of Classical Warfare to the Second World War.* London: Eyre and Spottiswoode, 1946.

Futrell, Robert Frank. *The United States Air Force in Korea, 1950–1953.* Rev. ed. Washington, DC: U.S. Air Force, Office of Air Force History, 1983.

———. *Ideas, Concepts, Doctrine: Basic Thinking in the United States Air Force.* Vol I, *1907–1960.* Maxwell Air Force Base, AL: Air University Press, 1989.

"The Future of NATO." *Journal of Strategic Studies* 17, no. 4 (December 1994).

Gaston, James C. *Planning the American Air War: Four Men and Nine Days in 1941, An Inside Narrative.* Washington, DC: National Defense University Press, 1982.

Geraghty, Tony. *Who Dares Wins: The Story of the Special Air Service, 1950–1982.* London: Fontana Books, 1983, rev. ed.

Gibbs, N. H. *History of the Second World War, Grand Strategy.* Vol. I, *Rearmament Policy.* London: HMSO, 1976.

Glaser, Charles L. "Why NATO Is Still Best: Future Security Arrangements for Europe." *International Security* 18, no. 1 (summer 1993): 5–50.

Gleick, James. *Chaos: Making a New Science.* New York: Penguin Books, 1988; first pub. 1987.

Goldman, Emily O. *Sunken Treaties: Naval Arms Control Between the Wars.* University Park: Pennsylvania State University Press, 1994.

Goldstein, Erik, and John Maurer, eds. *The Washington Conference, 1921–22: Naval Rivalry, East Asian Stability, and the Road to Pearl Harbor.* London: Frank Cass, 1994.

Gordon, John W. "Wingate." In John Keegan, ed., *Churchill's Generals*, 277–97. New York: Grove Weidenfeld, 1991.

Gordon, Michael R., and Bernard E. Trainor. *The Generals' War: The Inside Story of the Conflict in the Gulf.* Boston: Little, Brown, 1995.

Graffis, Judy M. "Strategic: Use with Care." *Airpower Journal* 8, special edition (1994): 4–10.

Gray, Colin S. *Strategic Studies and Public Policy: The American Experience.* Lexington: University Press of Kentucky, 1982.

———. "War Fighting for Deterrence." *Journal of Strategic Studies* 7, no. 1 (March 1984): 5–28.

———. *Nuclear Strategy and National Style.* Lanham, MD: Hamilton Press, 1986.

———. *War, Peace, and Victory: Strategy and Statecraft for the Next Century.* New York: Simon and Schuster, 1990.

———. *House of Cards: Why Arms Control Must Fail.* Ithaca, NY: Cornell University Press, 1992.

———. *The Leverage of Sea Power: The Strategic Advantage of Navies in War.* New York: Free Press, 1992.

———. *Weapons Don't Make War: Policy, Strategy, and Military Technology.* Lawrence: University Press of Kansas, 1993.

———. "Global Security and Economic Well-Being: A Strategic Perspective." *Political Studies* 42, no. 1 (March 1994): 25–39.

———. *The Navy in the Post–Cold War World: The Uses and Value of Strategic Sea Power.* University Park: Pennsylvania State University Press, 1994.

———. "Off the Map: Defense Planning after the Soviet Threat." *Strategic Review* 22, no. 2 (spring 1994): 26–35.

———. "Strategy in the Nuclear Age: The United States, 1945–1991." In Williamson Murray, MacGregor Knox, and Alvin Bernstein, eds., *The Making of Strategy: Rulers, States, and War*, 579–613. Cambridge: Cambridge University Press, 1994.

———, ed. *Special Operations: What Succeeds and Why? Lessons of Experience, Phase I.* Final Report. Fairfax, VA: National Institute for Public Policy, June 1992.

Griffith, Paddy. *Battle Tactics of the Western Front: The British Army's Art of Attack, 1916–18.* New Haven, CT: Yale University Press, 1994.

Grove, Eric. *The Future of Sea Power.* Annapolis, MD: Naval Institute Press, 1990.

Haffa, Robert P., Jr. *Rational Methods, Prudent Choices: Planning U.S. Forces.* Washington, DC: National Defense University Press, 1988.

Hall, Christopher. *Britain, America and Arms Control, 1921–37.* New York: St. Martin's Press, 1987.

Hallion, Richard P. *Rise of the Fighter Aircraft, 1914–1918.* Baltimore, MD: Nautical and Aviation Publishing Company of America, 1984.

———. *Strike from the Sky: The History of Battlefield Air Attack, 1911–1945.* Washington, DC: Smithsonian Institution Press, 1989.

———. *Storm over Iraq: Air Power and the Gulf War.* Washington, DC: Smithsonian Institution Press, 1992.

Handel, Michael I. *Masters of War: Sun Tzu, Clausewitz and Jomini.* London: Frank Cass, 1992.

Harvey, A. D. *Collision of Empires: Britain in Three World Wars, 1793–1945.* London: Hambledon Press, 1992.

Hattendorf, John B., and Robert S. Jordan, eds. *Maritime Strategy and the Balance of Power: Britain and America in the Twentieth Century.* New York: St. Martin's Press, 1989.

Hayden, H. T. *Warfighting: Maneuver Warfare in the U.S. Marine Corps.* Mechanicsburg, PA: Stackpole Books, 1995.

Heilbrunn, Otto. *Warfare in the Enemy's Rear.* London: George Allen and Unwin, 1963.

Hobkirk, Michael D. *Land, Sea or Air? Military Priorities, Historical Choices.* London: Macmillan, 1992.

Hogan, David W., Jr. *U.S. Army Special Operations in World War II.* Washington, DC: Department of the Army, Center of Military History, 1992.

Holley, I. B., Jr. *Ideas and Weapons: Exploitation of the Aerial Weapon by the United States During World War I: A Study in the Relationship of Technological Advance, Military Doctrine, and the Development of Weapons.* Hamden, CT: Archon Books, 1971; first pub. 1953.

Holsti, Kalevi J. *Peace and War: Armed Conflicts and International Order, 1648–1989.* Cambridge: Cambridge University Press, 1991.

Hooker, Richard D., Jr., ed. *Maneuver Warfare: An Anthology.* Novato, CA: Presidio Press, 1993.

"Horizon," *The I-Bomb.* Text adapted from the program transmitted on 27 March 1995. London: BBC, 1995.

Hough, Richard, and Denis Richards. *The Battle of Britain: The Greatest Air Battle of World War II.* New York: W. W. Norton, 1989.

Howard Michael. *The Continental Commitment: The Dilemma of British Defence Policy in the Era of the Two World Wars.* London: Temple Smith, 1972.

———. "The Forgotten Dimensions of Strategy." *Foreign Affairs* 57, no. 5 (summer 1979): 975–86.

——. *The Causes of Wars and Other Essays*. London: Counterpoint, 1984; first pub. 1983.

Huntington, Samuel P. "National Policy and the Transoceanic Navy." U.S. Naval Institute *Proceedings* 80, no. 5 (May 1954): 483–93.

——. *American Military Strategy*. Policy Papers in International Affairs, no. 28. Berkeley: University of California, Institute of International Studies, 1986.

——. "Playing to Win." *National Interest*, no. 3 (spring 1986): 8–16.

——. "The Clash of Civilizations." *Foreign Affairs* 72, no. 3 (summer 1993): 22–49.

Huth, Paul K. *Extended Deterrence and the Prevention of War*. New Haven, CT: Yale University Press, 1988.

Jablonsky, David. "U.S. Military Doctrine and the Revolution in Military Affairs." *Parameters* 24, no. 3 (autumn 1994): 18–36.

Jensen, Owen E. "Information Warfare: Principles of Third-Wave War." *Airpower Journal* 8, no. 4 (winter 1994): 35–43.

Jervis, Robert. "Cooperation under the Security Dilemma." *World Politics* 30, no. 2 (January 1978): 167–214.

——. *The Illogic of American Nuclear Strategy*. Ithaca, NY: Cornell University Press, 1984.

——. *The Meaning of the Nuclear Revolution: Statecraft and the Prospect of Armageddon*. Ithaca, NY: Cornell University Press, 1989.

——. "The Future of World Politics: Will It Resemble the Past?" *International Security* 16, no. 3 (winter 1991/92): 39–73.

Jervis, Robert, Richard Ned Lebow, and Janice Gross Stein. *Psychology and Deterrence*. Baltimore, MD: Johns Hopkins University Press, 1985.

Johnston, Alastair Iain. "Thinking about Strategic Culture." *International Security* 19, no. 4 (spring 1995): 32–64.

Jomini, Antoine Henri de. *The Art of War*. London: Greenhill Books, 1992; first pub. 1862.

Jones, John F. "Giulio Douhet Vindicated: Desert Storm, 1991." *Naval War College Review* 45, no. 4 (autumn 1992): 97–101.

Kagan, Donald. *The Fall of the Athenian Empire*. Ithaca, NY: Cornell University Press, 1987.

Kahn, David. *Seizing the Enigma: The Race to Break the German U-Boat Codes, 1939–1943*. Boston: Houghton Mifflin, 1991.

Kahn, Herman. *On Thermonuclear War*. Princeton, NJ: Princeton University Press, 1960.

——. *On Escalation: Metaphors and Scenarios*. New York: Praeger, 1965.

Kaufmann, William W. "The Requirements of Deterrence." In William W. Kaufmann, ed., *Military Policy and National Security*, 12–38. Princeton, NJ: Princeton University Press, 1956.

Keaney, Thomas A., and Eliot A. Cohen. *Gulf War Air Power Summary Report*. Washington, DC: U.S. Government Printing Office, 1993.

Kennedy, Paul. *The Rise and Fall of British Naval Mastery*. New York: Charles Scribner's Sons, 1976.

——. *The Rise and Fall of the Great Powers: Economic Change and Military Conflict from 1500 to 2000.* New York: Random House, 1987.

——. "The Influence and the Limitations of Sea Power." *International History Review* 10, no. 1 (February 1988): 2–17.

Kennett, Lee. *The First Air War, 1914–1918.* New York: Free Press, 1991.

Kent, Glenn A., Randall J. DeValk, and David E. Thaler. *A Calculus of First-Strike Stability: A Criterion for Evaluating Strategic Forces.* N-2526-AF. Santa Monica, CA: RAND, June 1988.

Kirtland, Michael A. "Planning Air Operations: Lessons from Operation Strangle in the Korean War." *Airpower Journal* 6, no. 2 (summer 1992): 37–46.

Klein, Bradley S. *Strategic Studies and World Order: The Global Politics of Deterrence.* Cambridge: Cambridge University Press, 1994.

Klein, Yitzhak. "A Theory of Strategic Culture." *Comparative Strategy* 10, no. 1 (1991): 3–23.

Kolkowicz, Roman, ed. *The Logic of Nuclear Terror.* Boston: Allen and Unwin, 1987.

Krepinevich, Andrew F. "Cavalry to Computer: The Pattern of Military Revolutions." *National Interest,* no. 37 (fall 1994): 30–42.

Lambakis, Steven. "Space Control in Desert Storm and Beyond." *Orbis* 39, no. 3 (summer 1995): 417–33.

Lawrence, T. E. *Seven Pillars of Wisdom: A Triumph.* New York: Anchor Books, 1991; first pub. 1935.

Levy, Jack S. *War in the Modern Great Power System, 1495–1975.* Lexington: University Press of Kentucky, 1983.

Liddell Hart, B. H. *The British Way in Warfare.* London: Faber and Faber, 1932.

——. *History of the First World War.* London: Pan Books, 1972; first pub. 1930.

Lucas, James. *Kommando: German Special Forces of World War Two.* New York: St. Martin's Press, 1986; first pub. 1985.

Lunt, James. *The Retreat from Burma, 1941–1942.* Newton Abbott, England: David and Charles Publishers, 1989; first pub. 1986.

Lupton, David E. *On Space Warfare: A Space Power Doctrine.* Maxwell Air Force Base, AL: Air University Press, June 1988.

Luttwak, Edward N. *On the Meaning of Victory: Essays on Strategy.* New York: Simon and Schuster, 1986.

——. *Strategy: The Logic of War and Peace.* Cambridge, MA: Harvard University Press, 1987.

——. "From Geopolitics to Geoeconomics: Logic of Conflict, Grammar of Commerce." *National Interest,* no. 20 (summer 1990): 17–23.

——. "Air Power in U.S. Military Strategy." In Richard H. Shultz, Jr., and Robert L. Pfaltzgraff, Jr., eds., *The Future of Air Power in the Aftermath of the Gulf War,* 17–38. Maxwell, Air Force Base, AL: Air University Press, July 1992.

Luttwak, Edward N., Steven L. Canby, and David L. Thomas. *A Systematic Review of "Commando" (Special) Operations, 1939–1980.* Potomac, MD: C and L Associates, 24 May 1982.

MacFarland, Stephen L., and Wesley Phillips Newton. *To Command the Sky: The Battle for Air Superiority over Germany, 1942–1944.* Washington, DC: Smithsonian Institution Press, 1991.

MacIsaac, David. "Voices from the Central Blue: The Air Power Theorists." In Peter Paret, ed., *Makers of Modern Strategy: From Machiavelli to the Nuclear Age,* 624–47. Princeton, NJ: Princeton University Press, 1986.

Macksey, Kenneth. *Commando Strike: The Story of Amphibious Raiding in World War II.* London: Leo Cooper, 1985.

McNab, Andy. *Bravo Two Zero.* London: BCA, 1993.

———. *Immediate Action.* London: Bantam Press, 1995.

McRaven, William H. *SPEC OPS: Case Studies in Special Operations Warfare: Theory and Practice.* Novato, CA: Presidio Press, 1995.

Mahan, Alfred Thayer. *The Influence of Sea Power upon the French Revolution and Empire, 1793–1812.* 2 vols. Boston: Little, Brown, 1898; first pub. 1892.

———. *Naval Strategy, Compared and Contrasted with the Principles and Practice of Military Operations on Land.* Boston: Little, Brown, 1919; first pub. 1911.

———. *The Influence of Sea Power upon History, 1660–1783.* London: Methuen, 1965; first pub. 1890.

Mann, Stephen R. "Chaos Theory and Strategic Thought." *Parameters* 22, no. 3 (autumn 1992): 54–68.

Marshall, Christopher. *Warfare in the Latin East, 1192–1291.* Cambridge: Cambridge University Press, 1992.

Maurice, Frederick. *British Strategy: A Study of the Application of the Principles of War.* London: Constable, 1927.

Millett, Allan R., and Peter Maslowski. *For the Common Defense: A Military History of the United States of America.* New York: Free Press, 1984.

Millet, Allan R., and Williamson Murray, eds. *Military Effectiveness.* 3 vols. Boston: Allen and Unwin, 1988.

Mitchell, William. *Winged Defense: The Development and Possibilities of Modern Air Power—Economic and Military.* New York: Dover Publications, 1988; first pub. 1925.

Momyer, William W. *Air Power in Three Wars.* Washington, DC: U.S. Government Printing Office, 1978.

Morgan, Patrick. *Deterrence: A Conceptual Enquiry.* Beverly Hills, CA: Sage Publications, 1977.

Morrow, John H., Jr. *The Great War in the Air: Military Aviation from 1909 to 1921.* Washington, DC: Smithsonian Institution Press, 1993.

Mueller, John. "The Essential Irrelevance of Nuclear Weapons: Stability in the Postwar World." *International Security* 13, no. 2 (fall 1988): 55–79.

Murray, Williamson. *German Military Effectiveness.* Baltimore, MD: Nautical and Aviation Publishing Company of America, 1992.

Naroll, Raoul, Vern L. Bullough, and Frada Naroll. *Military Deterrence in History: A Pilot Cross-Historical Survey.* Albany: State University of New York Press, 1974.

Nicholls, David, and Todor D. Tagarev. "What Does Chaos Theory Mean for Warfare?" *Airpower Journal* 8, no. 3 (fall 1994): 48–57.

Nye, Joseph S., Jr. "Old Wars and Future Wars: Causation and Prevention." In Robert I. Rotberg and Theodore K. Rabb, eds., *The Origin and Prevention of Major Wars*, 3–12. Cambridge: Cambridge University Press, 1989.

Offer, Avner. *The First World War: An Agrarian Interpretation.* Oxford: Clarendon Press, 1989.

Osgood, Robert E. *Limited War: The Challenge to American Strategy.* Chicago: University of Chicago Press, 1957.

Overy, R. J. *The Air War, 1939–1945.* New York: Stein and Day, 1985; first pub. 1980.

Paddock, Alfred H., Jr. *U.S. Army Special Warfare, Its Origins: Psychological and Unconventional Warfare, 1941–1952.* Washington, DC: National Defense University Press, 1982.

Pape, Robert A., Jr. "Coercive Air Power in the Vietnam War." *International Security* 15, no. 2 (fall 1990): 103–46.

———. "Coercion and Military Strategy: Why Denial Works and Punishment Doesn't." *Journal of Strategic Studies* 15, no. 4 (December 1992): 423–75.

Paret, Peter. *Clausewitz and the State.* New York: Oxford University Press, 1976.

———, ed. *Makers of Modern Strategy: From Machiavelli to the Nuclear Age.* Princeton, NJ: Princeton University Press, 1986.

Parker, Geoffrey. *The Military Revolution: Military Innovation and the Rise of the West, 1500–1800.* Cambridge: Cambridge University Press, 1988.

Parker, R. A. C. *Struggle for Survival: The History of the Second World War.* Oxford: Oxford University Press, 1989.

Perret, Geoffrey. *A Country Made by War: From the Revolution to Vietnam—The Story of America's Rise to Power.* New York: Vintage Books, 1990; first pub. 1989.

Perry, William J. (secretary of defense). *Annual Report to the President and the Congress.* Washington, DC: U.S. Government Printing Office, February 1995.

"The Rational Deterrence Debate: A Symposium." *World Politics* 41, no. 2 (January 1989): 143–237.

Ray, John. *The Battle of Britain, New Perspectives: Behind the Scenes of the Great Air War.* London: Arms and Armour Press, 1994.

Record, Jeffrey. *Hollow Victory: A Contrary View of the Gulf War.* Washington, DC: Brassey's (US), 1993.

Rhodes, Edward. *Power and MADness: The Logic of Nuclear Coercion.* New York: Columbia University Press, 1989.

Rice, Donald B. *The Air Force and U.S. National Security: Global Reach—Global Power.* White paper. Washington, DC: Department of the Air Force, June 1990.

Richards, Denis. *Royal Air Force, 1939–1945.* Vol. I, *The Fight at Odds.* London: HMSO, 1953.

Roberts, Brad. "From Nonproliferation to Antiproliferation." *International Security* 18, no. 1 (summer 1993): 139–73.

Rodger, N. A. M. "The Continental Commitment in the Eighteenth Century." In Lawrence Freedman, Paul Hayes, and Robert T. O'Neill, eds., *War, Strategy, and International Politics: Essays in Honour of Sir Michael Howard*, 39–55. Oxford: Clarendon Press, 1993.

Ryan, Donald F. "Implications of Information-Based Warfare." *Joint Force Quarterly*, no. 6 (autumn/winter 1994/95): 114–16.

Sagan, Scott D. *Moving Targets: Nuclear Strategy and National Security*. Princeton, NJ: Princeton University Press, 1993.

———. *The Limits of Safety: Organizations, Accidents, and Nuclear Weapons*. Princeton, NJ: Princeton University Press, 1993.

Sagan, Scott D., and Kenneth N. Waltz. *The Spread of Nuclear Weapons: A Debate*. New York: W. W. Norton, 1995.

Samuels, Martin. *Doctrine and Dogma: German and British Infantry Tactics in the First World War*. Westport, CT: Greenwood Press, 1992.

Schelling, Thomas C. "Surprise Attack and Disarmament." In Klaus Knorr, ed., *NATO and American Security*, 176–208. Princeton, NJ: Princeton University Press, 1959.

———. *Arms and Influence*. New Haven, CT: Yale University Press, 1966.

Schelling, Thomas C., and Morton H. Halperin. *Strategy and Arms Control*. New York: Twentieth Century Fund, 1961.

Schemmer, Benjamin F. *The Raid*. New York: Avon Books, 1976.

Schlesinger, James. "New Instabilities, New Priorities." *Foreign Policy*, no. 85 (winter 1991/92): 3–24.

Schwartz, David N. *NATO's Nuclear Dilemmas*. Washington, DC: Brookings Institution, 1983.

Segal, Gerald, ed. *New Directions in Strategic Studies: A Chatham House Debate*. RIIA Discussion Papers, no. 17. London: Royal Institute of International Affairs, 1989.

Segré, Claudio G. "Giulio Douhet: Strategist, Theorist, Prophet?" *Journal of Strategic Studies* 15, no. 3 (September 1992): 351–66.

Seversky, Alexander P. de. *Victory Through Air Power*. New York: Simon and Schuster, 1942.

Showalter, Dennis E. "Total War for Limited Objectives: An Interpretation of German Grand Strategy." In Paul Kennedy, ed., *Grand Strategies in War and Peace*, 105–23. New Haven, CT: Yale University Press, 1991.

Shultz, Richard H., Jr. "Compellence and the Role of Air Power as a Political Instrument." In Richard H. Schultz, Jr., and Robert L. Pfaltzgraff, Jr., *The Future of Air Power in the Aftermath of the Gulf War*, 171–91. Maxwell Air Force Base, AL: Air University Press, July 1992.

Shy, John. *A People Numerous and Armed: Reflections on the Military Struggle for American Independence*. London: Oxford University Press, 1976.

———. "The Cultural Approach to the History of War." *Journal of Military History* 57, no. 5, special issue (October 1993): 13–26.

Skorzeny, Otto. *Skorzeny's Secret Missions: War Memoirs of the Most Dangerous Man in Europe*. New York: E. P. Dutton, 1950.

Slim, Field-Marshal Viscount. *Defeat into Victory*. London: Papermac, 1986; first pub. 1956.

Smith, Paul A., Jr. *On Political War.* Washington, DC: National Defense University Press, 1989.

Snyder, Glenn. *Deterrence and Defense.* Princeton, NJ: Princeton University Press, 1961.

Spector, Ronald H. *After Tet: The Bloodiest Year in Vietnam.* New York: Free Press, 1993.

Spykman, Nicholas J. *America's Strategy in World Politics: The United States and the Balance of Power.* Hamden, CT: Archon Books, 1970; first pub. 1942.

Strachan, Hew. "The British Way in Warfare." In David Chandler, ed., *The Oxford Illustrated History of the British Army,* 417–34. Oxford: Oxford University Press, 1994.

Stratton, Ray E., and August G. Jannarone. "Toward a Strategic Targeting Doctrine for Special Operations Forces." *Air University Review* 36, no. 5 (July/August 1985): 24–29.

Summers, Harry G. *On Strategy: A Critical Analysis of the Vietnam War.* Novato, CA: Presidio Press, 1982.

Sun Tzu. *The Art of War.* Translated by Ralph D. Sawyer. Boulder, CO: Westview Press, 1994.

Taylor, Telford. *The March of Conquest: The German Victories in Western Europe, 1940.* Baltimore, MD: Nautical and Aviation Publishing Company of America, 1991; first pub. 1958.

Terraine, John. *White Heat: The New Warfare, 1914–18.* London: Sidgwick and Jackson, 1982.

———. *A Time for Courage: The Royal Air Force in the European War, 1939–1945.* New York: Macmillan, 1985.

———. *Business in Great Waters: The U-Boat Wars, 1916–1945.* London: Leo Cooper, 1989.

Thomas, David. "The Importance of Commando Operations in Modern Warfare, 1939–82." *Journal of Contemporary History* 18, no. 4 (October 1983): 689–717.

Tilford, Earl H., Jr. *Crosswinds: The Air Force's Setup in Vietnam.* College Station: Texas A and M University Press, 1993.

Toffler, Alvin, and Heidi Toffler. *The Third Wave.* New York: Bantam Books, 1980.

———. *War and Anti-War: Survival at the Dawn of the 21st Century.* Boston: Little, Brown, 1993.

Trachtenberg, Marc. *History and Strategy.* Princeton, NJ: Princeton University Press, 1991.

Travers, Tim. *How the War Was Won: Command and Technology in the British Army on the Western Front, 1917–1918.* London: Routledge, 1992.

Tucker, Robert W., and David C. Hendrickson. *The Imperial Temptation: The New World Order and America's Purpose.* New York: Council on Foreign Relations Press, 1992.

Tugwell, Maurice, and David Charters. "Special Operations and the Threats to United States Interests in the 1980's." In Frank R. Barnett, B. Hugh Tovar, and Richard H. Shultz, Jr., eds., *Special Operations in U.S. Strategy,* 27–43. Washington, DC: National Defense University Press, 1984.

Underwood, Jeffrey S. *The Wings of Democracy: The Influence of Air Power on the Roosevelt Administration, 1933–1941.* College Station: Texas A and M University Press, 1991.

Vegetius. *Epitome of Military Science.* Translated by N. P. Milner. Liverpool, England: Liverpool University Press, 1993.

Waltz, Kenneth N. "Nuclear Myths and Political Realities." *American Political Science Review* 84, no. 3 (September 1990): 731–45.

Warden, John A., III. *The Air Campaign: Planning for Combat.* Washington, DC: Pergamon-Brassey's, 1989; first pub. 1988.

———. "Employing Air Power in the Twenty-First Century." In Richard H. Shultz, Jr., and Robert L. Pfaltzgraff, Jr., eds., *The Future of Air Power in the Aftermath of the Gulf War,* 57–82. Maxwell Air Force Base, AL: Air University Press, July 1992.

Webster, Charles, and Noble Frankland. *The Strategic Air Offensive Against Germany, 1939–1945.* 4 vols. London: HMSO, 1961.

Weigley, Russell F. *The American Way of War: A History of United States Strategy and Policy.* New York: Macmillan, 1973.

Weinberg, Gerhard L. *A World at Arms: A Global History of World War II.* Cambridge: Cambridge University Press, 1994.

Wheeler, Nicholas J., and Ken Booth. "The Security Dilemma." In John Baylis and N. J. Rengger, eds., *Dilemmas of World Politics: International Issues in a Changing World,* 29–60. Oxford: Clarendon Press, 1992.

Williams, Michael C. "Neo-Realism and the Future of Strategy." *Review of International Studies* 19, no. 2 (April 1993): 103–21.

Willmott, H. P. *The Barrier and the Javelin: Japanese and Allied Pacific Strategies, February to June 1942.* Annapolis, MD: Naval Institute Press, 1983.

———. *The Great Crusade: A New Complete History of the Second World War.* New York: Free Press, 1989.

Wohlstetter, Albert J. "The Delicate Balance of Terror." *Foreign Affairs* 37, no. 2 (January 1959): 211–34.

———. "Bishops, Statesmen, and Other Strategists on the Bombing of Innocents." *Commentary* 75, no. 6 (June 1983): 15–35.

Wylie, J. C. *Military Strategy: A General Theory of Power Control.* Annapolis, MD: Naval Institute Press, 1989; first pub. 1967.

Index

ABOUT THE AUTHOR

COLIN S. GRAY is a strategic theorist and defense analyst who has worked in Britain, Canada, and the United States. He has written pioneering and controversial studies of nuclear strategy, arms control, maritime strategy, and geopolitics.

ISBN 0-313-29510-7

90000>

EAN

9 780313 295102

HARDCOVER BAR CODE